The Küng Dialogue

A documentation on the efforts of
the Congregation for the
Doctrine of the Faith
and of
the Conference of German Bishops
to achieve an appropriate clarification
of the controversial views of
Dr. Hans Küng (Tübingen)

United States Catholic Conference

PUBLICATIONS OFFICE
UNITED STATES CATHOLIC CONFERENCE
1312 MASSACHUSETTS AVENUE
WASHINGTON, D.C. 20005

Table of Contents

Preface

News reports and comments on the controversy involving the Sacred Congregation for the Doctrine of the Faith and Father Hans Küng have generated considerable debate. Often the impression has been given that the process was unfair or discriminatory towards Hans Küng. In the interests of a fuller understanding of the events and issues, the NCCB Committee on Doctrine here presents the extensive documentation on this matter first issued by the German Bishops' Conference.

Although some of these items have already appeared in full or in part in this country, this constitutes the fullest collection of these documents. It is intended for theologians, teachers of theology and religion, and all who share responsibility for the accurate presentation of the deposit of faith.

The documentation may be divided into four general sections: 1) a first part that has as its focus Hans Küng's book *The Church;* 2) a section that refers to the issues at stake in the infallibility discussion; 3) a section that refers to the discussion surrounding Hans Küng's book *On Being A Christian;* and 4) a section that deals with the final stage of the discussion.

In the second section the reader will note that Hans Küng's position on infallibility drew detailed critical comments from the Congregation for the Doctrine of the Faith. Enclosures nn.19 to 40 present that exchange. Enclosures nn.35 and 36 present declarations of the Congregation and of the German Bishops' Conference. Enclosures nn.30 and 31 have as one of their focuses the procedural norms of the Congregation.

In the third section the reader will note that enclosures nn.41 to 54 focus on the Christological positions in Hans Küng's book *On Being A Christian.* Enclosures nn.46/2 and 49/2 are declarations of the German Bishops' Conference on this matter.

Enclosure n.55 in Hans Küng's Preface to August Hasler's book *Wie der Papst Unfehlbar weirde* and n.56 is the postface to the book *The Church—Maintained in the Truth.*

For the assistance of readers, the Committee has added the statement of the *Congregation Mysterium Ecclesiae* and its declaration of December 19, 1979. The volume also includes, as a service to English-speaking readers, the recent letter of Pope John Paul II to the West German Bishops Conference on the matter and the statements of the President of the NCCB, of Cardinal Baum, former Chairman of the Committee on Doctrine of the NCCB and presently Prefect of the Sacred Congregation for Catholic Education, and of Cardinal G. Emmett Carter, Archbishop of Toronto.

The Committee wishes to thank His Eminence, Cardinal John Krol, Archbishop of Philadelphia, for his invaluable support and assistance in the accomplishment of this project, and the Executive Director of the Committee on Doctrine, Monsignor Richard Malone, for his interest in this undertaking.

Most Rev. James A. Hickey
Archbishop of Washington
Chairman, NCCB Committee on Doctrine

INTRODUCTION

THE FIRST DISCUSSIONS (1967-1973)

The discussions began with the publication of *Die Kirche* (Freiburg/Basel/Wien, 1967) and continued with the publication of *Unfehlbar ? Eine Anfrage* (Einsiedeln: Benzinger, 1970).

Exchange of Letters Concerning the Book Die Kirche

In a letter of April 30, 1968, the Congregation for the Doctrine of the Faith informed Professor Küng that it was examining the book *Die Kirche.* In connection with this examination, it invited Professor Küng to a discussion scheduled for May 8, 1968 **[Enclosure 1]**. On May 8, 1968, Professor Küng informed the Congregation for the Doctrine of the Faith that he was prevented from coming and that a letter would follow **[Enclosure 2]**.

On May 30, 1968, Professor Küng wrote **[Enclosure 3]** and declared himself ready to engage in the proposed discussion. However, he asked for a clarification concerning the conditions to be met if this discussion was to take place: access of his dossier; the list of the questions to be discussed; participation of competent experts; German as the language of the proceedings; reimbursement of expenses.

The Congregation for the Doctrine of the Faith replied with a letter dated July 8, 1968 **[Enclosure 4]**, mentioning some of the conditions. It asked which dates were convenient for the discussion and gave assurances that the expenses would be reimbursed. In his letter of July 28, 1968 **[Enclosure 5]**, Professor Küng repeated his willingness in principle to take part in the discussion, but made his participation contingent on the fulfillment of the remaining conditions previously mentioned. In its answer, dated August 31, 1968 **[Enclosure 6]**, the Congregation for the Doctrine of the Faith disclosed the names of those who were to take part in the proposed discussion.

On December 6, 1969, Professor Küng worte to Mr. A. H. M. van den Boogaard, President of the foundation Concilium **[Enclosure 7]** and reported on the exchange of letters and the discussion with the Congregation for the Doctrine of the Faith. He also sent a copy of this letter to the Congregation for the Doctrine of the Faith. In a letter dated January 24, 1970 **[Enclosure 8]**, the Congregation for the Doctrine of the Faith corrected Professor Küng concerning some points in his letter to Mr. van den Boogaard. Professor Küng replied on June 1, 1970 **[Enclosure 9]**. After thanking the Congregation for the Doctrine of the Faith for its clarifications, he wrote: "For various reasons I am of the opinion that the proceedings, already underway for two years, should be terminated. The discussion could still take place apart from these. Unencumbered by these proceedings, the discussion would turn out to be all the more fruitful."

"Invitation to Self-Help" by Professor Küng

Professor Küng commented on the motu proprio of Pope Paul VI concerning mixed marriages in the *Frankfurter Allgemeine Zeitung* of May 9, 1970 **[Enclosure 10]**. On May 19, 1970 the Conference of German Bishops released a statement in which it voiced its dismay "that a Catholic theologian . . . should take, with regard to the motu proprio, a stand which is not only polemical and offensive in part, but should also openly invite people to violate the stipulations of the law." Professor Küng replied on May 27, 1970 (for both statements, cf. **Enclosure 11**).

Exchange of Letters concerning Unfehlbar ? Eine Anfrage

The Conference of German Bishops issued a statement on this book February 4, 1971 **[Enclosure 12]**. It said in part: "In the book . . . basic questions of principle are raised concerning the possibility of a normative assertion of the faith which affect in part fundamental tenets in the Catholic understanding of faith and of the Church. The Conference of German Bishops believes that some of these tenets are not safeguarded in the aforementioned book. These concerns have not been removed even after further declarations by the author and after a discussion with him mandated by the episcopal conference. It is not the task of bishops to take a stand on the controversial questions, technical-theological in nature, which, because of this book, are now again at issue. However, the Conference of German Bishops feels obligated to draw attention to some unnegotiable givens which theology cannot deny if it is to remain Catholic." The Conference of German Bishops then went on to mention these "unnegotiable givens." Professor Küng replied on February 9, 1971 **[Enclosure 13]**. The Conference of German Bishops responded on March 4, 1971 **[Enclosure 14]** that "the genuine content of the infallibility of the Church . . . in Küng is, to say the least, obscured." He speaks of "propositions whose infallibility is guaranteed a priori. . . For this reason, a contradiction exists between the assertions of the episcopal conference and what one must derive from the book and from subsequent statements of Professor Küng."

In a letter dated February 12, 1971 **[Enclosure 15]**, the Congregation for the Doctrine of the Faith warned Professor Küng "to reflect on the position you occupy in the Church and on the impact and consequences of your undertaking. I hope that you will come to the conclusion that in this way one cannot truly love and serve the Church." Professor Küng replied on February 26, 1971 **[Enclosure 16]** by adverting to a manuscript of his, prepared independently of the letter of the Congregation for the Doctrine of the Faith. On May 6, 1971, the Congregation for the Doctrine of the Faith called to Professor Küng's attention the propositions "which are contained in your book and which the Congregation regards as erroneous or dangerous." The Congregation for the Doctrine of the Faith indicated that it expected a written statement about these propositions within a month **[Enclosure 17]**. Professor Küng replied on June 21, 1971

[Enclosure 18] by taking a stand on the questions raised by the Congregation for the Doctrine of the Faith. On July 12, 1971, the Congregation for the Doctrine of the Faith informed Professor Küng that it had initiated doctrinal proceedings against the book *Unfehlbar ?* , and transmitted the list of the theses to "which the Congregation for the Doctrine of the Faith finds difficult to give a Catholic interpretation. I request that you explain to the Congregation in writing within thirty days whether and in what way you believe that these theses and opinions can be reconciled with Catholic doctrine." **[Enclosure 19]** Professor Küng replied on July 19, 1971 from Moscow **[Enclosure 20]** that he would not be able to respond to the letter until his return. On December 17, 1971 **[Enclosure 21]**, the Congregation for the Doctrine of the Faith sent a reminder with regard to the letter of July 12, 1971. Professor Küng answered on January 24, 1972 **[Enclosure 22]**, taking exception in principle to the proceedings of the Congregation and making "preliminary remarks on the questions raised by the Congregation."

A FIRST ATTEMPT AT ENDING THE DISCUSSIONS WITH PROFESSOR KÜNG IN CONJUNCTION WITH THE DECLARATION MYSTERIUM ECCLESIAE, JUNE 24, 1973

This document does not intend to offer a comprehensive exposition of church doctrine on the mystery of the Church, but only to present and clarify some basic truths which had been the object of particular public discussions and theological debate between Vatican II and the publication of the declaration *Mysterium Ecclesiae.* What is involved here is not primarily a theological discussion with Professor Küng. Rather it is a stand taken with regard to changes and shifts in the faith consciousness of the whole Church, The normative understanding of the Church and of the foundations of the common faith is set forth.

(The text of the Declaration *Mysterium Ecclesiae,* edited with introduction and commentary by Karl Lehmann appears in the series *"Nachkonziliare Dokumentation"* Vol. 43; Trier: Paulinus-Verlag, 1975)

Regarding *Mysterium Ecclesiae,* issued June 24, 1973, the Congregation for the Doctrine of the Faith declared on July 4, 1973 **[Enclosure 23]** while referring to both proceedings: "Your letters have been examined by this Congregation. On April 26, 1972, it was decided, with the approval of the Holy Father, to prepare a declaration which would interpret Catholic doctrine for the benefit of the whole ecclesial community against today's erroneous opinions in the domain of ecclesiology.

"In regard to the doctrinal proceedings relative to the examination of your two books mentioned above, two options are open to you. First, the order of procedure provides for the possibility of a discussion with the representatives of the Congregation for the Doctrine of the Faith on the doctrinal points contained in the two letters of this Congregation. Or, second, you might accept at once the doctrine contained in the declaration. In this case, the doctrinal proceedings now in progress concerning your two books would be terminated."

In an additional statement relative to *Mysterium Ecclesiae* on July 5, 1973 **[Enclosure 24]**, Archbishop J. Schröffer, speaking on behalf of the Congregation for the Doctrine of the Faith, observed that a discussion with Professor Küng "can still take place. Should Professor Küng assent to the declaration *Mysterium Ecclesiae* of June 24, 1973, the doctrinal proceedings in progress would be terminated."

On July 5, 1973, Professor Küng released a declaration concerning the publication of *Mysterium Ecclesiae* **[Enclosure 25]**. As President of the Conference of German Bishops, Cardinal Döpfner responded on July 7, 1973 **[Enclosure 26]**: "In a first statement of his position dated July 5, 1973, Professor Küng has unfortunately made more difficult the continuation of an objective discussion through poorly supported and disparaging statements concerning the Congregation for the Doctrine of the Faith. As President of the Conference of German Bishops, I repudiate Professor Küng's assertions concerning the Congregation for the Doctrine of the Faith; in part, they are defamatory. Considering the importance of this matter, I expect that Professor Küng, through substantive cooperation, will execute a satisfactory clarification. This is the only way in which greater harm can be prevented."

On July 10, 1973, Cardinal Volk wrote to Professor Küng as follows **[Enclosure 27]**: "My concern now is rather to end this quarrel. I believe we do have a chance. In your article, you yourself acknowledge that in the Roman declaration a new element is clearly contained. . . I sincerely ask you . . . to speak with Rome." Professor Küng replied in an extensive letter **[Enclosure 28]** in which he wrote in part: "I have always been willing to discuss and will remain willing in the future, no matter what happens." On August 16, 1973 **[Enclosure 29]**, the Congregation for the Doctrine of the Faith sent Professor Küng a reminder concerning an answer to its letter of July 4, 1973 (cf. Enclosure 23 in this documentation). The Congregation said it expected an answer by September 20, 1973. On September 22, 1973 **[Enclosure 30]**, Professor Küng answered the letter of the Congregation for the Doctrine of the Faith dated July 4 and August 16, 1973. Again raising "a fundamental objection against the proceedings of your Congregation," he took up "questions on the theological problematic" and addressed "a personal word" to the Congregation for the Doctrine of the Faith: "Wouldn't this be the time to drop the questions between us and leave to history the task of judging what the answer should be?" On March 30, 1974 **[Enclosure 31]**, the Congregation for the Doctrine of the Faith replied in a detailed letter in which it explained that it could not accept Professor Küng's proposal. A discussion was still an open possibility. On September 4, 1974, Professor Küng answered **[Enclosure 32]**. In this letter he did not exclude the possibility that, given adequate time for in-depth study, he might bring his views in line with the doctrine of the authentic magisterium. In an extensive letter, dated December 23, 1974 **[Enclosure 33]**, Cardinal Höffner asked Professor Küng this question: "By what authority do you profess your opinions?" Professor Küng replied on Janaury 10, 1975 **[Enclosure 34]** and answered: "By the authority of the Word of God which, as a theologian, I must serve."

A NEW ATTEMPT AT A PROPER CLARIFICATION THROUGH THE DECLARATION OF THE CONGREGATION OF THE DOCTRINE OF THE FAITH, FEBRUARY 15, 1975 (Enclosure 35]

In this Declaration, the Congregation for the Doctrine of the Faith, referring to Professor Küng's two books, *Die Kirche* and *Unfehlbar ? Eine Anfrage,* pointed out three opinions which cannot be reconciled with the doctrine of the Church. (1) Küng's view concerning the dogma of the infallibility of the Church contradicts the doctrine defined by Vatican I and confirmed by Vatican II. (2) Küng's view of the Magisterium of the Church "does not use the genuine concept of authentic Magisterium. According to this concept, the bishops are "authentic teachers, that is, teachers endowed with the authority of Christ, who preach to the people committed to them the faith they must believe and put into practice" (Vatican II; Dogmatic Constitution *Lumen gentium*, 25 [Abbott, 47]). (3) The view professed by Professor Küng in the book *Die Kirche* "that, at least in case of necessity, the Eucharist can be validly consecrated by a non-ordained baptized person" cannot be reconciled with the doctrine of the Fourth Lateran Council and of Vatican II. The declaration went on to say: "In his letter of September 4, 1974, Professor Küng does not at all exclude the possibility that, given adequate time for thorough study, he could bring his views in line with the authentic doctrine of the magisterium of the Church. In view of this, and in spite of the importance of these doctrines, the Congregation, so directed by Pope Paul VI, *for the time being* imparts to Professor Küng the admonition not to advocate these doctrines any longer. It reminds him that the ecclesiastical authority has authorized him to teach theology in the spirit of the Christian doctrine, but not to advocate views which distort that doctrine, or call it in doubt." At the end of the declaration it was explicitly stated that with this declaration "the proceedings of the Congregation for the Doctrine of the Faith in this matter are *for the time being* terminated."

On its side, the Conference of German Bishops issued on February 17, 1975 a comprehensive statement concerning this declaration of the Congregation for the Doctrine of the Faith **[Enclosure 36]**. It said, in part: "The Conference of German Bishops concurs with the admonition of the Congregation for the Doctrine of the Faith, and expects Professor Küng no longer to advocate the positions which the magisterium of the Church has repeatedly disavowed." In addition, the Conference of German Bishops recalled in this statement certain principles which belong to the basic understanding of what Catholic theology is, and which are not, in its opinion, sufficiently observed in some theological works of Professor Küng, These are: (1) the normative significance of the tradition of the Church; (2) the relationship between magisterium and theology; (3) the concrete normativeness of faith. The statement concluded: "The Conference of German Bishops, therefore, addresses an urgent appeal to Professor Küng to reexamine the method and the objectionable assertions of his theology in the light of the principles presented here."

On February 17, 1975, Cardinal Döpfner forwarded this statement of the Conference of German Bishops with a covering letter **[Enclosure 37]**. He said, in part: "The bishops beg you insistently to consider and observe these principles (enunciated in the statement of the Conference of German Bishops) in your further work. These principles are not unknown to you; they have been pointed out to you in many discussions. It makes good sense that they now have been articulated in writing. . . We fervently hope that you in turn will be willing to contribute the share which is required on your part, so that this business may be settled permanently. We would be very grateful if this declaration should signal the end of a an era of confrontations, an era which has not done much good to our Church in the eyes of the world nor to our common task as theologians and bishops."

On February 20, 1975 **[Enclosure 38]**, Professor Küng released a statement on the termination of the doctrinal proceedings. He said, in part: "My concern is not that, in the debated questions of infallibility and Church order, I should be proved right against Rome and the bishops. . . Not even these declarations have disproved any of the things I have to say on theological grounds. The declaration of the Roman authorities is rather the public admission that the secret proceedings against me have proved unworkable, and have now been terminated. Such inquisitorial proceedings also contradict the Gospel, human rights, and the spirit of the 'Holy Year of Reconciliation' . . . I will certainly go on reflecting anew on the method and contents of my theology in the spirit of theological accountability. Hopefully, the Roman Curia will also take to heart the theological principles of the Conference of German Bishops, even if this is bound to entail important consequences for the method and content of Roman theology."

In a personal letter dated February 26, 1975 **[Enclosure 39]**, Professor Küng thanked Cardinal Döpfner for his personal efforts to bring about the termination of the doctrinal proceedings of the Congregation for the Doctrine of the Faith. He wrote, in part: "This time I would like to write you a personal letter, since, unless I hear differently from you, the two declarations do not necessarily require that I respond officially. In this way I need not return to the unpleasant shortcomings in the proceedings, nor to the questions which the two documents fail to answer."

After various statements and letters, Cardinal Döpfner, as President of the Conference of German Bishops, answered Professor Küng on May 6, 1975 **[Enclosure 40]** in a personal letter. He said, in part: "What concerns me most is what lies behind your more theologically oriented comments, both in your statement to the press on February 20, 1975 and in your letter of February 26, 1975. I find it unacceptable that you continue to reduce the faith-question addressed in the proceedings to the level of Church politics (in the broadest sense of the word), and that you make a pragmatic and tactical issue of it all. This begins with the expression 'offer of a standstill' and permeates also the tone of your letter. Therefore, I beg you again to consider deeply and seriously how matters precisely stand. If we had to quarrel once more over these difficulties and no rapprochement were in sight, I would be at my wit's end."

In an extensive letter dated April 27, 1976 **[Enclosure 41]**, Professor Küng informed Cardinal Döpfner of his conversations with the Congregation for the Doctrine of the Faith. He also informed the Cardinal that he had to reply "in a serious newspaper of wider circulation" to those critics who have attacked his book *Christ sein.* "All the same, this article is not supposed to be my last word in the matter. I hope to find time in the near future to address anew in scholarly fashion the exegetical, historical, systematic, and hermeneutical questions raised in the volume and elsewhere. It goes without saying that a renewed theological consideration of the subject matter includes clarifications and corrections, completions and deepenings of my own position, too. As already stated in the book itself, I am convinced that a positive updating is quite possible, and indeed desirable, with regard to various doctrinal points — also and especially with regard to those which the Congregation for the Doctrine of the Faith finds objectionable." Professor Küng pointed out certain assertions in *Christ sein* which the critiques of the book had failed to take seriously enough. He concluded: "I would be grateful to Your Eminence and to the German Bishops if I could be permitted to do my theological work in peace and quiet. I hope that, by my restraint and also by means of this letter, I may have said something which will bring us closer to a proper resolution of the present situation."

On June 24, 1976, Cardinal Döpfner again directed a letter to Professor Küng **[Enclosure 42]**. He mentioned easpecially Küng's "Reply to My Critics," published in the *Frankfurter Allgemeine Zeitung* May 22, 1976, which has been a rather great disappointment for him. He had expected "the reply to be to the point. . . You do indeed say in your letter that you intend to take up in scholarly fashion the questions and concerns of your critics; you expressly emphasize that 'clarifications and corrections, completions and deepenings' of your position are entirely possible. My dear Professor Küng, these clarifications have kept me waiting now for a long time. In recent years, you have made such a promise time and again in various connections. Your reply to the critics would have offered you an extremely favorable opportunity to make good on this promise. I must, therefore, remind you of the urgent appeal which the Conference of German Bishops addressed to you at the end of their declaration of February 17, 1975, a declaration you know. You were asked to 'reexamine the method and the objectionable assertions of your theology in the light of the above principles.' But when you respect your 'critics' as little as your reply in the *Frankfurter Allgemeine Zeitung* shows, it is hard to believe that, well over a year later, this reexamination has been started at all. I have always looked on such serious reexamination as a non-negotiable component of the 'new style' in the clarification of doctrines which can be misunderstood or are to be described as false. This much I am entitled to expect from you. . . Through all this, you create a new situation for the bishops. I hardly need to emphasize that I regret this very much. I, therefore, insistently urge you once again to reflect seriously and reexamine the method objected to in the declaration of the Conference of German Bishops, Febraury 17, 1975, and the assertions called in question."

In the same letter, Cardinal Döpfner mentioned that he had forwarded the letter of Professor Küng dated April 27, 1976, "to the chairman of the faith-commission, with the request that the faith-commission discuss the questions which have emerged anew in the debate."

On July 23, 1976, Cardinal Döpfner died. The day before his death he drafted a letter to Professor Küng. On August 31, 1976, this letter **[Enclosure 43]** was sent by the new President of the Conference of German Bishops, Cardinal Höffner. In this letter a proposal was made to hold a discussion "aimed at clarifying some key questions relative to *Christ sein.*"

The discussion took place January 22, 1977 in Stuttgart. For various reasons, Professor Küng felt that he would not be in a position to undertake in the near future the desired clarifications of certain key Christological questions. On January 28, 1977, Bishop Moser of Rottenburg-Stuttgart, who is Professor Küng's ordinary and within whose jurisdiction the University of Tübingen is located, sent Professor Küng a letter **[Enclosure 44]**. He urgently requested him to send the Conference of German Bishops a clarifying letter. Professor Küng wrote this letter to the President of the Conference of German Bishops on February 21, 1977 **[Enclosure 45]**.

In their spring meeting of 1977, the bishops considered both the outcome of the discussion in Stuttgart and the letter of Professor Küng of February 21, 1977. They felt that in this letter their questions had not been answered. This was stated by Cardinal Höffner in a letter dated March 4, 1977 **[Enclosure 46]**. (Note that to this letter was added the statement released to the press by the Conference of German Bishops on March 3, 1977.) On April 22, 1977, Cardinal Höffner sent Professor Küng the concrete questions that had been announced, together with a request that he answer them **[Enclosure 47]**. At the end of the letter, he said: "I, therefore, urge you, in spite of the many and sundry tasks of a semester in progress, to answer these questions in writing by June 15, 1977. You do realize that your answer is of decisive importance for the Conference of German Bishops."

An exchange of letters ensued **[Enclosure 48]** in which Professor Küng postponed the requested answer because of other commitments.

STATMENT OF THE CONFERENCE OF GERMAN BISHOPS CONCERNING THE BOOK CHRIST SEIN

Cardinal Höffner sent this statement to Professor Küng on November 17, 1977 **[Enclosure 49]**. In closing, he said: "As shown in the discussion of January 22, 1977, and as I stated more precisely in my letter of April 4, 1977, your book *Christ sein* contains assertions on essential contents of our faith which, in the opinion of the bishops, fails to do justice to the traditional doctrine of the faith. Since you refuse to deliver a more precise version of these assertions, the bishops feel that they must provide these essential clarifications in a communication addressed to all the faithful. I emphatically recall to your mind the declaration issued February 17, 1975 by the Conference of German Bishops, and the request to reexamine your theological method in keeping with the principles set forth in that declaration."

On November 18, 1977 Professor Küng, in a statement to the Deutsche Press Agentur **[Enclosure 50]**, called the statement of the Conference of German Bishops "a doctrinaire self-justification without self-criticism." In a footnote in his book, *Existiert Gott ?* (München: Verlag Piper, 1978), he referred again to this position of the Conference of the German Bishops **[Enclosure 51]**.

In 1978, Walter Jens published documentation under the title *Um nichts als die Wahrheit* (München/Zürich: R. Piper). The president of the Conference of German Bishops responded to this documentation in a letter to Professor Küng on February 22, 1978 **[Enclosure 52]**. He enclosed a transcript of his statement to the press concerning the documentation of Walter Jens.

On February 10, 1978 **[Enclosure 53]**, Professor Küng asked the Bishop of Rottenburg, Dr. Georg Moser, to support and circulate the "Appell zur

Verständigung" contained in Walter Jens' publication *Un nichts als ·die Wahrheit.* On April 3, 1978, Bishop Moser replied **[Enclosure 54]** in part: "I regret that I am not in a position to accede to your wish to undertake the dissemination of the 'Appell zur Verständigung' which you have enclosed. In my opinion, Walter Jens' documentation *Um nichts als die Wahrheit* which closes with this 'Appell' is anything but documentation of mutual understanding. In the editor's preface, there is no evidence of any willingness to promote mutual understanding. What comes through is the determination to engage in open confrontation. I cannot pry your own text loose from the whole context."

PROFESSOR KÜNG REITERATES HIS VIEWS ON THE INFALLIBILITY OF THE CHURCH

In a preface to the book *Wie der Papst unfehlbar wurde* by A. B. Hasler (München: Piper-Verlag, 1979) [Cf. **Enclosure 55]**, as well as in a piece of writing entitled "kirche—gehalten in der Wahrheit?" (Benzinger Verlag, 1979; Cf. especially pp. 73-75 **[Enclosure 56]**, Professor Küng explicitly reiterated his views concerning the infallibility of the Church, views which contradict both Vatican Councils.

In a letter dated February 19, 1979 **[Enclosure 57]**, Professor Küng informed the Bishop of Rottenburg, Dr. Moser, concerning these two publications, and said, in part: "This meditation, too, merely clarifies what I have set forth in the above-mentioned conclusive statement" (last chapter of *Fehlbar ?*). He emphasized the following: "No new infallibility debate should be provoked by my preface and by the theological meditation that accompanies it. Yet it is important to me, now as before, that the infallibility issue should be explored exegetically, historically, and systematically with objectivity and scholarly honesty."

Bishop Moser answered with a letter dated April 5, 1979 **[Enclosure 58]**. He wrote: "I will not hide from you that the reading of your two contributions to the question of papal infallibility have affected me very deeply. I find there again very sharply formulated only the theses which were objected to on February 15, 1975 by the Congregation for the Doctrine of the Faith, and which were deemed in need of revision and reexamination by the Conference of German Bishops on February 17, 1975. For this reason, I am entirely unable to understand how you can possibly think that your present utterances should not provoke a new infallibility debate. In my opinion, your conduct cannot be understood as anything but as a provocation. I, therefore, assume that unpleasant consequences are inevitable and that great difficulties will ensue.

"Although I do not at the moment know where we should go from here, especially in view of the fact that, as a theology teacher, you are still involved in the formation of the theologians of our diocese, I am still as prepared as ever to talk and to seek a tenable reconciliation."

* * * * *

This documentation may be summarized as follows:

1. From the start, that is, from 1968 until the present, the Congregation for the Doctrine of the Faith, as well as the Conference of German Bishops,

endeavored with great patience to achieve an appropriate resolution of the conflict with Professor Küng. After other efforts at clarification failed, *Mysterium Ecclesiae* was issued in 1973. This declaration offered a presentation of the doctrine of the Catholic Church designed to meet the questions and the findings of contemporary theology. No disciplinary measure was taken there, nor in fact was any mentioned. Professor Küng was rather offered the opportunity for a new discussion. He was advised that his assent to this declaration would bring about the termination of the proceedings.

In the declaration of 1975, the errors of Professor Küng were set forth, and a statement was made that, with this, the proceedings were "for the time being" terminated. Professor Küng was urged no longer to profess the objectionable theses and to take pains to achieve conformity with Church doctrine. In the additional statement of the Conference of German Bishops of February 1975, Professor Küng was urged to reexamine his theological method. In a 1977 declaration, the Conference of German Bishops in turn set forth and corrected the obscurities and questionable utterances contained in the book *Christ sein.* This was done because, in spite of repeated discussions and written requests, Professor Küng was not prepared adequately to do so himself.

2. In spite of repeated and urgent entreaties, requests and exhortations from the Congregation for the Doctrine of the Faith and the Conference of German Bishops to answer the questions put to him and to reexamine his theological method and in spite of personal efforts on the part of Cardinal Döpfner, for example, and especially of Dr. Moser, Bishop of Rottenburg-Stuttgart, Professor Küng entirely failed to comply.

3. Recently, Professor Küng has instead explicitly reiterated and in many respects sharpened his opinions, especially in regard to the infallibility of the Church, and this in spite of the fact that, in 1975, the doctrinal proceedings against these theses were terminated on condition that he would no longer profess his doctrines and would intead seek to conform with the explicit doctrine of the Church.

Bonn, December 18, 1979

CHRONOLOGICAL TABLE OF THE ENCLOSURES

ENCLOSURES

The documents which follow cover the most important phases of the discussions with Professor Küng concerning his ecclesiological and socio-Christological doctrines from 1967 to 1979.

A great number of documents are being made available here, and yet, this is only a selection. Omitted are statements to the press, the exchange of letters concerning the modalities of a discussion being planned concerning the volume, *Diskussion über Hans Küngs Christ sein,* and the transcript of the discussion between the Conference of German Bishops and Professor Küng in Stuttgart, January 22, 1977.

The documents omitted here are available in the following publications:

Erklärung Mysterium Ecclesiae zur Katholischen Lehre über die Kirche ("Nachkonziliare Dokumentation" Band 43; Trier: Paulinus-Verlag, 1975)

Walter Jens (ed.), *Um nichts als die Wahrheit. Deutsche Bischofskonferenz contra Hans Küng* (Munchen: Piper-Verlag, 1978)

For the sake of convenience, when several pieces relate to the same event, they are numbered as one.

Enclosure 1

LETTER OF THE CONGREGATION FOR THE DOCTRINE OF THE FAITH TO PROFESSOR KÜNG, April 30, 1968

399/57/i *April 30, 1968*

Prof. Dr. Hans Küng
Faculty of Catholic Theology
University of Tübingen
Germany

Dear Professor Küng:

The Congregation for the Doctrine of the Faith is examining your book, *Die Kirche.*

According to the norms of the Motu Proprio *Integrae servandae,* a discussion with the author should be held. I ask you, dear Professor Küng, to come to this discussion on Thursday, May 9, at 9:30 A.M. in the Palazzo del S. Uffizio in Rome.

Respectfully,
(no signature)

Enclosure 2

TELEGRAM OF PROFESSOR KÜNG TO THE CONGREGATION FOR THE DOCTRINE OF THE FAITH, May 8, 1978

STATO CITTA DEL VATICANO
TELEGRAMMA

CVAT73 X20 113 Reutlingen Telephone de Tuebingen 9 8 1442

UNFORTUNATELY PREVENTED LETTER FOLLOWS KÜNG

Enclosure 3

LETTER OF PROFESSOR KÜNG TO THE CONGREGATION FOR THE DOCTRINE OF THE FAITH, May 30, 1968

May 30, 1968

His Excellency
Archbishop Paul Philippe, O. P.
Secretary of the Sacred Congregation for the Doctrine of the Faith
Vatican City

Your Excellency:

As I advised you by telegram on May 8, I was unfortunately prevented from appearing at the discussion scheduled for May 9. In the meantime, I have taken pains to ponder carefully my answer to your letter and to discuss the same with other competent professors and ecclesiastics.

At the outset, I would like to state that, in principle, I am prepared to take part in a discussion. I consider the invitation to a discussion as notable progress compared to the procedure customary in the past. I am convinced that, through an open and congenial exchange of views, future difficulties and ambiguities can be entirely clarified. In the post-conciliar era, the dialogue among Catholics is at least as important as the dialogue with other Christian churches and with the modern world. You can be assured of my cooperation.

At the same time, I cannot hide my amazement at the way in which this invitation has been issued to me. Viewing the fact that the date for a discussion ought to be arranged by mutual agreement, I cannot understand how this invitation could have been issued on such short notice. I do not know whether this has been taken into account in your Congregation. Your letter is dated April 30. It was handed to me Saturday, May 4. In order to be present at the discussion in Rome on May 9, I would have had to leave May 8. In my opinion, this was a downright imposition. Apparently, people are hardly aware of the work load a university professor carries. Due precisely to my work load, I was even forced at that same time to decline the invitation of a Catholic university in the U. S. A. to receive an honorary doctorate. You will, therefore, understand that an unplanned journey to Rome is out of the question as long as the semester at the University of Tübingen is in progress. Besides, it must be your concern as well as mine that the conditions for a fruitful and successful discussion be agreed upon before my departure. In this connection, the following seems to be essential.

1. In your letter of April 30, 1968, as well as in earlier letters of the Congregation, there is a reference to your dossier 399/57/i, which obviously concerns me. If I am to engage intelligently in a discussion, it is indispensable that I should have unrestricted access to the official documents and free perusal of my dossier which, to judge by the number, was already started by the Index. In my view, the discussion cannot be fair, unless I am fully cognizant of the official documents that concern me and free to use them without restrictions of any sort. I hardly need to mention that, in all civilized states of the West, even criminals are guaranteed complete access to the dossiers that pertain to them. I, therefore, request written assurance that I shall be allowed unlimited perusal of the official documents relative to me.

2. The letter of your Congregation to the Bishop of Rottenburg of December 19, 1967, No. 399/57, already deals with me and my work, *Die Kirche.* In this letter, it is stated that the examination of my book by your Congregation had been concluded and had led to the publication of a decree on November 29, which, however, has not been made public in the meantime. Your latest letter of April 30, 1968 says, on the contrary, that the Congregation for the Doctrine of the Faith "is" still "examining" my book. If so, the earlier statement must be regarded as immaterial. Likewise, the "authoritative invitation" mentioned at that time to renounce my right to further disseminate my book, would, as a consequence, also be immaterial since the proceedings are obviously still in progress, and the examination continues. I am glad to be able to take part in your discussion free from this burden which, by the way, contrary to the motu proprio of Pope Paul VI *Integrae servandae* of December 7, 1965, was imposed without the author and the local ordinary being heard. The discussion will hopefully reveal that the Bishop of Rottenburg did not grant the Imprimatur irresponsibly, as has been alleged, but rather in keeping with canonical norms.

3. Your Congregation, I presume, is interested in definite points in my book. You will no doubt understand that it is important for me to be informed beforehand about the questions to be discussed, and the ambiguities you find difficult to understand. This is what *Integrae servandae* stipulates. In this way, I can prepare my answers, which in turn will make for a pointed and fruitful discussion. I, therefore, ask you to provide me with a written statement of your position in the matter.

4. Since my book is not a piece of vulgarization but a scholarly, technical, and theological treatise, I can expect that the discussion will take place with competent experts. An expert judgment on the book, *Die Kirche*, presupposes specialized and precise exegetical, historical, and dogmatic knowledge. As I know from prior experience, it makes poor sense to deliberate exegetical, historical, and dogmatic questions with a canon lawyer who is not well-informed in such matters. I, therefore, ask you to let me know in writing the names of my partners in the discussion.

5. The motu proprio of Pope Paul VI *Pro comperto sane* of August 6, 1967, stipulates that the Curia may now conduct business in modern languages. I want to make use of this right. Since this discussion concerns a German book of an author who speaks German, I wish to use my mother tongue, that is, German. I ask you to advise me whether you agree to this request.

6. For the sake of this discussion, I am being required to travel to Rome. You will understand, no doubt, that I regard as inequitable the expenses entailed. I, therefore, ask to be assured in writing that all the expenses in connection with this discussion be reimbursed to me by the Congregation for the Doctrine of the Faith. Should this solution be unacceptable, the conversation could certainly take place in Tübingen. My house would be at your disposal.

It seems to me that it would be an advantage to all concerned if this matter could be disposed of without causing a public uproar; otherwise, harm would come to the Church, which my whole theological work intends to serve. Assuring you once more that I am willing to cooperate, I convey my greetings to your Excellency.

Most respectfully,
(signed) Hans Küng

cc.
Dr. Carl-Joseph Leiprecht, Bishop of Rottenburg
Prof. Dr. Joseph Ratzinger, Dean of the Faculty of Catholic Theology, University of Tübingen

Enclosure 4

LETTER OF THE CONGREGATION FOR THE DOCTRINE OF THE FAITH TO PROFESSOR KÜNG, July 8, 1968

Prot. No. 399/57/i *Rome, July 8, 1968*
Piazza del S. Uffizio 11

Prof. Dr. Hans Küng
Nauklerstrasse 37 a
D--74 Tübingen
Germany

Dear Professor Küng:

In reply to your letter of May 30, 1968, be advised that, in a decree issued July 3, 1968, their Eminences the Cardinals of the Congregation for the Doctrine of the Faith have decided the following:

1. The Congregation for the Doctrine of the Faith asks you to submit dates on which you would be able to come to Rome.
2. This Congregation intends to reimburse you for travel expenses, etc.
3. Here we are not dealing with a *trial* but with a *discussion* [''Kolloquium''] on some of the theses advocated in your book, *Die Kirche,* as provided for by the norms of the motu proprio *Integrae servandae.* Access to the dossier 399/57/i, to which you refer, is not necessary. The dossier does not pertain to the matter at hand.

Respectfully,

PAOLO PHILIPPE
Secretary

LETTER OF PROFESSOR KÜNG TO THE CONGREGATION FOR THE DOCTRINE OF THE FAITH, July 27, 1968

Tübingen, July 27, 1968
Nauklerstrasse 37a

His Excellency
Archbishop Paul Philippe, O. P.
Secretary of the Congregation
for the Doctrine of the Faith
Vatican City

Your Excellency:

After receiving your letter of July 8, I would like to confirm that I am willing to come to Rome and to participate in the discussion you require.

After a conversation with you in Rome, Archbishop Clarizio, Apostolic Delegate to Canada, wrote me that my letter of May 30 has made a polemical impression. It was not my intention to cause such an impression. My concern was to give an objective answer to an objective letter. Before the Council, I had emphasized what a curse it was that, for centuries on end, Catholics and Protestants should meet only to argue. After the Council, I have pointed out time and again how important it is now for Catholics to understand each other. The intra-Church dialogue is of fundamental importance if we are to overcome present-day difficulties. Nor do I need to stress that I am no friend of "psychological" or similar schisms. On the contrary. I have often and publicly branded the "private excommunication" meted out to those who think differently in the same Church as a basic evil of Protestantism. I have advocated a further "catholicizing" of the Roman Curia (nationalities *and* mentalities). Thus, I belong to the number of those who would never let themselves be guided by an anti-Roman sentiment, but to those who have sought in various ways to dialogue with Roman authorities. May I here remark in all modesty that, in my theology, I have advocated the necessity and usefulness of a Petrine office in today's world more effectively perhaps than all the apologists of another stripe to whom no one lends an ear any more. I would, therefore, beg Your Excellency to understand that, as I wrote in my letter, my one and only concern was to make sure that a *genuine* discussion should come about, that is, a discussion in which all the marks of the Inquisition trials are removed.

I am, therefore, sincerely glad that, on various points, agreement has already been reached. I thank Your Excellency for taking kindly into account the difficulties connected with my schedule. I am gladly prepared to indicate the times when I can come to Rome. I am also grateful for your willingness to sustain my travel expenses.

On my part, I would like also to show good will where I have the opportunity of doing so. Should it prove difficult to find appropriate discussion partners with a command of the German language, I am prepared to conduct the discussion in other modern languages (English, French, Spanish, and Italian). I am also convinced that agreement is attainable with regard to the remaining points. In this connection, allow me to come back to what I have already mentioned.

In my letter to Your Excellency, I had asked that you provide me with the names of my eventual discussion partners. In your letter you made no mention of this request. I reiterate my request. Would you let me know *with which experts* the discussion will take place. I stress again that competence in exegesis and history is especially important.

It is also important to know ahead of time *what* precisely is to be discussed. I do not need to reiterate that only if this condition be fulfilled can a meaningful and fruitful discussion take place, adequate preparation made, and the discussion conducted without waste of time. In your letter you limit yourself to saying that the discussion is to deal with "some" theses from my book, *Die Kirche.* On account of your earlier letter, I already had to assume that this would be the case. However, it would be easy for the Congregation for the Doctrine of the Faith to delimit with precision which are the theses from my book which cause difficulties for you, and why they do so. For the sake of the business at hand, I, therefore, ask you again not to deny me this.

I would also be grateful if you would send me the order of procedure of your Congregation, worked out on the basis of *Integrae servandae.*

You emphasize in your letter that you regard as "unnecessary" the perusal of the documents of your Congregation pertaining to me. Not to make this letter too burdensome, I postpone at this stage of the preparations for the planned discussion my request in this matter until such time as mutual understanding has been achieved on the items mentioned above.

In the last month, the Italian press of the extreme right has been disseminating false allegations against me. The Roman newspaper *Il Tempo* has asserted, in connection with the first meeting of the Cardinals of the Curia, that I had offended the Pope, and that, for this reason, the Pope himself had ordered the Cardinals to take measures against me (cf. *Il Tempo,* June 12, 1968). The Vatican correspondent "Lo Svizzero" of *Il Borghese* (July 4, 1968) stated that the Vatican was proceeding against me because of an alleged "heretical attitude." Since *Il Tempo* and Lo Svizzero of *Il Borghese* are reported to be closely connected with certain circles in the Curia, the grave allegations against me were taken up by the German press (cf., for example, the *Frankfurter Allgemeine Zeitung,* June 13-14; *Der Spiegel,* June 24). I had to enter a strong protest against these reports. I would have been grateful if the press office of your Congregation had intervened in an appropriate manner against these offensive doings. But since no official dementi or anything like it appeared in Rome, I, the injured party, was forced to make clear in the press what was false and what was correct in these press reports.

In spite of this publicity campaign originating in Rome, I will not allow myself to grow bitter. I will do whatever may help the cause and make possible the discussion you desire. As once again I assure Your Excellency of my readiness, I convey my greetings to you.

Respectfully,
(signed) Hans Küng

Enclosure 6

LETTER OF THE CONGREGATION FOR THE DOCTRINE OF THE FAITH TO PROFESSOR KÜNG, August 31, 1968

399/57/i *August 31, 1968*

Professor Dr. Hans Küng
Tübingen

Dear Professor Küng:

This Sacred Congregation acknowledges receipt of your letter of July 27, 1968. With satisfaction, it takes cognizance of the fact that you are prepared to take part in the discussion not only in German but also in other modern languages.

The following reverend gentlemen are to take part in the discussion, as representatives of the Sacred Cognregation: the Very Reverend Father E. Dhanis, S. J., the Very Reverend Father J. Witte, S. J., the Very Reverend Father B. Ahern, Passionist.

The topics to be discussed will be imparted to you soon.

An order of procedure has been worked out on the basis of *Integrae servandae.* It is, however, only *ad experimentum,* and not *publici juris.*

Respectfully,
(no signature)

Enclosure 7

LETTER OF PROFESSOR KÜNG TO Mr. A. H. M. van der BOOGAARD, December 6, 1969

Tübingen
Nauklerstrasse 37 a
December 6, 1969

Mr. A. H. M. van den Boogaard
President of the Foundation Concilium
Nijmegen

Dear Mr. van den Boogaard:

It has not been for lack of good will that I am only now replying to your letter. I have been away from Tübingen for several months. At the beginning of the winter semester, I have been extraordinarily busy. By this time I had promised to complete a major scholarly work. Everything else had to be put off until then, last but not least my mail which, for me, has almost become unmanageable. Besides, the negotiations with Rome have not proceeded so fast as to force me to state my position in a hurry.

At the outset, I would like to voice my satisfaction at the fact that Monsignor Carlo Colombo works so hard on behalf of our discussion with the Roman authorities. During a short stay in Milan, I have also ascertained his fairness and objectivity in the public discussion of my book, *Die Kirche.* In a personal conversation with him, I became convinced that his intentions are positive. He would like to contribute constructively to a better relationship between Rome and the theology represented by Concilium. These efforts deserve every support. I would, therefore, ask you explicitly to convey to Monsignor Colombo my sincere thanks for his assistance.

I may further express my satisfaction that, judging by the latest utterances, Rome is now more willing to discuss than seemed the case in an earlier phase of these lengthy negotiations. To anyone in Rome who endeavors to bring about a better rapport with contemporary theology, everyone of us shall be sincerely grateful. Our opinions may and do often differ, and yet all of us ultimately work for the one and the same Church. With regard to the subject matter itself, as far as it concerns my name, I would like to submit a few remarks, together with a few enclosures.

1. I am not a persona grata in Rome, now no more than in the past. I, therefore, insistently beg you and the colleagues on the board of Concilium not to make the discussion with the Roman authorities contingent on my participation in it, as a conditio sine qua non. I would be glad if the discussion were conducted without me by our colleagues Congar, Rahner and Schillebeeckx. I am convinced they would best represent in Rome that about which you and I are concerned. You may also rest assured that the fact of not being a party to this discussion neither vexes nor embitters me. I am rather glad if, in this way at least, the rapport between Rome and Concilium should grow a little friendlier.

2. Concerning the letter of Monsignor Colombo, I would like to *correct* a few errors. These are not to be charged to Monsignor Colombo personally, but are due no doubt to the fact that the Secretariat of State has not been sufficiently informed by the Congregation for the Doctrine of the Faith about my case. In the letter of Monsignor Colombo there are three statements that concern me. None of them agrees with the facts.

a. It is not correct to say that I have refused ("rifiuto") to participate in an interview with the Congregation for the Doctrine of the Faith. What is correct is this: From the beginning, I have explicitly voiced my willingness to participate in a discussion (cf. my letter to Monsignor Paul Philippe, Secretary of the Congregation for the Doctrine of the Faith, dated May 30, 1968).

b. It is not correct to say that this refusal is "a fact known far and wide" ("un fatto publicamente conosciuto"). What is correct is this: Press reports which are supposed to get their information from the Vatican have openly hurt my good name as a Catholic and as a theologian. They have reported from the Vatican that the Pope feels he has been offended by me, and that a meeting of the heads of Congregations concerned itself with my case. These press reports were picked up by the international press. They have never been denied by the Vatican. Only for this reason, did I release a short and moderate communiqué to the press to publicly set the record straight in my own defense. Apparently not even this has been taken into account in Rome; otherwise, they would no longer speak of a "fact known far and wide" ("un fatto publicamente conosciuto").

c. It is not correct to say that my "refusal" constitutes "a sort of challenge to the authority of the Holy See" ("una specie di sfida all'autorità della Santa Sede"). What is correct is this: Prescinding from the fact no one can say that I have refused to engage in a discussion, it can scarcely constitute a "challenge" to the Holy See if one sets conditions which have long been taken for granted in civilized countries (cf. again my letter to Monsignor Philippe, May 30, 1968). Besides, these conditions are supported in part by the utterances and instructions of Pope Paul VI himself. Further, they coincide with the conditions set forth in a petition forwarded to the Holy See on April 8, 1969 by 1360 renowned Catholic theologians from 53 countries to better safeguard the freedom of theology and theologians. Neither my letter nor this petition are a "challenge" ("sfida") to the Holy See. They are rather serious efforts at enhancing the credibility of the Holy See and especially of the Congregation for the Doctrine of the Faith in the Church and in the world. Few things do as much damage to the Catholic Church in the eyes of people today as repeated inquisitorial encroachments.

3. The course of the negotiations has developed as follows:

a. In a letter dated July 8, 1968, Monsignor Philippe granted item six in my letter of May 30, 1968 (reimbursement of expenses). Tacitly, he also granted item two (no conditions attached to the discussion).

b. In a letter of July 27, in which I reiterated my readiness to participate in a discussion, I also made a concession. I dropped item five (German as the language to be used in the proceedings). At the same time, I asked that the other items be regulated.

c. In a letter of August 31, 1968, Monsignor Philippe conceded item four (notification concerning the discussion partners: Father Dhanis, Witte, and Ahern), and item three (notification concerning the discussion topics). Basically then, only item one (access to my dossier, No. 399/57/i, and the order of procedure of the Congregation for the Doctrine of the Faith to be sent to me) is still pending.

d. As far as the present state of affairs is concerned, the decisive fact is this: On August 31, 1968, Monsignor Philippe informed me: "The topics to be discussed will be delivered to you soon." Yet these topics have not, until now, been given to me. If the discussion has failed to take place, the Congregation for the Doctrine of the Faith is alone responsible. Since 15 months have passed since this communication was issued, I cannot be far wrong if I assume that the proceedings against my book, *Die Kirche,* have, in fact, been terminated.

4. This does not mean at all that the matter is closed as far as I am concerned. With respect to my book, *Die Kirche,* accusations have been made, many decrees have been issued by the Congregation for the Doctrine of the Faith, and measures have been threatened. In many circles of the Catholic Church, my reputation as a Catholic theologian has been dealt a severe blow because of the interventions of the Congregation for the Doctrine of the Faith. Rumors, imputations, and calumnies have reached the world press, but the Holy See has never issued a dementi. Besides, I have not the slightest guarantee that the proceedings will not be resumed at some appropriate time, or that similar proceedings will not be initiated. All the more so in view of the fact that,

very recently, inquisitorial measures have been taken (Illich, Girardi) which have brought discredit on our Church before the eyes of the public at large. Likewise, the order of procedure of the Congregation for the Doctrine of the Faith has not been made public, contrary to the instructions of the Pope.

Since I must regard the proceedings of the Congregation for the Doctrine of the Faith as a "challenge" ("sfida") against me, I have, understandably enough, received with mixed feelings the suggestion to make "a good will gesture" ("un gesto di buona volontà"). It seems to me that it is rather the Congregation for the Doctrine of the Faith that should make a "good will gesture." However, since the whole affair has already done enough damage to our Church, I would not want to be petty. For the sake of the Church, I would like this to count as my good will gesture: I do not insist that I be publicly given total satisfaction. The only thing I am entitled to and must expect of the Congregation for the Doctrine of the Faith is a short official communication to the effect that the proceedings against my book, *Die Kirche,* have been terminated. Even with regard to this point, I do not ask for anything more than what in civilized countries today is a matter of custom and law in any legal action. As soon as such a communication on the part of the Congregation for the Doctrine of the Faith is released to the public, there will be no obstacles on my side to a discussion with the representatives of the Congregation for the Doctrine of the Faith before, during, or after an eventual discussion between the theologians of Concilium and the Roman authorities.

It was important for me, dear Mr. van den Boogaard, that I should give you and the colleagues of Concilium an objective account of the situation as it presents itself to me. I may emphasize once more that I consider it as important that a discussion should come about between the Roman authorities and theologians from Concilium, even if I should not take part in it. All the participants ought to have in mind only the good of the Church and of the people who constitute the Church. Permit me to add a personal word in this connection. My dossier at the Congregation for the Doctrine of the Faith, formerly the Holy Office, was started already in 1957, the year in which I received my doctorate in theology. The years since have been spent almost day in and day out in the service of the Church, working for the good of this our Church, often with my last energies. I have never regarded theology as anything but pastoral care, and this has given me much joy. I did not expect Rome to be grateful to me. However, this much I did expect: Not to be unjustly suspected over and over again by Roman authorities, attacked and condemned. Often I am being asked how one can manage, in spite of it all, to work constantly for our Church in the world, at the university, among our students. One does it because the message of Christ and the Church, as the community of believers, are entitled to expect from us the commitment of all our energies.

In the hope that this letter may serve to clarify the situation, I convey to you, Dear Mr. van den Boogaard, my friendly greetings.

Yours,
(signed) Hans Küng

cc.
Professors Congar, Rahner, Schillebeeckx

Enclosures:
1. Letter of Monsignor Philippe, April 30, 1968
2. Letter of Hans Küng, May 30, 1968
3. Letter of Monsignor Philippe, July 8, 1968
4. Letter of Hans Küng, July 27, 1968
5. Letter of Monsignor Philippe, August 31, 1968

Enclosure 8

LETTER OF THE CONGREGATION FOR THE DOCTRINE OF FAITH TO PROFESSOR KÜNG, January 24, 1970

399/57/i *January 24, 1970*

Dear Professor Küng:

The Congregation for the Doctrine of the Faith has received a copy of your letter of December 6, 1969, to Mr. van den Boogaard, President of the Foundation Concilium. Mr. van den Boogaard had sent your letter to the Secretariat of State, where preparations are in progress for an eventual meeting of representatives of the Holy See with representatives of the Foundation Concilium.

In the letters relative to this meeting, some misunderstandings have obviously arisen. For this reason and in order to inform you concerning the inquiry being conducted here about your work, *Die Kirche,* I give you the following information:

The Congregation for the Doctrine of the Faith has circulated no reports of any sort about the inquiry now in progress on your book, *Die Kirche,* or about you yourself. Nor is the Congregation responsible for what has been divulged concerning you in the press in and outside Rome.

Neither directly nor indirectly has the Congregation required of you a"good will gesture." Because the date for the discussion on your book, *Die Kirche,* had first been set on short notice, you were prevented by your schedule from attending the meeting. The Congregation did not, however, regard this fact as a refusal on your part to come and take part in any discussion. The Congregation only had reservations about some of your proposals relative to the discussion and rejected these; it accepted others. Thus, the names of the three discussion partners were sent to you, and you were promised to be informed about the items to be discussed.

True, the discussion has not yet taken place and indeed, for reasons for which you are not responsible. Perhaps you may know that one of the participants is not stationed in Europe. He happened to be staying in Rome on May 9, 1968. This was the reason why on April 30, 1968 an invitation was issued to you on short notice. Moreover, we intended to impart to you the order of procedure, as you wished. However, this could not be done until the order of procedure, which was being used experimentally, was printed. This is to be done soon.

As you see, the Congregation for the Doctrine of the Faith considers it as a matter of importance that you should be acquainted with the order of procedure before the discussion takes place, and that you should be convinced that the Congregation will proceed with loyalty, equity, and without arbitrariness. The foregoing shows that you are mistaken in your assumption that the examination of your book has been terminated. There is, then, no point to your request that the Congregation for the Doctrine of the Faith release an official declaration that the proceedings have been terminated.

After the *Modus procedendi in examine doctrinali* is published, you will receive another communication about the items still pending.

The Congregation for the Doctrine of the Faith asks you to share this letter with the persons to whom you addressed yourself in your letter of December 6, 1969; that is, Mr. van den Boogaard, Fathers Congar, Rahner and Schillebeeckx, so that these gentlemen, too, may be convinced that the intentions of this Congregation are loyal.

With the expression of my singular respect,

Devotedly yours,
(no signature)
[Card. Franjo Seper]

Enclosure 9

LETTER OF PROFESSOR KÜNG TO THE CONGREGATION FOR THE DOCTRINE OF THE FAITH, June 1, 1970

June 1, 1970

His Eminence
Cardinal Franjo Seper
Prefect of the Congregation for the Doctrine of the Faith
Vatican City

Your Eminence:

After a lengthy stay in Belgium, Holland, England, and the United States, I have come back to Tübingen at the beginning of the summer term. I can now answer your friendly letter. I am sorry that I was unable to answer it earlier.

In such a clear, objective, and benevolent way you have addressed the misunderstandings which have arisen in connection with the future discussion with your Congregation. For this, I am sincerely grateful. I gladly acknowledge that your Congregation is not responsible for the indiscretions and rumors circulated in the press concerning me. I am also glad to learn that your Congregation has not requested of me, directly or indirectly "a good will gesture." In particular, it is very important for me that you unambiguously state that the Congregation has never regarded as a refusal the fact that I was prevented by my schedule from taking part in the proposed discussion (in fact, I have repeated many times over that I was prepared to take part), and that I am not responsible for the postponement of the discussion.

No need to underline in particular that I have, with the greatest satisfaction, taken cognizance of the statement that, to use your own words, the Congregation will proceed with loyalty, equity, and without arbitrariness, and that the order of procedure of the Congregation is to be made public before the discussion and made available to me. I may no doubt assume that in formulating this order of procedure, attention will be paid to the constructive proposals which were worked out by various theologians connected with the publication Concilium and endorsed by 1,360 professors of theology all over the world.

A termination of the proceedings would have been welcome all the same. The book, *Die Kirche*, is entirely orthodox. Of this I am convinced now even more than three years ago when the book was published. The book strikes a middle course between a legalistic institutionalism and a fanaticism that rebels in principle against anything institutional, a fanaticism which is being espoused today within the Church, by way of a somewhat understandable over-reaction. The reason why I would have welcomed the termination of the proceedings is rather that I worry that the resumption of the proceedings will inflict additional harm on the Church, and further impair the credibility of the Roman authorities. Wherever I go, in Europe and elsewhere in the world, people speak to me about these proceedings. We cannot ignore the fact that the proposed discussion is linked to earlier decisions of the Congregation on the same book for which Your Eminence is not responsible, but which, contrary to the present intention of the Congregation, were not loyal, equitable and free from arbitrariness. I had to regard these as rather inquisitorial and discriminatory. It is true that, at present, the Inquisition is being repudiated in Rome (the letter of Your Eminence is a valuable confirmation of this); yet I am certainly entitled to sympathetic understanding if I again insist on the conditions for a discussion as set forth in the first letter I wrote to the Congregation concerning this matter.

This, then, is the reason why I still would welcome the termination of the proceedings, which were initiated under an unlucky star. The discussion could still take place independently of these proceedings, unburdened by the events of the past, and in the new spirit of loyalty, equity, and mutual understanding to which you refer.

However, I do not intend to give the Congregation for the Doctrine of the Faith orders as to how it should conduct its business. No matter how it all turns out, I am grateful that your letter has brought about a basic clarification. What comes of it, as particularly important for the negotiations between the Foundation Concilium and the Secretariat of State, is this: There is no reason why, because of me, a meeting between representatives of the Holy See and of the Foundation Concilium should not take place.

I, myself, have not desired this meeting, but neither have I opposed it. In view of what has happened, I would have had enough grounds for doing so. Rather, I have from the beginning explicitly agreed to it, which could be construed as "a good will gesture" on my part. Such a meeting could perhaps bring about a better understanding at a time when, more so than in the past, the Church needs the unity of all people of good will, and especially friendly rapport between the Curia and theologians in the Church. It is true that, on the basis of the Christian message itself, and together with many others, I hold the view that I must stand up for a broader and deeper understanding of what the papacy should be. And yet, as my book, *Die Kirche*, shows, I am deeply convinced that a renewed Petrine office is the source of many blessings in the Church. In this connection, if I may say this again with all modesty, I am also convinced that, through the critical and constructive theological positions I have taken in the book, *Die Kirche*, and in other publications, I have rendered the Pope a greater service among Catholics and non-Catholics than the numerous shallow-minded defenders and comfortable eulogizers of the Pope. I have no part in that basic anti-Roman sentiment which, because of various Roman interventions, is widespread in our Church. My concern was not and is not subversion and revolution, but thorough reform and renewal in the spirit of the Gospel of Jesus Christ. No matter how sharp my criticism of Rome had to be and, I am sorry to say, still has to be, whatever emerges from Rome in the spirit of the Gospel can always count on my cheerful support. Especially in Rome my criticisms may now and then sound harsh indeed and lacking in compassion (they come from the "periphery" and from a younger generation). Because of the plight of so many, steps that are by far too short and the slow pace of post-conciliar renewal put my patience to a hard test. I ask, if not for approval, at least for some understanding. It is important to me that, even in the Congregation for the Doctrine of the Faith, there should be no doubts about my fundamental attitude toward the Church. With God's grace, I hope to remain forever loyal to the Church. Besides, I do not regard myself as infallible. I submit all my theological views to public scrutiny in the Church. These criticisms, which I mean to ponder over, will help me not to grow rigid, as I thrust forward, but to remain always, even as a theology teacher, a learner of theology.

If I may summarize my letter: I sincerely thank Your Eminence for your clarifying and friendly letter. I conclude from it that you have never held the view that I had refused to participate in a discussion with the Congregation for the Doctrine of the Faith, and that I had been responsible for the postponement of the discussion. Now as before, I am agreeable to take part in a fair discussion. But I do suggest that the discussion should be separated from the proceedings which apparently are still in progress against me. For various reasons, I am of the opinion that these proceedings, begun two years ago, should be terminated. The discussion could take place apart from these. Unencumbered by these proceedings, the discussion would turn out to be all the more fruitful. Finally, I thank you that my case is being completely separated from the discussion being planned between the representatives of the Foundation Concilium and those of the Holy See. I have clearly said that I renounce taking part personally in this discussion if my person should prove to be an obstacle to the project. I would not want anyone to use me as an excuse to cancel this meeting. I am grateful to you for having said clearly enough that the idea to make me look the stumbling block cannot be attributed to you.

In keeping with your wishes, I have immediately shared your benevolent letter with the members of the Foundation Concilium whom you name. I will also share this letter with them. With the expression of my singular esteem, I convey to Your Eminence my greetings.

Devotedly yours,
(signed) Hans Küng

Enclosure 10

DECLARATION OF PROFESSOR KÜNG IN THE *Frankfurter Allgemeine Zeitung*, May 9, 1970

SUMMONS TO SELF-HELP

Concerning the Decree of the Pope on Mixed Marriages

Professor Hans Küng, a Catholic theologian at the University of Tübingen, known as a strong champion of conciliar theology, takes a wholly negative position with regard to the motu proprio of the Pope on mixed marriages. Here, he expounds his views for our readers.

The authority of the Church is still being sold down the river. After the abortive decisions concerning birth control, the law of celibacy, civil divorce, after the various attempts at restoring pre-conciliar theology (Encyclical on the Eucharist, the Papal Credo, the Dutch Catechism), and in view of a Roman "ecumenism" that limits itself to gestures and junkets, the motu proprio of Paul VI comes as a surprise only to those who had expected that, under this pontificate, serious steps would be taken toward the renewal of the Church and the attainment of ecumenical agreement. I do not mean to dispute the good intentions of the Pope nor the small improvements in the Roman system. And yet, once again, Rome takes positions which, theologically and practically, are out of date even within the Catholic Church, and which, in the long run, cannot be sustained. All of this damages the credibility of the Church and of authority of the Church, since it harms the people who are affected by it. By this I do not mean only married couples, but also people engaged in the care of souls. In the struggle of everyday life, these people are forced to eat up what a remote bureaucracy dishes out to them.

In this product of Roman legalism, there is hardly any trace of the liberating power of the message of Jesus. For him, the commandments are for the sake of people, not people for the sake of the commandments. As the time goes by, theology becomes less and less willing to render the Church leadership the dubious service that consists in trying to make such documents sound harmless, to pretty them up, and to "interpret" them so that the whole thing looks like a "historic turning point" and an "ecumenical breakthrough." This is what we read in episcopal press conferences. I leave to apologists the task of extracting from this document the "advances" it represents, when compared to earlier legislation. The Latin text of this obscure, clause-ridden, and vague decree no doubt offers much elbow room to legal hermeneutics. But this is precisely where its inner lack of veracity lies. Now as before, the mind remains closed to a clear, fundamental, theological and ecumenical solution. But when canon lawyers and episcopal conferences choose to make use of certain back doors, many things which, according to the decree, are a sin, can presumably be converted into virtue by means of individual dispensations. The decisive difference from previous legislation is that the power to dispense has moved from Rome to the bishops. Given the notorious conservatism of many bishops, episcopal conferences, and official advisers in matters of this kind, only the future will tell how this will all work out.

What remains important, when compared to all the improvements, possible or impossible, depending on how they are interpreted, is this: The fundamental solution of the question of mixed marriages has been once more indefinitely deferred. Such a solution ought to have included three things:

1. All mixed marriages ought to be recognized as valid, including those which are contracted without observing the canonical form. (In Germany, almost two thirds of the mixed marriages — in 1966, almost 71,000 out of 122,000 — are invalid. According to canon law, which otherwise shows little understanding for divorce, these marriages can be dissolved any time, since, according to canonical legislation,they are not sacramentally indissoluble marriages). The Decree is opposed to this recognition. It states: "Mixed marriages must be entered into in keeping with the canonical form. This form is indispensable to their validity" (No. 8). Dispensation (No. 9) does not solve the problem, since it requires the "sincere promise" that the children will be brought up as Catholics (cf. No. 4 and 15), a promise which in numberless cases cannot be made, not even with the greatest of efforts ("pro viribus").

2. An ecumenical rite for the celebration of marriage which, in some concrete way or other, takes the other church as an equal partner. The Decree is against this. It states: "The celebration of marriage before a Catholic priest or deacon and a non-Catholic clergyman, both performing together their respective rites, is prohibited. Nor is it permitted to have a religious wedding before or after the Catholic wedding for the giving or the renewal of consent" (No. 13). Understandably, no church is interested in a rite in which its representative may not officiate as an equal partner.

3. The decision concerning the baptism and upbringing of the offspring ought to be left to the conscience of the spouses. The Decree is against this: "In order to obtain from the bishop the dispensation from the impediment, the Catholic spouse must declare that he or she is prepared to remove the danger of defection from the faith. In addition, he or she has the strict obligation to honestly promise that, to the best of his or her ability, he or she will do everything to have all the children baptized and brought up in the Catholic Church" (No. 4). That such a promise is exacted only from the Catholic spouse does not constitute the recognition of the freedom of conscience for the spouse in such a conflict situation.

It sounds downright paradoxical when, in the preface to the Decree, spouses in a mixed marriage are reproachfully blamed for the fact that a mixed marriage introduces "a certain split into the living cell of the Church, as the Christian family is rightly called." As if mixed marriages were not the consequence but the cause of the separation of the churches, for which, as everyone knows, members of the hierarchy itself were largely responsible. To that extent, the first sentence in the motu proprio must be looked upon not only as a bitter irony but also as a formal error. It reads: "In keeping with her mandate, the Church has from time immemorial bestowed special care on mixed marriages."

But let us put aisde any further minute critique of this document. Let us ask ourselves the decisive question for the future: What are we to do now? Two things stand out:

1. Theologically. — The time has come to ask at least from what source the Church leadership actually derives the right to pronounce on the validity and lack of validity of marriages. From the standpoint of today's theology, it does not seem as if this right can be grounded. According to the Roman Decree itself, "to marry and to have children is a human right grounded on nature." It may be presumed that no bishop or pope may prevent two human beings from exercising this right.

When the sacramentality of marriage is invoked to justify the Church's right to pronounce on the validity of marriage, we counter: a. In contemporary theology, there is a dispute as to what extent marriage can be called a sacrament by comparison with baptism and the Lord's Supper. b. In any case, sacraments are for the sake of people. They do not abolish human rights. c. Even according to traditional Catholic doctrine, it is not the official of the Church (in the Decree he is referred to in pre-conciliar language as "the Church") who administers the "sacrament." The spouses do. Church officials perform mere auxiliary services, and these give them no power over the "sacrament."

2. Practically. — Over ten years have passed since the convocation of Vatican II, and over five years since the end of it. According to Pope John XXIII, the great goal of the Council was supposed to be the attainment of ecumenical understanding. Today, we are no longer satisfied when we notice "fruitful starts toward a solution." What we want now is the solution itself. In view of the fact that an irresponsible ecclesiastical legislation causes millions of people to have an uneasy conscience and to suffer disparagement, a solution cannot be deferred to any later time. Not only spouses are involved in a conflict of conscience, but also the most sensitive among the pastors and parish associates, who see the plight, want to help, and because of juridical stipulations cannot do so.

What are we then to do? The same as the bishops recommended with regard to birth-control: act according to conscience, and all the more so, since this very law attributes such great importance to the responsibility of conscience! For pastors, this means: use whatever latitude the law allows for, as extensively as possible. If this is not enough in a particular case, make concessions to the spouses as much as possible, even contrary to juridical stipulations.

In view of the fact that the problem becomes steadily more urgent even in German-speaking countries, a point could be reached where pastors no longer apply for dispensation. Elsewhere, and especially in the United States of America, this is already happening. In this way, the problem would be solved *via facti.* Some years ago, the question of fasting before communion was likewise resolved in this same way — *via facti.* As soon as this practice will prevail, Rome too will gain insight. As experience shows, it will ratify by law the new *status quo.*

Granted, in the question of responsible mixed marriages, as in the question of responsible parenthood, self-help is not the ideal or the desirable way of settling the problem. It is, however, the renewed failure of the leadership of the Catholic Church to solve an urgent problem of today that many times will not permit any other option.

We shall reach a basic turning point toward improvement only if a new self-understanding of the Catholic Church, permeated by the Gospel, prevails also in the various ranks of the "hierarchy." Only then will such secondary questions as mixed marriage, birth control, celibacy no longer conceal and displace time and again the Church's great errand, namely, what the reality of God should mean to people.

Enclosure 11/1

DECLARATION OF THE CONFERENCE OF GERMAN BISHOPS, May 19, 1970

Declaration of the Conference of German Bishops on May 19, 1970 on Professor Küng's article "Summons to Self-Help" in the Frankfurter Allgemeine Zeitung, *May 9, 1970*

In the first days after its publication, the motu proprio of Pope Paul VI "On the Juridical Regulation of Mixed Marriages" has encountered mixed acceptance. Obviously, a number of very critical positions were traceable to an inadequate translation prematurely issued and to hurried critical commentaries based on inadequate acquaintance with the matter at hand. Meanwhile important statements have been made, even in non-Catholic circles, which do, on the whole, amount to a positive assessment, in spite of the many criticisms.

This makes it all the more difficult to understand how, in the *Frankfurter Allgemeine Zeitung* of May 9, 1970, Hans Küng, a Catholic theologian and professor of theology at the University of Tübingen, should take, with regard to the motu propio of the Pope, a stand which is not only polemical and offensive in parts, but does not hesitate to invite people to disregard stipulations of the law.

The Conference of German Bishops feels under obligation to disavow in every way the view advocated in this article. The motu proprio goes back to the clear decisions of the First Synod of Bishops. The wishes of the episcopal conferences were extensively taken into account in the final revision. To go against the stipulations of a document so well grounded cannot truly serve the cause of reform in the Church. The bishops expect that, guided by an ecclesial sentiment, the priests will endeavor to understand the difficult and complex questions, and that, in their pastoral ministry, they will conduct themselves in keeping with the instructions of the motu proprio.

RESPONSE OF PROFESSOR KÜNG, May 27, 1970

To the criticisms directed in the name of the Conference of German Bishops and by individual Bishops to his comments on Rome's new Decree on mixed marriages, Professor Küng replied on May 27, 1970 with the following declaration:

One would have expected the bishops to respond to my article on the new Decree on mixed marriages with an understanding and helpful word for the totally unnecessary juridical predicament of mixed marriages and for the pastors involved in this predicament. What we have instead is "Declarations" and pedantic lectures, which attack the critic personally, without producing any arguments, or sulk without letting anyone know why.

In Vatican II, the decision concerning the question of mixed marriages was by a strong majority remanded to the Pope for definitive resolution. In the 1967 Synod of Bishops, in contrast to Cardinal Döpfner (acting in the name of a large majority of German bishops), about one third of the bishops together with Cardinal Alfrink favored removing the impediment of mixed religion, including the unilaterally demanded promise to educate the children in the Catholic faith. This view did not prevail. As is often the case, what prevailed instead was a compromise proposal. And yet, even the decisions of bishops, no more than the statements of theologians, can claim to be exempt from all criticism in society and in the Church.

The new papal Decree does not solve the decisive problems: validity of mixed marriages, ecumenical rite for weddings based on equal rights for both confessions, decision concerning baptism and upbringing left to the conscience of the spouses. This is a fact that not even bishops can deny. To attribute the "mixed acceptance" with which, according to the bishops, the Decree has been received also in Germany and the number of very critical positions to an "inadequate translation" (as far as I know, the translation comes from the papal Secretariat of State) and "to hurried critical commentaries based on inadequate acquaintance with the matter at hand" (last but not least, these come from canonists and theologians), conceals the true grounds of the criticism. My own article was based on the original Latin text.

The predicament which Church law conjures up for the conscience of spouses and involved pastors is not eliminated by the new Decree. This is shown by a new promissory formula published this week by the chancery office of an otherwise sensitive bishop. Hiddenly, and yet in a clear way, this formula again lays upon the marriages of the future the burden of conflict.

"a. Declaration and promise of the Catholic spouse.—I am instructed concerning my responsibility to have the children baptized and brought up as Catholics. I acknowledge that this is an obligation binding in conscience. I sincerely promise that I will, to the best of my ability, take pains that the children born of our marriage will be baptized and brought up in the Catholic Church. Given the present attitude of my non-Catholic spouse, I cannot tell in advance to what extent I can fulfil this promise. My Protestant spouse knows, however, that I cannot be released from that promise.—Signature of the Catholic spouse.

b. Declaration of the non-Catholic spouse.—I am instructed as to the obligation binding upon the conscience of my Catholic spouse relative to the baptism and upbringing of our children.—Signature of the non-Catholic spouse.

c. I certify the signature of the spouses.—Signature of the pastor."

This writer is not alone in his prognosis as to the further development of mixed marriages. In his significant speech, at the first session of the Papal Theological Commission (cf. *Frankfurter Allgemeine Zeitung,* April 8, 1970), no less a man than Karl Rahner, a man whose complete Catholic orthodoxy no bishop in Germany will impugn, said the following: "Today, the question of mixed marriages is still largely unresolved. Many questions relative to this topic are not yet sufficiently attended to. In the praxis, truly divine right and merely ecclesiastical law are often confused one with the other. In addition, it is often mistakenly presupposed that all depends here on the free concession on the part of the authority of the Church, without the thing itself, and the concrete circumstances of our time imposing any norms and limits to that authority. Unless, after thorough and yet prompt reflection, laws are enacted which are simple, really easy to understand and unencumbered by numberless exceptions and legalistic procedures, nothing will happen, except that people in general, and the younger clergy itself, will no longer bother with the laws."

A summons to act according to conscience under difficult circumstances, and even against specific legal stipulations, means neither rebellion against the leadership of the Church, nor "open disobedience" (Archbishop Schäufele). The Conference of German Bishops has advocated acting according to conscience against *Humanae Vitae* in the matter of birth-control. It would then also be affected by this reproach. With regard to the relationship between Magisterium and theology, the topic of Archbishop Schäufele's sermon on Pentecost Day (including the naming of names), I plan to address this issue shortly in a separate publication. Five years after the end of the Council, and after all too many negative experiences, time has come to take up this issue of the authority of the Church in matters of doctrine and to speak a clear word about it.

If, unlike in the celibacy issue, the Conference of German Bishops should decide to be of service to the freedom of the Christian conscience and help it to achieve a breakthrough, at least by means of a very generous interpretation of the Roman Decree, *(secundum, praeter,* or, under certain circumstances, *contra legem),* my article would have achieved its purpose. This article is written in such sharp yet objective language for no other reason than to rouse from sleep the leadership of the Church. In this manner, too, the public expects not lone resolutions of episcopal conferences, but confident cooperation of the bishops with all the theologians, all the canonists, the pastors, the leadership of the Protestant denominations, the mixed marriage circles, the associations of priests, and with all those who have made special efforts to resolve the issue. Needless to say, the writer will not be stingy in his praise and recognition if, in the service of people, the leadership of the Church "should, for God's sake, perform an act of courage" (Zwingli).

DECLARATION OF THE CONFERENCE OF GERMAN BISHOPS, February 4, 1971

Declaration of the Conference of German Bishops concerning the book of Professor Dr. Hans Küng, Unfehlbar ? Eine Anfrage, *February 4, 1971*

In the book, *Unfehlbar ? Eine Anfrage* (Einsiedeln: Benzinger Verlag, 1970), fundamental questions are raised concerning the possibility of there being in the Church a normative statement of faith. These touch, in part, on basic tenets of the Catholic understanding of the faith and of the Church. The Conference of German Bishops believes that some of these tenets are not being safeguarded in the aforementioned book. These concerns are not removed even after further declarations by the author and after a discussion with him mandated by the Episcopal Conference. It is not the task of bishops to take a stand on the controversial questions, technical and theological in nature, which are again at issue because of this book. However, the Conference of German Bishops feels obligated to mention some non-negotiable givens which no theology can deny if it is to remain Catholic.

1. The faith in the Word of God, attested to in the Bible and confessed by the Church in the Creed, presupposes that even there, in spite of the ambiguity and historical mutability of human language, there should exist in principle the possibility of statements:

a. which are true and recognizable as true, and

b. whose meaning remains the same, and whose validity remains unrescindable, while thought patterns and speech undergo historical change.

2. The normativeness proper to God's word of revelation finds its concrete expression in the Creed of the Church. In it, the Church responds to God's Word attested to in the Bible and makes this Word her own. True, the faith of the Church always needs to be reflected upon afresh. To this extent, it remains open-ended until the end of history. And yet, it includes an unchangeable Yes and an unchangeable No. The Yes and the No are not interchangeable, one for the other. Otherwise, the Church could not remain in the truth of Jesus Christ.

3. With regard to questions raised anew in given historical situations, it is the right and the duty of the Church, on the one hand, to make room for a thorough reflection on faith, and, on the other, to give expression, whenever necessary, to her unchangeable Yes and No. "Dogmas" is the name we give to formulations which help to clarify the Creed, thus providing, in fact, an interpretation of the witness intended by the Scriptures. These are set forth by the Church with truly ultimate normativeness.

4. A dogma does not draw its own proper normativeness from the outcome of the theological debate, nor from the assent of a majority in the Church, but from the charism given to the Church to maintain the Word, once proclaimed in the force of its own truth, and to interpret it unerringly. The task of insuring that, through binding statements of faith, the Church should remain in the truth of the Gospel is entrusted, in a special way of its own, to the Magisterium. Reception in the Church of any such dogmatic statements may be important as

a sign of the Church's agreement with the normative source, but it is not the basis of either the truth or the authority of the statements.

5. According to the common and clear doctrine of the Roman Catholic Church and of the Eastern Churches, the power to issue such ultimately binding statements pertains first and foremost to the ecumenical councils, as representing the whole episcopacy. Together with Vatican I and II and with the tradition to which these two councils gave concrete expression, the Catholic Church also believes that the exercise of this power pertains also to the bishop of Rome, as successor of Peter and head of the college of bishops. The conditions required for such authoritative utterances are derived from the tradition of the Church, and are set forth in both Vatican Councils.

February 4, 1971
(Published, February 8, 1971)

Enclosure 13

DECLARATION OF PROFESSOR HANS KÜNG, February 9, 1971

Professor Hans Küng on the declaration of the Conference of German Bishops of February 8, 1971

In its declaration of my book, *Unfehlbar ? Eine Anfrage,* the Conference of German Bishops happily refrains from any condemnation. The five points which the bishops make allow for different interpretations. To a large extent, they support my concern. However, the question raised in the book concerning the possibility of propositions not only true but guaranteed as infallible is avoided. Significantly, the word "infallible" does not occur once in the whole declaration. This means that the bishops allow room to a further constructive discussion of this issue, which is of fundamental importance for today's Church.

Tübingen, February 9, 1971

Enclosure 14

DECLARATION OF THE CONFERENCE OF GERMAN BISHOPS, March 4, 1971

Reply of the Conference of German Bishops to the statement of Professor Dr. Hans Küng with regard to the declaration of the Conference of German Bishops of February 4, 1971 [see above, enclosures 12 and 13]

The Epsicopal Conference dealt also with the statement of Professor Küng in its own declaration on his book, *Unfehlbar ?* Among other things, this declaration also contains the statement that in his book some basic tenets of the Chris-

tian understanding of the faith appear not to be safeguarded. The Conference is glad to notice that, in his reply to the President of the Conference, Professor Küng does not contradict this declaration. The Conference must, however, reject his view that the infallibility question is not being touched upon in this declaration. The text makes it clear that the Magisterium of the Church has the specific power to interpret normatively the faith of the Church. With this, the proper content of the doctrine of infallibility is expressed, a doctrine which in Professor Küng is at least obscured. He speaks of "propositions whose infallibility is guaranteed a priori," a formulation which is alien to the tradition of the Church. The declaration of the bishops has avoided the word "infallible" and used other formulations, the word "unerringly" for example, so as not to be identified with the distorted interpretation of Küng. For this reason, a contradiction exists between the statements of the Episcopal Conference, what one must derive from the book and from subsequent utterances of Professor Küng.
Bad Honnef, March 4, 1971

Enclosure 15

LETTER OF THE CONGREGATION FOR THE DOCTRINE OF THE FAITH TO PROFESSOR KÜNG, February 12, 1971

399/57/i *February 12, 1971*

Dear Professor Küng:

Your book, *Unfehlbar ? Eine Anfrage,* published by Benzinger and also translated into Italian under the title, *Infallibile ? Una domanda* (Brescia: Quiriniana), carries no Imprimatur. According to canon 1385, paragraph 1 and 2, the Imprimatur is required. Moreover, you maintain in the body of the book itself that you have deliberately dispensed with the Church's permission to publish because you yourself are of the opinion that your book is still Catholic.

Prescinding from the question whether or not a Catholic may at all raise the questions you raise in your book, it is necessary to state the following: unambiguously, and not for the first time, you have brushed aside a valid prescription of the Church which, in spite of many discussions, is by no means abrogated. You use your reputation to urge publicly people to disobey legitimate authorities, as for example in the question of mixed marriages. Allow me to invite you to reflect on the position which you hold in the Church and the impact and consequences of your undertaking.

In the hope that you will then come to the conclusion that in this way one cannot truly love and serve the Church, I remain,

Devotedly yours,
(no signature)

Enclosure 16

LETTER OF PROFESSOR KÜNG TO THE CONGREGATION FOR THE DOCTRINE OF THE FAITH, February 26, 1971

February 26, 1971

His Eminence
Cardinal Franjo Seper
Prefect of the Congregation for the Doctrine of the Faith
Piazza del S. Uffizio, 11
Vatican City

Your Eminence:

I have undertaken cognizance of your friendly letter of February 12, 1971.

I wil gladly think over your exhortations. With regard to the question of the Imprimatur, Dr. O. Bettschart, Director of the Publishing House Benzinger, has already submitted a detailed statement in a letter to you dated February 10, 1971. You invite me, in addition, to reflect well about my position in the Church. May I, then, take the liberty to send you a manuscript which originated independently of your letter, and yet summarizes my thoughts in this connection. It should emerge from this manuscript that, in everything, and even when I must be uncomfortable, my concern is to be of service to the Church.

I do not intend to impose my personal views on the Church or to issue a call to rebellion. What I want instead is to make a contribution to the renewal of the Church in obedience to the critical norm of the Gospel of Jesus Christ, and this, if you will, in season and out of season. I make myself available for any discussion in which arguments are brought forth, not just verdicts. Evidence of this will be found in a little volume of discussions of the book, *Die Kirche*, which collects the most important reactions and reviews, gives an account of the debate, and states the author's position. I hope to be able to send you this volume soon for your information.

I send you friendly greetings.

Very devotedly yours,
(signed) Hans Küng

LETTER OF THE CONGREGATION FOR THE DOCTRINE OF THE FAITH TO PROFESSOR KÜNG, May 6, 1971

399/57/i *May 6, 1971*

Professor Dr. Hans Küng
Tübingen
Germany

Dear Profesor Küng:

As you have already been informed, the Congregation for the Doctrine of the Faith is examining your book, *Die Kirche.* In accordance with the new procedural norms of the Congregation, "Ratio agendi in doctrinarum examine," a copy of which I enclose, we are sending you in the enclosure the theses contained in your book which the Congregation for the Doctrine of the Faith regards as erroneous or dangerous.

I ask you to reply to these theses in writing within a month (cf. the Norms of Procedure, No. 13).

Respectfully,
(no signature)

(two enclosures)

ON THE BOOK OF HANS KÜNG, DIE KIRCHE

The Congregation for the Doctrine of the Faith has some difficulties concerning the book of Professor Hans Küng, *Die Kirche* (1967). Although the Congregation regrets that the book often speaks too negatively about the Church, it does acknowledge that the merits of the book are not slight. It highly praises the author's copious erudition, the synthetic power of his presentation, and the ecumenical spirit of the same.

The difficulties concern primarily two points: first, the unity of the Church; second, the necessity of the sacrament of orders for a valid consecration of the Eucharist.

I. THE UNITY OF THE CHURCH
(*Die Kirche,* pp. 313-352)

Does the author understand the doctrine of Vatican II according to which the Church "subsists" ["subsistit"] in the Catholic Church, governed by the successor of Peter and the bishops united with him? (*Lumen Gentium,* 8 [Abbott, 23]) He translates "subsistit in" by "exists in" ["existiert in"], and seems to identify "church *elements* which are present elsewhere" with the other "churches and ecclesial communities" (p. 337). This could easily favor the conclusion that the Church of Christ exists, according to its primary element, in the Catholic Church, and, according to its other elements, in the other churches of ecclesial communities. The Council reads: "This Church [of Christ] . . . subsists in the Catholic Church . . . although *many elements of sanctification and truth can be found outside her visible structure.* These elements, however, as gifts properly belonging to the Church of Christ, possess an inner dynamism toward Catholic unity" (ibid.). These "elements" are not the churches and ecclesial communities, but some sacraments, perhaps, or some revealed truths.

It seems as if the author's mind is attracted to the notion that the Church of Christ, whose unity is torn asunder, consists of all the churches and ecclesial communities. Cf. "Eine Kirche," pp. 312-352. We have noticed that, unless we are mistaken, the author does not acknowledge the following: "For it is through Christ's Catholic Church *alone* . . . that *the fullness of the means of salvation can be obtained.* It was to the apostolic college *alone,* of which Peter is the head, that we believe our Lord entrusted all the blessings of the New Covenant" (*Unitatis redintegratio,* 3 [Abbott, 346]). "For although the Catholic Church has been endowed with all divinely revealed truth and all means of grace. . ." (*Unitatis redintegratio,* 4 [Abbott, 348])

II. NECESSITY OF THE SACRAMENT OF ORDERS FOR THE VALID CELEBRATION OF THE EUCHARIST (*Die Kirche,* pp. 519-522)

Chiefly on the basis of an argument from silence, the author believes that at the time when First Corinthians was written the faithful in the Corinthian church celebrated the Eucharist without conferring the priestly office by the imposition of hands. From this belief, from the doctrine of sacraments received by desire ("in voto"), and from the doctrine of the priesthood of the faithful (with the addition of remarks of minor importance), the author conjectures that, in abnormal cases, the Eucharist may be consecrated by non-ordained baptized persons. For this reason, he maintains that the celebration of the Eucharist in many Protestant communities is invalid due to the lack of an ordained priesthood. Vatican II speaks differently. Cf. *Unitatis redintegratio,* 22 [Abbott, 363-364].

We know that other theologians (most of them later than the author) have expressed such views as these, at least conjecturally. However, the arguments of the author do not appear valid to us. We feel that, in this matter, he should take into consideration that the Magisterium teaches, especially, Fourth Lateran, Trent, and Vatican II.

Enclosure 18

LETTER OF PROFESSOR KÜNG TO THE CONGREGATION FOR THE DOCTRINE OF THE FAITH, June 21, 1971

June 21, 1971

His Eminence
Cardinal Franjo Seper
Prefect of the Congregation for the Doctrine of the Faith
Vatican City

Your Eminence:

Various obligations in the course of an arduous semester have prevented me from replying earlier to your letter of May 6, 1971. I beg for your indulgence.

Replying to your letter would have been an easier task for me if the new norms of procedure had cleared away the objections which I have raised against the procedure of your Congregation in my letter of May 30, 1968, and have since repeated in various letters. Unfortunately, this has not happened. I applaud the publication of the norms. I have studied these carefully. As the Congregation for the Doctrine of the Faith no doubt knows, these norms have aroused sharp criticism among Catholics and non-Catholics, and in my opinion rightly so. There are improvements in particular points, and these I gladly acknowledge. However, the norms are not at all free of the spirit of the Inquisition. They certainly fall short of the very moderate claims which the 1360 theology professors the world over have set forth in a declaration intended to promote the freedom of theology.

In your letter of January 24, 1970, you informed me that "the Congregation will proceed with loyalty, equity, and without arbitrariness." But I cannot regard these proceedings as loyal, equitable and free from arbitrariness, since I am still being denied access to official documents, since I am kept entirely in the dark as to the course of the still secret proceedings, and since I cannot choose my own "defender" (relator "pro auctore") who is, in fact, entirely unknown to me. Besides, within these "ordinary proceedings", "extraordinary" ones are possible any time beyond the pale of legality. One merely needs to compare the new procedural norms with the norms which are routine in constitutional states to notice immediately that the norms of the Congregation for the Doctrine of the Faith must, unfortunately, still be regarded as inquisitional and discriminatory. I consider it my duty to uphold in every respect my objections against such norms and to confirm these objections. In my letter of June 1, 1970, I have already made it abundantly clear that I do this impelled by an ecclesial spirit, Here I need only to refer to what was said there.

Meanwhile, I would not want to fail to acknowledge with gratitude that, for the first time, the Congregation for the Doctrine of the Faith has recognized that "the merits of the book are not slight." With regard to the two difficulties of the Congregation, I would respond as follows:

1. Concerning the Unity of the Church.—

My interpretation of the expression "subsistit in" (*Lumen Gentium,* 8) as meaning "exists in" is based on the interpretation which I personally discussed in the Council with Monsignor Gerard Philips (Louvain), the second secretary of the Theological Commission of Vatican II. I further refer to the Commentary of Professor A. Grillmeier, S. J., another expert in the Commission, in the Supplement to the *Lexikon für Theologie und Kirche,* Part I. On p. 175, he writes: "No absolute, exclusive judgment of identity is uttered, such as, for instance, that the Church of Christ "is" the Catholic Church. . . . Hence the one true Church of Christ does exist. It is recognizable, and visible in its own way. . . . But "ecclesiality" does not simply coincide with the Catholic Church, because ecclesial elements of sanctification and truth can be found outside it. This brings up the question of the "ecclesiality" of the Churches and communities apart from the Catholic, which involves on the one hand their quality as mediators of salvation, and on the other hand, the necessity of the Catholic Church for salvation. These problems are not fully discussed here." [ET; *Commentary on the Documents of Vatican II,* Vol. I, p. 150] The pertinent section in my book, *Die Kirche,* was meant to carry forward the clarification of these problems.

2. The necessity of ordination for the valid consecration of the Eucharist.—

It is not the contention that an ordained presbyter is lacking in the community of Corinth that seems to rest on an argument from silence, but the contention that one is present. I raised the question because it emerges from the texts, because it was ignored in pre-conciliar Catholic literature, and it could not be answered by competent Council theologians whom I queried during the Council. If one could name me one serious theologian who does offer a serious argument for the presence in Corinth of an ordained presbyter, I would be grateful. Unfortunately, not even *Unitatis redintegratio,* 22 answers this question. At the end of the pertinent passage, it says explicitly: "For these reasons, dialogue should be undertaken concerning the true meaning of the Lord's Supper, the other sacraments, and the Church's worship and ministry" [Abbott, 364]. In the aforementioned Commentary [Part II, p. 118f.; ET, Vol. II, p. 155], Professor Joseph Feiner, consultant of the Secretariat for the Unity of Christians, writes in this connection: "Neither the Reformation Churches nor the Catholic Church may regard the present state of their understanding in the field of the sacraments as something final and complete. Consequently, the last sentence of the article stresses the necessity of dialogue between the churches on this subject in the hope that it will lead to a more profound understanding of faith and to the drawing together of the churches." This is precisely what I have tried to do in my book. In fact, the dialogue on this question has made considerable progress in the meantime, as it appears from the volume edited by Hermann Häring and Josef Nolte, *Diskussion um Hans Küng DIE KIRCHE* (1971). There, other exegetes and theologians and I discuss thoroughly and constructively the exegetical and dogmatic questions that have been raised. I may, therefore, draw your attention to this volume, which I sent to Your Eminence right after its publication. Should it have failed to arrive, please let me know. I would gladly send you a second copy.

Your Eminence, I hope that these remarks will satisfactorily solve the difficulties of the Congregation.

With the expression of my singular esteem, I remain,

Devotedly yours,
(signed) Hans Küng

Enclosure 19

LETTER OF THE CONGREGATION FOR THE DOCTRINE OF THE FAITH TO PROFESSOR KÜNG, July 12, 1971

399/57/i *July 12, 1971*

Professor Dr. Hans Küng
Waldhäuserstrasse 23
D 74 Tübingen
GERMANY

Dear Professor Küng:

The Congregation for the Doctrine of the Faith has initiated doctrinal proceedings against your book, *Unfehlbar ? Eine Anfrage.*

By a decree of June 23, 1971, approved by the Holy Father on June 25, 1971, the plenary assembly of this Congregation has decided that you should be informed in writing of the theses in this book which, in the basis of the inquiry conducted by this Congregation, seem to conflict with Catholic doctrine.

In the enclosure, I am sending you the list of these theses which cause difficulties to the Congregation as far as a Catholic interpretation is concerned. I ask you to explain to the Congregation in writing within thirty days whether and in what way you believe that these theses and opinions can be reconciled with the Catholic faith.

With the expression of my esteem, I remain,

Devotedly yours,
(no signature)

QUESTIONS ON THE BOOK *UNFEHLBAR ? EINE ANFRAGE* By HANS KÜNG (Zurich, 1970)

In the implementation of its office, the Sacred Congregation for the Doctrine of the Faith requests Professor Hans Küng to explain certain statements in his book, *Unfehlbar ?* and to answer some questions relative to these. The Congregation for the Doctrine of the Faith has noticed that, on the one hand, Professor Küng advances his opinions as if they were open to discussion, and on the other he maintains that these opinions, even when advocated by the Catholic theologian in this tentative manner, remain within the boundaries of Catholic doctrine.

I. ON THE AUTHENTIC MAGISTERIUM IN THE CHURCH

The author writes: "Certainly some popes in recent times . . . have continually attempted absolutely and exclusively to reserve to themselves (and, when it suited them, also to the bishops) the 'authentic' explanation of the 'deposit of faith'. . . . From all that has been said in this book, from beginning to end, it is clear that the Holy Spirit is not given only to pope and bishops in authentic fashion for the salvation of the Church, . . . [and] that the 'authentic' proclamation and exposition of the Christian message is not 'reserved' to anyone" (p. 191 [ET by E. Quinn, Hans Küng, *Infallible ? An Inquiry* (Garden City: Doubleday, 1971) p. 234]).

This Sacred Congregation remarks:

(1) "Authentic Magisterium" is a technical expression which refers to the Magisterium of those who "endowed with the authority of Christ . . . preach to the people committed to them the faith they must believe and put into practice. By the light of the Holy Spirit, they make that faith clear . . ." (*Lumen Gentium,* 25 [Abbott, 47]). Precisely because it is the Magisterium of those who are *endowed with the authority of Christ* in various ways and degrees, according to the way in which it is exercised, the faithful "are . . . to adhere to it with a religious assent of soul" (ibid. [Abbott, 48]).

(2) According to the Constitution *Dei Verbum,* "The task of authentically interpreting the word of God, whether written or handed down, has been entrusted exclusively to the living teaching office of the Church, whose authority is exercised in the name of Jesus Christ" (*Dei Verbum,* 10 [Abbott, 117-118]).

(3) The Constitution *Lumen Gentium* credits the authentic Magisterium to no one except the bishops and the pope (art. 25). However, it clearly acknowledges that the Holy Spirit through the "sense of the faith" arouses and sustains the whole people of God (art. 12 [Abbott, 29]).

(4) All this is traditional in the Church. The theologian is not being prevented by this from devoting himself to scholarly teaching, which is not to be confused with "authentic" teaching. Nor is the theologian's task suppressed by the fact that the Magisterium has the task of looking into the inquiries of theologians and the spiritual lights of "charismatics."

(5) The author denies that the authentic Magisterium *is reserved* to "some", that is, "to the bishops and the pope."

How can a Catholic theologian do this?

II. ON THE INFALLIBILITY OF THE COLLEGE OF BISHOPS AND OF THE POPE

The author writes:

(1) ". . . The statements about an infallibility of the college of bishops, based on traditional, unhistorical theory of a direct and exclusive apostolic succession

of the bishops, exegetically, historically, theologically, have feet of clay. That is to say, unless the substantiation were to be supplied by the basic source to which Vatican II, in article 25 on the infallibility of pope and bishops constantly refers" (p. 68 [ET, 86]).

(2) "If the foundations of neoscholastic doctrine on infallibility are so fragile and its expression, both in connection with the pope (Vatican I) and in connection with the episcopate (Vatican II), creates so many unsolved and perhaps insoluble problems, would not the simplest and best solution be to abandon altogether the whole doctrine of ecclesiastical infallibility?" (p. 151 [ET, 125]).

This Sacred Congregation believes that, at least by expressing doubt, such assertions as these conflict with the doctrine of Vatican II, and with the constant practice of the Church, starting with the first ecumenical councils. In regard to the pope, that doctrine has been defined. The author seems to be denying the infallibility of the ecumenical councils.

If this interpretation of the author is correct, how can he justify his opinion?

III. INDEFECTIBILITY INSTEAD OF INFALLIBILITY

The author would prefer to admit the "indefectibility" rather than the "infallibility" of the Church. He describes indefectibility as follows: "A fundamental remaining of the Church in truth, which is not annulled by individual errors" (p. 148 [ET, 181]).

This Sacred Congregation believes that this ought to be said: The "particular errors" which, according to the author, "indefectibility" would allow for, *either* do not, *or* do, refer to what the supreme Magisterium of the Church defines as doctrine of faith. If the author maintains that they do not, he preserves Catholic doctrine. If the author maintains that they do, (the context inclines in this direction), he departs from the doctrine of Vatican I (DS, 3011) and of Vatican II (*Lumen Gentium,* 25 [Abbott, 47-48]). Can a Catholic theologian think that he is permitted to do this?

IV. ON INFALLIBLE PROPOSITIONS

The author admits that the faith of the Church needs propositions to be believed, since one section of his book bears the caption "The faith of the Church is dependent on propositions of faith" (p. 116 [ET, 144]). However, he adds that it cannot be proved that faith needs infallible propositions. He writes: "It has not been proved that faith is dependent on infallible propositions" (p. 122 [ET, 150]). But for centuries the Church has been requiring that symbols and professions of faith be assented to with the firmness of an assent absolutely certain. Does this not show that in these symbols and professions of faith infallible propositions are set forth, that is, definitions? The author explains that the faithful can "throughout all perhaps ambiguous or perhaps in particular even false propositions, commit themselves in their whole existence to the message, to the person proclaimed: they can believe *in* Jesus Christ. It is this faith alone," he adds, "that can give certainty: the peace that surpasses all reason" (p. 156 [ET, 192]).

However, this *Sacred Congregation* notes that, in many professions of faith, the Church demands a very firm statement of faith, even to specific propositions, especially concerning the person of Christ. (All these contribute to an extent to exhibiting the mystery of God which saves us through the Christ.) The formula *Quicumque* may serve as an example. It begins: "Anyone who wants to be saved must first of all hold the Catholic faith. Unless this faith be preserved in its integrity and inviolability, one will most certainly incur eternal damnation" (DS, 75). Consider also Lateran IV: "We firmly believe and unambiguously profess that . . ." (DS, 800). Likewise, the Tridentine formula of faith says: "I, N., believe with a firm faith and profess each and every doctrine contained in the (Constantinopolitan) symbol of faith" (DS, 1862).

We request of the author that, even with regard to this question, he submit an explanation.

Enclosure 20

LETTER OF PROFESSOR KÜNG TO THE CONGREGATION FOR THE DOCTRINE OF THE FAITH, July 19, 1971

399/57 *Moscow, July 19, 1971*

Your Eminence:

Your letter reached me a few hours before my departure for a journey around the world. I am writing from my first stop, where I am engaging in conversations with the Russian-Orthodox Church. Unfortunately, for the time being, it is totally impossible for me to answer your letter in a manner commensurate to the seriousness of the business at hand. I will have the possibility of doing this only after I return home and look at the records. I, therefore, beg you to wait until that time.

With sincere regard, I remain,

Devotedly yours,
(signed) Hans Küng

Enclosure 21

LETTER OF THE CONGREGATION FOR THE DOCTRINE OF THE FAITH TO PROFESSOR KÜNG, December 17, 1971

399/57/i *December 17, 1971*

Professor Dr. Hans Küng
Waldhäuserstrasse, 23
D 74 Tübingen
GERMANY

Dear Professor Küng:

On July 12, 1971, I sent you various questions, with the request to answer them for the Congregation for the Doctrine of the Faith. These questions concerned your book, *Unfehlbar ? Eine Anfrage.*

In a letter from Moscow on July 19, 1971, you answered that you were travelling, and you asked for patience until your return.

I hereby request again that you answer the questions put to you within thirty days after receiving this letter.

With the expression of my esteem, I remain,

Devotedly yours,
(no signature)

Enclosure 22

LETTER OF PROFESSOR KÜNG TO THE CONGREGATION FOR THE DOCTRINE OF THE FAITH, January 24, 1972

Tübingen
January 24, 1972

His Eminence
Cardinal Franjo Seper
Prefect of the Congregation for the Doctrine of the Faith
Vatican City

Your Eminence:

In a registered, special delivery, letter of July 12, 1971 you informed me that the Congregation for the Doctrine of the Faith had initiated doctrinal proceedings against my book, *Unfehlbar ? Eine Anfrage,* and that, in a decree of June 23, 1971, approved by the Holy Father on June 25, 1971, the plenary assembly of the Congregation for the Doctrine of the Faith had decided to inform me in writing of the theses which, on the basis of an inquiry conducted by the Congregation, seemed to conflict with Catholic doctrine. Within thirty days, I would have to explain in writing whether and in what way these theses and opinions can, in my opinion, be reconciled with Catholic doctrine.

In a letter from Moscow, dated July 15, 1971, [July 19, 1971; translator's correction], I advised you that your letter had reached me a few hours before my departure for a tour of lectures and study around the world, and that it would not be possible during this journey to reply to your letter in a manner commensurate to the seriousness of the business at hand. I had to beg you to wait until I could return home and examine the records.

I returned to Tübingen December 6. I had already drafted this reply when I received your reminder of December 17, 1971. This letter arrived at Christmas time, just as the letter which, four years ago, your predecessor, Cardinal Ottaviani, wrote to me to interdict the further dissemination and translation of my book, *Die Kirche.*

I have not taken lightly the task of responding to your letter. I would like to respond in two parts.

I. FUNDAMENTAL OBJECTIONS AGAINST THE PROCEEDINGS OF THE CONGREGATION

Already on May 6 of the same year, 1971, you sent me a letter of like tenor about my book, *Die Kirche,* which was published as far back as 1967. I answered this letter on June 21, and again raised fundamental objections about the manner in which the Congregation was proceeding. You have not responded to my objections. You notify me instead that other doctrinal proceedings have been initiated against my book, *Unfehlbar ? Eine Anfrage.* In view of all this, I cannot refrain from reiterating my objections against this manner of "doctrinal proceedings." If possible, I would like to bring these objections to expression with even greater clarity.

You refer to my letter to the Secretary of your Congregation, Archbishop Paul Philippe, O. P., dated May 30, 1968, where I voiced my objections and gave my reasons for them. In the meantime, in an exchange of letters with the Congregation, some of these objections were cleared away. Others still remain in force. The new order of procedure of the Congregation of January 15, 1971, which I have desired and welcomed, does not, unfortunately, address these objections. This is not only my own personal opinion. It is no doubt known in your Congregation that this order of procedure has aroused sharp criticism among both Catholics and non-Catholics.

Therefore, I must say again: in spite of improvements in matters of detail, this order of procedure is not free of the spirit of the Inquisition. In any case, it is far short of the very moderate requests which, some time ago, 1,360 theology professors the world over set forth for the sake of the freedom of theology.

I, therefore, ask myself how these proceedings can be compatible with your communication of January 24, 1970. There you state "that the Congregation will proceed with loyalty, equity, and without arbitrariness." Let me prescind here from the fact that, next to these "ordinary" proceedings, "extraordinary" ones are still possible any time. In the latter proceedings, the Congregation is not even bound to observe the norms of procedure it has itself stiplated. This leaves the door open to inquisitorial arbitrariness. With regard to the "ordinary" proceedings in question here, I must state that I cannot acknowledge as "loyal, equitable and free from arbitrariness" proceedings which:

(1) do not allow me access to the official records;

(2) prescribe a relator "pro auctore" not of my own choice;

(3) do not clearly limit competence and makes no provision for any appeal;

(4) are bound only by time-limits set by one side.

Assessed against the modern understanding of legality, these proceedings of the Congregation for the Doctrine of the Faith must, I am sorry to say, still be described as inquisitorial and discriminatory. What I did in regard to the proceedings against my book, *Die Kirche,* in my letter of June 21, 1971, I must now do with regard to the new proceedings against the book, *Unfehlbar ? Eine Anfrage. I protest such proceedings in principle, and even underscore the protest.* In my letter of July 1, 1970, I have already made it abundantly clear that I am not prompted to do this by animosity against the Church, but rather by a deeply ecclesial sentiment. Here, then, I can refer to what was said there.

As far as the book, *Die Kirche,* is concerned, I have answered the questions of the Congregation while presupposing that my fundamental objections against the proceedings in the Congregation would be taken seriously. Now that further proceedings against *Unfehlbar ?* have been initiated, I realize that my hope was mistaken. Under these circumstances, you will no doubt understand that I can look upon the proceedings of your Congregation as meaningful only if my complaints are heard, and the following conditions are met:

1. In all your communications you keep referring to your dossier No. 399/57/i which, obviously, concerns me. Only if I be granted *complete access and free perusal of my records* can I regard the proceedings as loyal, equitable, and free from arbitrariness. In this connection, one thing strikes me: In your letter of July 12, you speak of a new decree of the assembly of the cardinals of your Congregation. You explicitly mention that, shortly afterwards, this decree was approved by the Pope. To this day I have received neither a copy of the decree, nor of the document which approved it. I must confess that I cannot understand how secret decrees can still be issued in this century without the slightest evidence of any effort to submit them at least to the person concerned. The secrecy regulations of your Congregation may have their reasons. However, the impression is given that this secrecy does not help the business at hand, nor does it help the person concerned; it helps rather your Congregation and its routines. In the last century, the old Congregation of the Index had still enough confidence in itself to impart its secret verdicts, which are the basis of these "secret decrees," to an author who had been put on the Index. The author would thus be informed about the arguments and the reasons and know where he stood. This is what I read in the *Journals* of the German Church historian Franz Xaver Kraus, published by H. Schiel (Cologne, 1957), p. 484. Why is one not permitted today to see the votes cast, if this was already possible in the past century? Inevitably, the impression will be left behind that your Congregation wants to hide something which it is afraid to bring out into the open. As I did in my letter of May 30, 1968, and time and again since, I beg you to state in writing that I will be given access to the decrees, votes, and official records.

2. The relator "pro auctore" for whom provision is made in the new procedural norms has, strangely enough, been provided with quotation marks. The

phrase is indeed ambiguous. If the relator "pro auctore" is appointed by the *Congregation* and acts in the name of the Congregation, which in turn has initiated the proceedings "against" (see the latter of July 12) the book of the author, the relator finds himself in an ambiguous position. He must at the same time act for and against the author. No matter how the Congregation looks at this judicial problem, I, as an author, cannot acknowledge that such a relator "pro auctore" whose name is being withheld from me speaks on my behalf. If the relator "pro auctore" is really to speak for the author, then the author ought to decide who is going to be his relator and work with him. I, therefore, ask that the Congregation modify accordingly the procedural norms it has itself decreed, so that the author will be entitled to choose the relator "pro auctore".

3. The opening of doctrinal proceedings in Rome raises the issues of the *limitation of competencies,* and of *the courts of appeal.*

a. Some episcopal conferences have already initiated such proceedings with regard to the book, *Unfehlbar ? Eine Anfrage* and concluded them in various ways. Now the Roman Congregation for the Doctrine of the Faith comes along with proceedings of its own. I ask: How many doctrinal proceedings will still be conducted against my book? Must I look upon the proceedings now in progress in Rome as a review, or perhaps as a second instance of the proceedings conducted by the doctrinal-commission of the Conference of German Bishops? Are the judgments of the different episcopal conferences, or their organs, ("the doctrinal-commissions"), being rescinded in accordance with the old principle, "*ne bis in idem*" [double jeopardy principle]? And how is the initiation of special Roman proceedings being legitimized in the first place? When, in the declaration mentioned earlier, the 1360 theologians requested, among other things, that limits be set to the competence of the episcopal and Roman doctrinal-commissions, I had no presentiment that in such a short time a case would occur in which one is faced with such overlapping competencies: the secret decree approved by the Pope, June 23, 1971, and at the same time a number of declarations by the parallel organs of the episcopal conferences.

b. But it seems as if overlapping competencies are not only the case between your Congregation and individual episcopal conferences. On the basis of many indications (cf. for instance, *Diskussion um Hans Küng DIE KIRCHE,* ed. H. Häring and J. Nolte [Freiburg/Basel/Wien, 1971], p. 31; 32 ff.), I had to realize that various curial authorities apparently believe that they are competent to take measures, to exercise pressure, and to take initiatives against publishers, etc. One must ask how many Holy Offices are there really in our time, and which is the court of last resort?

c. The following is particularly important for the person concerned: Is there a guarantee that I will in the end be able to file an appeal against the various proceedings, including the one conducted by your Congregation? Can an appeal be filed at the Apostolic Signature, which, since the reform of the Curia, is called the highest court of appeal? I would have found it loyal and fair if I had not only been notified that secret proceedings had been initiated and secret decrees issued, but if I had also been told what appeals were available to me. Or is the Congregation for the Doctrine of the Faith not at all competent to do this? Should I address myself to the Apostolic Signature?

4. A fourth aspect of the proceedings of your Congregation concerns the *duration* of the proceedings and the *deadlines.* I speak with the benefit of ten

years of experience with the old Holy Office and the present Congregation for the Doctrine of the Faith. My experience includes discussions, decrees, prohibitions, interventions, and letters addressed to me by this body. With all possible clarity, I want to say that I regard the duration of these proceedings as an imposition. The only deadline which the procedural norms of the Congregation mention concerns the thirty days within which the author is to return definite answers to the Congregation. But which are the deadlines which the Congregation itself is obliged to observe? Is it entitled to drag on proceedings indefinitely? In the norms of procedure I find no reference to such deadlines. Even traditional canon law knows, among other things, a statute of limitations. It makes provisions for a reasonable duration of the proceedings. To be kept in suspense for years about the outcome of proceedings can be a form of injustice. This may well be the reason why, last year, Pope Paul VI advised the Roman Rota to shorten considerably the duration of their proceedings. With regard to the proceedings of the Roman Congregation for the Doctrine of the Faith something equivalent is urgently needed in the interest of justice and loyalty. Permit me to recall this experience: In 1967, the Congregation for the Doctrine of the Faith issued a secret decree concerning my book, *Die Kirche*. In 1971, four years later, after the book has been translated in various languages and issued in many editions, the Congregation sends me the questions which then must be answered within thirty days. More than six months have passed since my reply of June 24. To this day, I still do not know whether the proceedings were subsequently terminated, whether new proceedings against my book have been initiated, whether everything has been prorogued, concluded, or whatever. Instead of leaving the author in the dark for years, which makes possible the pressures and the meddlings of various snipers, as mentioned, the Congregation should from the start set deadlines for itself in terms of which its proceedings must be initiated and concluded. Failing this, they must be considered terminated or they must be started anew. This aspect, too, is included in the requests which I consider indispensable if the proceedings are to be equitable, loyal, and acceptable to the author. Neither in the practice of the Congregation for the Doctrine of the Faith, nor in its order of procedure, is there any evidence that this request is being honored.

I will not, in this context, address other important questions connected with the way the proceedings are conducted and concerning the norms of procedure, as for instance the eventual prejudices of an expert or a member of the bodies which are to make decisions. However, I may be permitted to point out that, according to today's jurisprudence, it must be established that those who are to pass judgment must be free of bias, even if they are not judges in the strict sense of the word. This condition must be fulfilled if the proceedings are to be incontestable. The foregoing may suffice to make the point that certain crucial regulations and practices conflict with today's understanding of legality. This is the reason why many people consider the present proceedings against my book as damaging to the reputation of the Catholic Church. Among other things, this is what comes to expression in a "Declaration of Solidarity" that was handed to your Congregation. This declaration came about without my having anything to do with it, in the summer of 1971, while I was away from Europe. In a short time, it collected over 300 signatures. Likewise, the public has been given the painful impression that *L'Osservatore Romano* has recently published many major articles against the author, without one single objective review of the contents of my book, *Unfehlbar ? Eine Anfrage.* Could this practice be the reason why, even in good Catholic circles, the Vatican sheet is time and again compared to Moscow's *Pravda?* Only at the end of these considerations about the way in which proceedings are conducted in Rome would I like to mention how much damage has been done to my theological reputation by the different questionable initiatives of the most diverse Roman organs. I am not the only one who is compelled to ask what Rome plans to do in order to compensate the author for this damage, and especially for the non-material one.

II. PRELIMINARY REMARKS ON THE QUESTIONS RAISED BY THE CONGREGATION

1. With regard to the questions raised by the Congregation about my book, *Unfehlbar ? Eine Anfrage,* I would like to note the following: In principle, the questions I have raised have been admitted. However, to affirm the opposite of what I affirm is, obviously, of little help to anyone, if not supported by arguments. In my book, my concern is precisely to ascertain *how* certain doctrinal statements, and especially the corresponding passages from Vatican I and II, are to be theologically grounded and responsibly supported. Especially my "inquiry" as to the possibility of infallible propositions was clearly articulated. If any official organ of the Catholic Church knows what response to make to this inquiry of mine and what reasons to give for that response, the Roman Congregation for the Doctrine of the Faith is the one. But to refer again to these doctrinal and magisterial documents to which my questions are addressed is a vicious circle. What is to be proved to be so, is in fact, assumed to be so. I will any time be convinced by arguments. Therefore, I beg the Congregation to produce at least in abbreviated form a substantiation that would prove the possibility of infallible propositions. In this substantiation, however, the difficulties I have raised concerning certain doctrinal and magisterial texts should not be ignored but addressed.

2. With this I have already made it clear that I do not at all refuse to participate in a discussion. The *discussion* is, in fact, in full swing. The book has been reviewed numberless times. In addition, in the short time after its publication, many volumes of discussions have appeared in print. I mention the volume of essays edited by Karl Rahner under the title, *Zum Problem der Unfehlbarkeit: Antworten auf die Anfrage von Hans Küng* (Freiburg/Basel/Wein, 1971). This volume contains many contributions, especially from German-speaking countries. There is also the volume published by G. Baum, G. Lindbeck, R. McBrien, and H. McSorley under the title, *The Infallibility Debate* (New York/Toronto, 1971), and especially the comprehensive issue of the *Journal of Ecumenical Studies* (1971, fascicle 4), which is devoted to the infallibility debate. Note likewise the important contributions by H. Stirnimann and A. Antweiler in the *Freiburger Zeitschrift für Philosophie und Theologie* (1973, fascicle 3), and by W. Kasper in *Stimmen der Zeit* (December, 1971). For me, it would be very worthwhile to know what the Congregation thinks of the whole discussion. According to my observations to date, this is the picture that emerges:

a. There are hardly any serious Catholic contributions to the discussion that do not affirm that my question is justified.

b. There are no serious Catholic contributions to the discussion that do not subject the traditional Roman view to sharp criticism. This is the case even if they do not agree with my solution, or only in part.

c. My critics often contradict each other, both with regard to the interpretation of the Roman doctrine on infallibility and to the answer to my *Inquiry*.

d. To date, not a single author has produced convincing arguments for the possibility of infallible propositions, and this is, in my opinion, of crucial importance for the outcome of the debate. This is evidenced in particular by the debate with Karl Rahner. Apparently, even this great theologian was unable to cite an argument for infallible propositions. I take the liberty of sending you by the same mail for your information my answer to Rahner in Italian. Together with my answers to M. Löhrer and K. Lehmann, this constitutes indirectly a contribution to the answer to the Congregation's own questions.

3. On my side, I will continue to subject to careful *study* all the answers to my book. In addition to articles which are apologetic in the traditional sense, as in the Rahner volume, very important contributions have appeared, which extend the issue considerably. This is the case, for instance, with a piece of historical research by Brian Tierney on the origins of papal infallibility. It is included, together with other contributions, in the issue of the *Journal of Ecumenical Studies* mentioned above. This piece of research fills a vacuum in my argumentation. According to the research, Peter Olivi seems to be the first advocate of papal infallibility. He was promptly condemned by the pope of the time. In the next summer term, I would like to hold a *graduate seminar* about the infallibility debate. The most important German opponents of my book will be thoroughly discussed. To make sure that the views of my opponents are expressed as clearly as those of the author, I shall personally invite each of them to the pertinent meeting of the seminar. The Institute of Ecumenical Research of the University of Tübingen is undertaking the funding. Should the Congregation for the Doctrine of the Faith be interested in sending one of its experts to this graduate seminar, we would, of course, offer him every opportunity to thoroughly expound his views and to give his reasons.

4. All this clearly shows that I am aware of what is at stake for the Church and Christianity in this infallibility issue. On the other hand, it will certainly be known in your Congregation that the issue will not be resolved by any onesided Roman statement. Such statements will, at best, add heat to the debate. The history of the decisions of the Congregation for the Doctrine of the Faith (and of the Holy Office) and of other Roman authorities from Galileo and the Rites Controversy down to the condemnation of historical-critical exegesis and of various theologians still living (who were then appointed periti in Vatican II), this history, I say, shows that a problem can be suppressed in the Church for a time or that it could be suppressed in the past, but that it does resurface in a more acute form. What is important to me personally is this: An *objective clarification* should be achieved about this question, which is of great importance for our Church both theoretically and practically. To my own theological position, I attach only slight importance. I am now busying myself with a thorough study of questions relative to the Christian message which are by far more crucially important. But since the question I had raised about infallibility

in *Strukturen der Kirche* (1962), *Theologie und Kirche* (1964), *Die Kirche* (1967), and *Unfehlbarkeit* (1968) had received no answer in Catholic theology, I saw it as my duty — not a particularly pleasant duty — not only to bring out the question with all modesty and fairness, but also with the decisiveness and sharpness required to make it impossible to ignore. This I have done "not for the undoing of the Church, but for her edification." In this sense, I would want to also apply this word from Acts 5/38 f. to my little book.

Your Eminence, I do not know how you assess the present situation of the Catholic Church. I am referring to the world-wide mistrust of clergy and lay people toward authorities in the Church, and most of all toward Rome. The negative repercussions of this mistrust cannot be anticipated. The source of it is not perversity but disappointment. This was brought home to me in thousands of conversations all over the world, in letters and statements which come to me from Catholic lay persons, seminarians and priests from the most diverse constituencies within the Church. Since Vatican II, Rome has suffered a dramatic loss of credibility, which may well be due mostly to the situation which originates in Rome itself. In our own Church, I must often stomach the reproachful questions why I waste so much time and energy with Rome and the institutional Church. I am being asked in particular why I should write a book on papal infallibility and take the trouble to exchange letters with Roman authorities. My answer has always been that I myself have not written Rome off and that I am not endeavoring to bring about the undoing of the Catholic Church. I am not of the opinion that practically everything must disintegrate before we can start to rebuild. In a declaration that was highly regarded and very positively received, I have publicly explained why, in spite of all my criticisms of certain institutions and events, I remain in this, my Church. In spite of all the attacks on my Catholic attitude, I intend to work within the Church cheerfully, as I have done until now. In a time when tens of thousands of priests and sisters have stopped ministering to the Church or left their communities, I have given in numberless individual letters, in conversations and lectures courage and hope to students, priests, religious and lay persons; so that they might persevere and recommit themselves to working in the Church, in the ministry, and in the religious communities. Even in my last journey of four months around the world, I have everywhere tried to battle energetically against boundless frustration and despondency by showing, on the basis of the Christian message itself and in spite of all the difficulties, that it makes very good sense to be a committed person. I have received moving testimonies from men and women who had gratefully, and with renewed energy and hope, said Yes once again to their existence in the Church.

Your Eminence, through radical renewal and convincing reforms in keeping with the very Gospel of Jesus Christ, Rome, too, could again inspire in Christians a new courage and a new trust. I do not consider myself infallible; I am not self-opinionated. I always let people correct me, if they should happen to know more than I do. I do not want to "demolish Rome," as certain circles reproach me of doing, nor do I delude myself of being able to do anything of the sort. Only Rome can demolish Rome through lack of understanding, ridigity, and backwardness. In my theology, I concern myself also with "Rome," even though other Catholics would not want to hear that word any longer. I am convinced that a Petrine Office is necessary and beneficial, not only for our Church, but also for the whole of Christianity. What I am striving for is a Church which, in the spirit of the Gospel of Jesus Christ, does for people today and for their cares and anxieties, more than she has done until now. For the sake of the Gospel and of the salvation of people, I engage in much extraordinary work and numerous exertions which my position does not require of me. For the same reason, I do bring my criticisms to bear on the Roman authorities, various conventions traditional in the Church, and on theological opinions. In my letter, I had to speak at some length about some formal questions and certain exigencies of justice and fairness in the Church and in the Roman Curia. All this, I say, is of minor importance for my theological work. And yet, it had to be said to you in this context, since you are the representative of one of the Roman authorities. The government of a Church which speaks so much about "justice in the world" must let humanness and justice have their day also; most of all, within her own walls, else she will enjoy no credibility in the world.

Your Eminence, may I conclude my long letter by requesting again that the Congregation send me positive answers both to the four formal questions I have raised, and especially to the substantive questions still outstanding.

With singular esteem, I remain,

Devotedly yours,
(signed) Hans Küng

cc.

Cardinal Dr. Julius Döpfner, President of the Conference of German Bishops
Dr. Carl Joseph Leiprecht, Bishop of Rottenburg
Professor Dr. Johannes Neumann, Rector of the University of Tübingen
Professor Dr. Walter Kasper, Dean of the Department of Catholic Theology, University of Tübingen

Enclosure 23

LETTER OF THE CONGREGATION FOR THE DOCTRINE OF THE FAITH TO PROFESSOR KÜNG, July 4, 1973

399/57/i *Rome, July 4, 1973*

Professor Dr. Hans Küng
Waldhauserstrasse 23
D 74 Tübingen
GERMANY

Dear Professor Küng:

In a letter of May 6, 1971, you gave your answer concerning theses advocated in your book, *Die Kirche,* which this Congregation has found incompatible with Catholic doctrine. Subsequently, in a letter dated January 24, 1972, you took a stand with regard to points in your book, *Unfehlbar ?,* which do not conform with the doctrine of the Church and to which the Congregation for the Doctrine of the Faith had objected.

Your letters have been examined by this Congregation. On April 26, 1972, it was decided, with the approval of the Holy Father, to prepare a Declaration which sets forth for the benefit of the whole ecclesial community Catholic doctrine over against today's erroneous opinions in the area of ecclesiology.

With regard to the doctrinal proceedings relative to the examination of your two books mentioned above, two options are open to you:

First, the order of procedure provides for the possibility of a discussion with the representatives of the Congregation for the Doctrine of the Faith on the doctrinal points contained in the two letters of this Congregation.

Second, you can accept immediately the doctrine contained in the Declaration. In this case, the doctrinal proceedings now in progress concerning your two books would be terminated.

Awaiting your prompt reply, and with the expression of our esteem, we remain,

Devotedly yours,
(signed) Franc. Card. Seper, Prefect
+ Jerome Hamer, O. P.

Enclosure 24

STATEMENT TO THE PRESS BY ARCHBISHOP J. SCHRÖFFER IN THE NAME OF THE CONGREGATION FOR THE DOCTRINE OF THE FAITH, July 5, 1973

1. In this Declaration ["Mysterium Ecclesiae" of June 24, 1973 — Translator's note], the Church has in mind to perform a much needed service for the benefit of all the faithful. It aims to safeguard the truth of the faith as condition for salvation in Christ. This is one of the gifts bestowed on the Church by the Holy Spirit, but it is a task which constantly requires renewed efforts just as much on the part of theology. This self-understanding of the Church and of her mission articulated by Vatican I and reaffirmed by Vatican II is called in question today by several authors and expecially by Küng.

2. The Congregation for the Doctrine of the Faith has been in written communication with Professor Küng as to the doctrinal proceedings relative to the examination of some of his theses and their incompatibility with the Catholic faith. In the order of procedure, provision is made for the possibility of a discussion.

3. Should Professor Küng assent to the Declaration *Mysterium Ecclesiae* of June 24, 1973, the doctrinal proceedings in progress would be terminated.

Enclosure 25

STATEMENT OF PROFESSOR KÜNG CONCERNING THE PUBLICATION OF MYSTERIUM ECCLESIAE, July 5, 1973

Through its action, the Roman Congregation for the Doctrine of the Faith has disqualified itself juridically and theologically. In 1967, it initiated secret proceedings against my book, *Die Kirche,* and in 1971 still other proceedings against *Unfehlbar ? Eine Anfrage.* In the same year 1971, Pope Paul VI promulgated norms of procedure for the Congregation for the Doctrine of the Faith, so that the notorious abuses of this old inquisitional board would be corrected.

In these many years, the Congregation for the Doctrine of the Faith did not apparently believe itself to be in a position to conduct and conclude these two proceedings according to the norm of law; that is, in keeping with the papal norms of procedure. Contrary to law and equity, it now intervenes in the proceedings in progress by means of a general and public Declaration concerning the questions raised in the two books.

This procedure and the Declaration — all assertions but no solid arguments — make it obvious that the Congregation for the Doctrine of the Faith is incapable of making a progressive contribution to the questions which are discussed today world-wide in Catholic theology and in ecumenical circles about the Church, its teaching office, and infallibility. Thus, once more, the one and the same Roman authority appears on the scene as both accuser and judge. By this whole initiative, the Congregation gives evidence now and before the world that the proceedings it had attempted were prejudiced.

Enclosure 26

DECLARATION OF CARDINAL DÖPFNER, PRESIDENT OF THE CONFERENCE OF GERMAN BISHOPS, July 7, 1973

July 7, 1973

Statement of the President of the Conference of German Bishops relative to the statement of Professor Küng of July 5, 1973 concerning the publication of Mysterium Ecclesiae

Although doctrinal proceedings were in progress, the Congregation for the Doctrine of the Faith has for a long time allowed the theological discussion on Professor Küng's book *Unfehlbar ? Eine Anfrage* (Einsiedeln, 1970) to take its course. In order to protect the faithful against further confusion and in fullfilment of the responsibility mandated to it, the Congregation for the Doctrine of the Faith issued a Declaration on July 5, 1973 in which it takes a stand on the questions at issue. The Congregation for the Doctrine of the Faith calls attention to errors in some positions of Professor Küng concerning the Catholic teaching on infallibility. In spite of this, the offer of a discussion between Professor Küng and the Congregation for the Doctrine of the Faith still stands.

In a first statement of his position, dated July 5, 1973, Professor Küng has unfortunately made considerably more difficult the continuation of an objective discussion through poorly supported and disparaging statements concerning the Congregation for the Doctrine of the Faith.

As President of the Conference of German Bishops, I decisively repudiate these statements of Professor Küng about the Congregation for the Doctrine of the Faith. In part, they are defamatory. Considering the importance of this matter, I expect Professor Küng to contribute, through substantive cooperation, to a satisfactory resolution. This is the only way in which greater harm can be prevented.

Julius Cardinal Döpfner
President of the Conference of
German Bishops

Enclosure 27

LETTER OF CARDINAL VOLK TO PROFESSOR KÜNG, July 10, 1973

65 Mainz, July 10, 1973

Professor Dr. Hans Küng
Tübingen
Waldhauserst. 23

Dear Professor Küng:

Many thanks for sending me your article in the *Frankfurter Allgemeine Zeitung*. I would not want at this time to battle with you over this article and other of your statements. My concern is rather to make an end of this quarrel. I believe we do have a chance. In your article, you acknowledge that in the Roman pronouncement a new element is clearly contained. It explicitly mentions the historical character of every faith assertion — including, therefore, today's assertions — and the limitations contingent on that historical character. It acknowledges that the theologian's work is therefore required. This is no small thing. In this connection, we can ask whether it is the task of such an authority to do the theologian's own work. Unless I am mistaken, the Roman Congregation does not regard this as its own task. A recognition of the theologians and their work may be seen in the fact that such an authority does not itself do this work in its own Declaration. The question, then, is always going to be to what extent the results of the theologians' work will be incorporated by that authority into its own declarations. On this question, opinions will forever differ. You are obviously convinced that your book *Unfehlbar* has definitely shown here what is no longer possible. But you also know that this is being contested by others. Obviously, an "operative agreement with Karl Rahner" is hardly equivalent to a substantive agreement. The substantive issue and the resolution of it, in which philosophical elements easily intrude, will necessarily require theological work in the future as well.

What is important now, and what I sincerely ask you to do, is that you speak with Rome. You know that the text itself does not mention your name and that it explicitly voices and confirms a willingness to engage in a discussion. The Declaration does not speak *de fide.* You should not, however, construe this as a sign of weakness or cowardice, but of a readiness to discuss. I, therefore, beg you most personally, please do take part in such a discussion.

Once you mentioned to me that you would be glad to turn your attention to other tasks. If I understood you correctly — I seem to remember that you mentioned then the Sunday obligation, which you would support — you were leaning strongly toward positive contributions. I, too, am convinced that there are many such positive tasks to be attended to. We are certainly not doing whatever is necessary when our prevalent concern is to say No to what is the case and to the way things are done. All of us should endeavor to contribute to what is indispensable to the deepening of faith and piety. For years it has been my contention up and down the land, and also in my sermons, that our time demands a deepening of faith and piety. There are times when, if faith does not grow, it perishes. I am convinced that we are now in such a time. I am convinced that highly important tasks await all of us.

I would, therefore, regret it very much if the business still pending could not be cleared out of the way enough to make possible for us to go ahead with our tasks in the areas where our work is very much needed. You will not be disappointed if you make your own personal contribution by engaging in discussion with Rome.

Cordial greetings.

Yours,
(signed) + Hermann Card. Volk

Enclosure 28

LETTER OF PROFESSOR KÜNG TO CARDINAL VOLK, July 27 1973

July 27, 1973

His Eminence
Cardinal Dr. Hermann Volk
Bishop of Mainz
Mainz

Your Eminence:

Within a week the coordinated initiative against me has brought me

— a Declaration of the Congregation for the Doctrine of the Faith (twice, once by messenger from the Nunciature and then by registered priority mail),

— two Vatican press conferences.
— two articles in *L'Osservatore Romano,*
— two declarations of the Conference of German Bishops,
— the visit of a bishop at your suggestion,
— and finally, also your own priority mail letter, to say nothing of numberless telephone calls, letters, discussions, press reports, radio broadcasts and telecasts. This is a bit much for one man facing a gigantic and powerful machinery.

When your letter was brought to my home by a messenger on July 12 at seven o'clock in the morning, you may understand how, against this whole background, I took cognizance of it with mixed feelings. It would have been easy for you long ago to get in touch with me peacefully and calmly. Since the proceedings of the Congregation for the Doctrine of the Faith, of which you have been a member until very recently, have been in progress for three years *(Unfehlbar ? Eine Anfrage),* or even for six years *(Die Kirche),* and since my last letter to the Congregation, dated January 24, 1972, was not answered (instead, already on April 26, 1972, it had been secretly decided to prepare the document which has now been published), I cannot quite understand why, five days after the publication of that document I should be honored with a special delivery letter. Even at the risk of being reproached again for lack of "savoir-faire", I voice my amazement at such methods. I must state that I feel exposed to the most massive pressure, even though, where I am concerned, pressure is not exactly the appropriate method to get anything accomplished.

I am convinced that, personally, you are well disposed. You are genuinely interested in bringing about a peaceful settlement of the issue which the Congregation for the Doctrine of the Faith has handled in that way. I was very happy to notice how friendly the tone of your letter is, and all the more so that it differs from another public statement to which I have replied only indirectly, in order not to exacerbate a situation which has already been made dramatic enough by the initiative Rome has taken. (Cf. enclosed statement to the press of July 10, 1973, and also the enclosed reprint of an interview to appear in the next issue of the *Herder-Korrespondenz.)*

It was more difficult for me to understand why you would urge me so strongly to devote myself to positive theological contributions. There should be no need for me to list my bibliography, beginning with *Rechtfertigung,* and *Konzil und Wiedervereinigung,* to *Die Kirche,* and *Menschwerdung Gottes.* I would like to stress that even critical writings such as *Wahrhaftigkeit, Unfehlbar ? Fehlbar ?,* serve a positive purpose and are being so understood by a great many people. In today's situation, that deepening of the faith and piety, which you so rightly urge, seems to me and to others to be meaningful only if its goes hand in hand with a critique of conditions and abuses in the Church. Nor should bishops leave this critique only to theologians and lay persons. Upon the occasion of your elevation to the cardinalate, I took the liberty of sending you a talk of mine which was well received everywhere, "What Must Remain in the Church." In this talk, I briefly show how, in my theology, the critical and the constructive concerns are necessarily intertwined. The one makes no sense without the other. I propose to keep to this course in season and out of season. I would already have completed work on an introduction to Christianity, if the volume of essays on the infallibility debate produced with the encouragement of the German doctrinal-commission and to which I was not permitted to contribute, had not forced me to produce a volume of essays of my own.

I can well understand why you so urgently desire a discussion with Rome. If the information coming to me from my German colleagues is correct, you are the one I should thank for the fact that the letter of the Congregation for the Doctrine of the Faith has kept open the possibility of a discussion. For this I am sincerely grateful. In this way, it was possible to avoid for the present a head-on confrontation with this body and all the inevitable consequences. For this reason, I can promptly respond to the wish you have expressed with such friendliness: I have always been willing to take part in a discussion with Rome, and I will remain willing in the future, no matter what happens. At the public urging of Cardinal Döpfner, I have also declared before the world that I am prepared to contribute through substantive cooperation to a satisfactory resolution.

Of course, substantive cooperation is needed on both sides. In this connection, I was amazed that neither the letter of the Congregation for the Doctrine of the Faith of July 4, 1973 nor your own letter should touch upon the key question of the just and fair conditions for such a discussion. These conditions I have already articulated in my letter of May 30, 1968 to the Congregation for the Doctrine of the Faith and reiterated in my letter of January 24, 1972 (published in *Fehlbar ?*). Time and again, I have made it clear in various ways that I am willing to take part in any genuine discussion, but that I will have no part in any kind of Inquisition. Twice in Germany, I have taken part in discussions with you, and this does prove that my willingness is genuine. As far as Rome is concerned, to this day it has not been possible to agree either on a date or on a list of topics. The questions I asked in my last letter concerning just and fair conditions have not been answered by the Congregation, not with one word. I am still being denied access to the records, adequate possibilities for defense, the name of the defender assigned to me by the Congregation, as well as appropriate time-limits binding on both sides. Instead, the Congregation now breaks sensationally into the proceedings in progress with a general and public Declaration on the questions raised in both books. Thus it plays the role of accuser, lawgiver, and judge, all at the same time. In spite of all these extraordinary events, I would like to stand by my willingness to engage in a discussion. However, since Rome has waited one year and a half before responding to my letter and since now the outcome of the discussion has been for no understandable reason prejudiced through an official Declaration, I must be permitted the time required for me to figure out what bearing this new and, both juridically and theologically, complex situation has on such a discussion. I, therefore, ask you to understand that, at present, I am not in a position to be more explicit in my statements in this regard. I am fully aware that the whole thing must be handled with the greatest caution, if yet greater harm to the credibility of the Catholic Church in Germany and in the world is to be prevented.

You will already have noticed that everywhere, and even in Italy, the Roman Declaration has had the worst possible press. It has not really "fared" well either with the clergy or with the people. Should the Declaration be "received" by the Church, which, of course, is not likely to happen, the repercussions on ecumenism would be devastating. This may explain why there has been widespread amazement at the fact that the German bishops have uncritically supported the initiative of Rome and gone against one of their own theologians. For the good of our Church, it is to be sincerely hoped that the bishops, who once again have not been consulted by Rome concerning the text of the document, would manage to achieve an unprejudiced view of things. In this as in other cases, Rome would want the bishops to get the chestnuts out of the fire for the Curia. From the declarations of the Episcopal Conference I conclude that, in Germany, bishops and theologians are agreed that the freedom of theological inquiry should not be suppressed, that the continuation of ecumenical efforts should not be impeded, and that the initial achievements of Vatican II should not be reversed.

As far as my position in this whole affair is concerned, it should be important even for Rome to know what I briefly state here: with all legitimate means at my disposal, I mean to struggle for my cause, which is indeed not only my own. Neither am I permitted to act against my own conscience, a conscience which, fallible to be sure, I try to form according to the Gospel. Nor can I disappoint numberless people the world over who pin their hopes for the future upon this course. They expect from me personally (as numberless letters and conversations have brought home to me in these days) that I should remain in the Church, and that I should be unpretentiously steadfast. After dealing with the Roman Inquisition for just about ten years, I may perhaps be believed if I say that if it has to be, I will, with God's help, persevere for ten more years. If I may be blunt, disciplinary measures would not in any case mean the end, but the beginning of the real confrontation, the end of which no one could foretell. I would not want to paint for you or for myself a picture of the consequences, pastoral consequences within the Church, civil and academic consequences, and finally also consequences in the area of ecumenism. In the preceding few weeks, you yourself have no doubt noticed how many people, men and women, within and without our Church, and especially how many priests, theology students are deeply troubled by the initiative which Rome, in the manner of a general staff, has mounted against me. I have made only limited use of the possibility of enlightening the public. Until now I have prevented further escalation, not merely by not encouraging but by preventing certain groups from making public statements and organizing manifestations of solidarity. In return, I would indeed be extremely grateful to the bishops, if on their side, in response to their pastoral responsibility, they would take a strong stand against Rome's own escalation, the consequences of which we would have to endure together. This much is obvious even in Rome: Against the will of the bishops, Rome cannot enforce any measures in Germany.

Your Eminence, may I, in conclusion, address you in a more personal vein. I sincerely regret that a more constructive cooperation has not actually materialized between you and me. Precisely in connection with this confrontation, disagreeable as it is on both sides, I would like to underscore that, when it comes to the foundations on which we stand and the goal we pursue, you and I are one. For many years you have known me well enough to know that in all that I do or not do to the best of my ability as a theologian, I am concerned with what is truly Christian in the Church and in the world. I have always resisted the erosion of Christianity, not only from the right but also from the left. This is the only reason why, fully conscious of my fallibility, I must speak about many things so clearly and unmistakably, even though this can of course be construed easily enough as pride, arrogance, and "infallibility" on my part. In this letter, too, I had to speak clearly. The seriousness of the moment does not admit pretense. All the same, I can promise you that, without regard for protocol or personal prestige, I wil gladly contribute to any honorable, honest, and just solution in a Christian spirit. At the same time, I ask that you and your fellow-bishops use your influence, so that in Rome too an effort will be made at achieving a honorable, honest, and just solution. Basically, I ask nothing more and nothing less than the freedom to inquire and learn in peace in compliance with my mandate as a teacher of theology in the Catholic Church. To theology I will forever remain completely loyal and unequivocally faithful.

Sincerely obligated to you, I convey to you my cordial greetings.

Devotedly yours,
(signed) Hans Küng

Enclosure 29

LETTER OF THE CONGREGATION FOR THE DOCTRINE OF THE FAITH TO PROFESSOR KÜNG, August 16, 1973

399/57/i

Rome, August 16, 1973
Palazzo del S. Uffizio, 11

Professor Dr. Hans Küng
Waldhauserstrasse 23
D-74 Tübingen
GERMANY

Dear Professor Küng:

In the letter we addressed to you on July 4, 1973, we expressed the expectation that we would soon receive your reply. Since we have not received such a reply to date, we feel that we should remind you of it and also set a deadline. We expect to receive your statement relative to our letter within one more month, by September 20, at the latest.

We are indeed of the opinion that a period of two months and a half ought to be sufficient for a statement on your part.

With the hope of receiving a positive answer from you, and with the expression of our regards,

Franc. Card. Seper, Prefect
Fr. Jérome Hamer, O. P., Secretary

Enclosure 30

LETTER OF PROFESSOR KÜNG TO THE CONGREGATION FOR THE DOCTRINE OF THE FAITH, September 22, 1973

September 22, 1973

His Eminence
Cardinal Franjo Seper
Prefect of the Congregation for the Doctrine of the Faith
Vatican City

Your Eminence:

Your letter, dated Rome, July 4, 1973, reached me in Tübingen on the morning of July 5. I will forgo a detailed account of the strange circumstances that surrounded this letter, circumstances which have been well noted even by the public.

— The letter was first brought to my house in Tübingen by a special messenger from the Nunciature in Bonn;

— half an hour later, it was conveyed to me by the postal service, registered mail from the Nuncio;

— one hour later, it was made known to the public, together with the Declaration *Mysterium Ecclesiae,* and its contents were commented upon by spokesmen of the Congregation for the Doctrine of the Faith in a Vatican press conference summoned especially for the occasion;

— it was flanked by articles in *L'Osservatore Romano,* and further by statements issued to the press by the Vatican;

— it was bolstered in Germany by two declarations of the Conference of German Bishops and through the personal interventions of many bishops also instigated by Rome.

One can only surmise what your Congregation and the other Vatican and episcopal bodies which were asked to join in wanted to achieve through this coordinated initiative. Be that as it may, I am entitled to ask for understanding if my answer is late. For me, an individual theologian who does not have at his disposal the mighty machinery of the Vatican and who has been exposed to a massive pressure of this kind, it would have been irresponsible, in such a situation, to comply immediately with your request to reply "soon". However, I did confirm at once receipt of your letter in a letter to the Nuncio in Bonn, Archbishop Basile. May I, in self-defense, remind you of how much time the Congregation itself has taken to answer my own letters:

— My answer to your letter relative to the proceedings against my book *Unfehlbar ? Eine Anfrage* is dated Janury 24, 1972. The Congregation required one year and a half to acknowledge receipt of this letter.

— My answer to your letter relative to the proceedings against my book *Die Kirche* is dated June 21, 1971. The Congregation has needed two years to confirm receipt of this letter.

— In a letter of August 31, 1968, the Congregation assured me that the "topics" for a discussion on my book *Die Kirche* would "soon" be given to me.

To date, that is, five years later, the Congregation has not sent me anything of the sort nor has it given me any reasons or explanation for not keeping its promise.

This being the case, I was certainly entitled to assume that you would give me more time to answer, especially during the summer vacations. But, after all the extraordinary demands made on me, your letter of August 6 came in the middle of my vacation, and demanded that, by September 20, I should answer your letter of July 4. Once more, your Congregation sets deadline unilaterally, similar to the earlier thirty day time limit, and within that deadline demands an answer in a manner that resembles an ultimatum.

Without relinquishing my objection against your unilateral deadlines, I would like to answer your letter today, September 22, since your admonition arrived at my summer address in Switzerland precisely one month ago.

By way of introduction, may I take the liberty to make the following point, which concerns the infallibility issue only indirectly: In your letter of July 4, an error has slipped in. You maintain that on May 6, 1961 I answered the Congregation concerning my book *Die Kirche.* A letter written by me on that date to your Congregation does not exist. I surmise that the letter in question is the one dated June 21, 1971.

With regard to your letter of July 4, I would like to declare my position under two headings:

I. FUNDAMENTAL PROTEST AGAINST THE PROCEEDINGS OF YOUR CONGREGATION

Your letter informs me that "the procedural norms" *(Ratio agendi)* of your Congregation make provisions for the possibility of a discussion on the doctrinal points contained in two letters of your Congregation, in case I should not want to subscribe "immediately" to the doctrine contained in the Declaration. This is exactly what was announced to the public in the press conference in the Vatican and commented upon in *L'Osservatore Romano.* This does raise several questions:

1. To my surprise, both spokesmen of the Congregation for the Doctrine of the Faith in the press conference failed to enlighten the public as to what is actually the case with the *discussion with the Congregation.* May I recall the following: The Congregation invited me to Rome five years ago to take part in a discussion on my book, *Die Kirche.* I declared, and later confirmed time and again, that I was willing in principle to do so (cf. especially my letter of May 30, 1968). A discussion ensued as to the just and fair conditions for such a discussion. Some questions could be settled to the satisfaction of both parties. Among other things, the Congregation promised to inform me soon about the list of topics to be discussed. The Congregation has never invited me to take part in a discussion on my book *Unfehlbar ?* until its Declaration was published. In this Declaration it was announced that a discussion was "possible." If the Congregation was of the opinion that the whole affair was worth a press conference, truth and veracity would have demanded that the true state of affairs should not be withheld from the public. Hence my question: Is the Congregation, which has imparted to the public the dissimulating and, in fact, deceitful information

mentioned above, prepared to inform the public with the same degree of emphasis how things actually stand?

2. To my even greater surprise, the latest letter of your Congregation on July 4 does not say a single word to take a stand on the question which has now been at issue for five years, namely, the question about the *just and fair conditions.* In contrast to earlier statements of the Congregation, this letter makes it all look as if these conditions had never been discussed. My last two letters to the Congregation, to which your letter explicitly refers, raised and underscored my fundamental reservations against the legality of the proceedings of your Congregation. On January 24, 1970, you were so kind as to assure me unrestrictedly "that the Congregation will proceed loyally, equitably, and without arbitrariness." In my last letter of January 24, 1972 (but see also my letter of May 30, 1968), I took the trouble to substantiate in many pages of writing what I do not need to repeat here in detail: I absolutely cannot regard as "loyal, equitable, and free from arbitrariness" proceedings which:

— allow me no access to official records;

— prescribe a relator "pro auctore" not of my choice and whose name I do not even know;

— neglect to clearly delimit competence and to provide for the possibility of appeal;

— are bound only by deadlines unilaterally set.

In my earlier letter (July 1, 197 and January 24, 1972), I already explained in detail that my fundamental protest against both proceedings, which I must reiterate and underscore here once again, is not to be traced to animosity against the Church, but rather to a deeply ecclesial sentiment. Here I need only refer to what was said there.

Hence my question: Is the Congregation prepared to accede to these wishes which, by the standards of our modern sense of legality go without saying? If it has to come to such proceedings, that is what the Congregation ought to do in order to proceed "loyally, equitably and without arbitrariness."

3. Since my last letter of January 22, the situation has worsened. I did not intend this to happen. It has happened because of the way the Congregation has acted publicly at various levels. Instead of responding to the objections I had expressed, the Congregation decided, as far back as April 26, 1972, to go public by way of a Declaration. Your letter makes it clear that this "Declaration concerning Catholic Doctrine on the Church to Be Defended Against Some Contemporary Errors" was prepared in connection with the two proceedings pending against me, and so comes through, in fact, as a "Lex Küng." It is clear, then, that, instead of standing by its own procedural norms, and contrary to right and equity, the Congregation is breaking into the proceedings still pending and undecided by a general and public declaration on the questions raised in both books. In so doing, the Congregation plays the role of law-giver, accuser, and judge, all at the same time, as it were.

In view of these events, highly extraordinary as they are in terms of modern legal sensitivity, and so difficult for the public within and without the Church to understand, it is not easy for me to stand by my own willingness to participate in a discussion. I have declared even in public how badly shaken is my confidence in the legitimacy of the way the Congregation is proceeding. It is only in order to preclude still greater harm to the credibility of the Catholic Church, and of

Rome in particular, and to show good will on my part, that, at the public urging of Cardinal Döpfner, I have already declared that I stand by my willingness to participate in a discussion, no matter what happens, and so to contribute through substantive cooperation to a satisfactory resolution.

This substantive cooperation, urged by Cardinal Döpfner for the sake of a satisfactory resolution, I am certainly entitled to expect also from the Congregation. But, since the action of the Congregation itself has shown that its present norms of procedure are obviously inadequate, a revision of the whole order of procedure seems to be needed. Already on April 1969, 1360 Catholic theologians from 53 countries — among them, some of the best known names in Catholic theology — submitted to the competent Roman authorities a "Declaration for the Freedom of Theology." All these theologians call on the teaching office of the Church to proceed differently with regard to the theologian. Unfortunately, the proposals of the theologians have been implemented only to a small extent in the "norms of procedure" adopted by the Congregation in January 1971. I would like, therefore, to renew my support for this declaration which is written "in complete loyalty and unequivocal fidelity to the Catholic Church." I would also like to request that the Congregation should do the same.

Hence my question: Is the Congregation for the Doctrine of the Faith prepared to accede to the wishes of the 1360 theologians "so that pope and bishops may, adequately and worthily, meet their responsibility also with regard to the function of theology in the Church"? I take the liberty of sending you the aforementioned declaration in German, Italian, French, English, and Spanish.

4. Finally, the conduct of the Congregation also raises the question whether the *proposed discussion makes sense* at all. You have not as yet made a proposal as to which topics should be addressed in this discussion. The question, then, is whether the published Declaration of the Congregation does not, in fact, so prejudice the outcome of the discussion that it turns into a "farce," as the press has surmised. Actually, you are proposing an alternative to the discussion, namely, that I should accept "immediately" the doctrine contained in the Declaration. In this case, the proceedings pending against my two books would be "concluded." Many find that this alternative is cynical, since any proceedings are "concluded" if the accused does "immediately" subscribe to his condemnation, even before the sentence is passed. I do not want to quarrel about this point. What I want to know is whether, under the present conditions, a genuine and fair discussion is at all possible. Until now I have taken part in every discussion on infallibility that held out a promise of success. I have done this not only in Frankfurt, Paris, Bern with theologians of a different persuasion, but also with bishops and theologians of the German doctrinal-commission in Stuttgart. In all these cases, a genuine dialogue was involved, a genuine speaking with one another, in which both sides could learn something. In Rome, too, I would like to engage in a genuine dialogue of that sort. On the contrary, a discussion in which one side demands the surrender of the other or which is only the veiled beginning of disciplinary measures is of no help either to the common cause or to me personally. It rather blocks a genuine solution of the question still pending and is prejudicial to the credibility of the Catholic Church.

Hence my questions:

a. Can the Congregation guarantee me a genuine discussion, or am I to expect a dictatorial act in which what is not being "immediately" subscribed to is *then* supposed to be endorsed? In other words, is the purpose of the discussion to ascertain the truth, or is it submission and the initiation of disciplinary measures? Is the Congregation prepared to implement the theologians' Declaration "For the Freedom of Theology"?

b. How does the Congregation explain the contradiction between its two letters? In its earlier letter of July 12, 1971, it speaks of theses in my book which "*seem* to conflict with Catholic doctrine" and "which cause *difficulties* for the Congregation as far as a Catholic interpretation is concerned." You ask me to explain "whether and in what way I believe that these theses and opinions can be reconciled with Catholic doctrine." And yet in your letter of July 4, 1973, the same Congregation speaks of "points which do not conform with the doctrine of the Church," as well as of "theses which this Congregation has found incompatible with Catholic doctrine." It seems as if, here too, the verdict is already being anticipated.

c. If the discussion is to be genuine, how are we to explain the statement of the spokesman of the Congregation in the press conference of July 5 1973, that anyone who does not subscribe to this Declaration of the Congregation is already "outside the Church"? How does this statement relate to the fact that the Declaration itself recoils from formulae of excommunication?

d. Is there any truth to the report which has appeared in Catholic sheets in Germany to the effect that the Congregation for the Doctrine of the Faith has opened further proceedings again my book, *Wozu Priester ? Eine Hilfe* (1971)?

Permit me to add a final remark relative to this composite of questions. For five years now — to say nothing about earlier proceedings — I have made all the efforts I could think of to reply to the various letters of your Congregation extensively and to the point. Time and again for five years, I have raised the same questions as to the legality of your procedure. But your Congregation does not answer, not even the most fundamental questions, about right and equity in the manner of procedure being forced upon me. The Congregation knows very well that we are dealing here with presuppositions in the absence of which a substantive discussion is out of the question. Under these circumstances, many would have stopped exchanging letters with your Congregation, which is what several people have advised me to do. But, because of the concern I have for the common cause of the Catholic Church, a cause to which you and I are dedicated, I have always examined your letters, I have informed you of my readiness to participate in a discussion, and I have taken pains to achieve scholarly resolution of outstanding problems from within a Catholic faith-conviction. The Congregation, on the contrary, has steadily escalated its own initiative, and in a way totally incomprehensible to me, it has carried it forward to the point of disqualifying me without a sentence. I ask whether the Congregation is sufficiently aware that, through its action, it is putting a strain on the patience, loyalty, and sense of faith of a Catholic theologian. At any rate, out of this section of my letter this much emerges with unmistakable clarity: Without a clarification of the essential preconditions, the discussion requested by the Congregation is senseless for both sides.

II. QUESTIONS ON THE THEOLOGICAL PROBLEMATIC

Because of the way the Congregation proceeds, I had to speak a great deal about questions of justice. I now come to the theological questions.

1. The Declaration of the Congregation does not aim to "prove" the dogma at issue "through an inquiry into the foundations of our faith," but only "to call to mind" what is already known especially from Vatican I and II. With this the Declaration bypasses the questions raised in my book without examining them in the least. The texts which the Declaration quotes from Vatican I and II are, of course, known to me. Not only did I take part in Vatican II in my capacity as *peritus,* but for over ten years I have submitted the pertinent conciliar texts to thorough historical and theological analysis. As I wrote to you in my letter of January 24, 1972, in my book I am trying to ascertain precisely *how* certain doctrinal statements, and especially the corresponding texts from Vatican I and II, are to be theologically grounded and responsibly supported. To merely refer to these doctrinal-magisterial documents, to which my questions are addressed, is a vicious circle. What is to be proved to be so is, in fact, assumed to be so. I will any time be convinced by arguments. This is why then I already begged the Congregation to produce, at least in abbreviated form, an argumentation that would prove the possibility of infallible propositions. In this argumentation, however, the difficulties I have raised concerning some doctrinal-magisterial texts should be addressed, not ignored.

After the publication of this Declaration, I have no choice but to reiterate with even greater insistence my request to the Congregation for an argumentation. As the reactions to my book and to the Declaration of the Congregation show, these questions are not only my own. The Declaration of the Congregation has been met with incomprehension in broad segments of the Catholic clergy and laity, due to the fact that it clarifies nothing. It only calls to mind what is in need of clarification. People expect arguments and what they get is assertions.

2. In connection with the latest Declaration of the Congregation, I am struck by a contradiction. The letter of the Congregation on July 12, 1971 contains a whole section on "infallible propositions" (Section IV. On Infallible Propositions [pp. 88-9 in this translation]). But that Declaration, in spite of everything it has to say about infallibility, nowhere speaks of "infallible propositions," which is indeed surprising. Should I take this silence to mean that there are no such "infallible propositions"? If so, my "inquiry" could be looked upon as substantially closed.

3. In the same connection, another question emerges. I am pleased to notice that the Declaration speaks in detail of the "historical condition" of doctrinal statements. It maintains that the articulations of the faith are contingent on the situation, that they are imperfect, perfectible, open to additions, replaceable. If so, a question emerges for the Magisterium to answer: If these articulations are in many ways historically conditioned, if they are contingent on the situation, if they are imperfect, perfectible, open to additions, and replaceable, why could they not, under certain circumstances, also depart from the truth? Why wouldn't "historical condition" entail in particular cases even the possibility of error, as in many ways history seems to show? To that extent is the assertion that, in determinate individual cases, the Holy Spirit absolutely prevents errors,

a form of theological wishful thinking, rather than an utterance grounded on "the foundations of our faith"?

4. It is obvious that the Declaration has not adequately taken cognizance of the most recent international *discussions* on infallibility. Unfortunately, the Congregation for the Doctrine of the Faith failed to respond to my invitation to send one of its representatives to our graduate seminar in Tübingen on the infallibility debate, a seminar which was attended by numerous experts from other universities; such as Professors H. Fries, K. Lehmann, K. Rahner, and J. Ratzinger. Thus, the Congregation missed a good opportunity for a genuine discussion. In this connection, I should not fail to mention that the Institute for Ecumenical Research at the University of Tübingen has established archives on the infallibility debate. Documents of the most various kinds which have come to us and relate to the infallibility debate are collected there and subjected to disciplined investigation.

As a sign of how much I have endeavored to be amenable to serious theological discussion, how I am gathering and responding to all the arguments against my book, and how I am trying to make my own views ever more precise, may I send you a 574 page volume on the infallibility debate which I edited. It is entitled, *Fehlbar ? Eine Bilanz.* This volume is dedicated to the Congregation, "not to the undoing but to the edification of the Church." This shows what sentiment is behind my book.

5. Parallel questions would have to be raised on the undifferentiated statements about the uniqueness of the Catholic Church, the apostolic succession, the Magisterium of the Church, the sacramental character and validity of the Eucharist. But in order not to prolong this already lengthy letter, I would like to defer these questions.

III. A PERSONAL WORD

Your Eminence, I am well aware that my various formal and substantive requests strive for a larger measure of freedom which the teaching office of the Church ought to guarantee to the theologians as they minister to the Church. But you yourself know that numberless true Catholics find that Rome's measures against Catholic theologians detract considerably from the credibility of the Catholic Church in today's society and put a strain on their own faith. On my side, I feel that I am being supported not only by numberless positive letters and encouragements, but also by the aforementioned declaration of 1360 theologians made public already five years ago. In its introduction, this declaration voices what concerns me most deeply in this whole affair:

"In complete loyalty and unequivocal fidelity to the Catholic Church, the undersigned theologians are impelled and obliged to point out publicly and in all seriousness that the freedom of theology and theologians in the service of the Church, which was won anew in Vatican II, ought not to be again endangered in our time. This freedom is a fruit and an exigency of the liberating message of Jesus himself. It remains an essential aspect of the freedom of the children of God in the Church, proclaimed and defended by St. Paul. Hence, it is incumbent on all the teachers in the Church to proclaim the Word in season and out of season.

For us theologians, this freedom goes hand in hand with the heavy responsibility not to jeoparidze the genuine unity and the true peace of the Church and all her members. We are well aware that we theologians can commit errors in our theology.

But we are convinced that erroneous theological opinions cannot be disposed of through coercive measures. In our world, they can be effectively corrected only through unrestricted, objective, and scholarly discussion, a discussion in which the truth will win the day by its own resources. With conviction, we say Yes to a teaching office of the Pope and the bishops which stands under the word of God and in the service of the Church and her proclamation. But we also know that this pastoral ministry of proclamation ought not to constrain or impede the scholarly teaching of the theologians. Any kind of inquisition, be it ever so subtle, harms not only the unfolding of a healthy theology; it also inflicts incalculable damage to the whole Church in the world. We, therefore, expect the pastoral office of proclamation of the Pope and the bishops to exhibit axiomatic confidence in our ecclesial attitude and to support without prejudice our theological work for the good of people in the Church and in the world. We would like to attend to our obligation to seek the truth and to tell it without being hampered by administrative measures and sanctions. We expect our freedom to be respected whenever, to the best of our ability, we voice or publish our founded theological convictions."

Although I do stand up for the freedom of theology, I am anxious to assure you that, in a Christian spirit, I will contribute my share to any honorable, honest, and just solution of this difficulty. A further escalation of this affair, an escalation which is being watched with the greatest anxiety by many bishops, priests, theology students, men and women the world over, could have incalculable negative consequences for our Church. I, therefore, insistently beg of you to see to it that in Rome, too, efforts are made to achieve an honorable, honest, and just solution. Basically, I ask nothing more and nothing less than to be permitted to inquire and teach without being suspected. As a theology teacher in the Catholic Church, this is my vocation. I will always preserve my complete loyalty and unequivocal fidelity to this, our Church.

In an effort at achieving a good solution, permit me to make the following proposal to your Congregation: Through its Declaration, the Congregation has publicly said about the matter at hand what it believed it ought to say. If what it has said is the truth, it will prevail by its own resources. On my side, I have taken a stand in copious publications concerning the discussion on *Die Kirche* and *Unfehlbar ?* Conscious of my fallibility, I will continue to be open to and grateful for criticisms directed at my views. I have already moved on to other and more central theological themes.

Under these circumstances, hasn't the time come to close this affair which is unpleasant on both sides and holds out no great promise for the future? Hasn't the time come to let Catholic theologians debate these difficult questions freely on the basis of the declarations issued to date?

Hasn't the time come to speak a final word of reconciliation, as I did in my exchange with Karl Rahner about the infallibility of the Church? What I wrote to Rahner I would like to write to Your Eminence and to your Congregation:

"Hasn't the time come to drop the question between you and me and leave to history the task of deciding what the answer should be? I am not particularly anxious to be right. If it was given to human beings to produce such [infallible] propositions with the help of the Holy Spirit why should that disturb me? If anything, I would ask that, for the sake of people, more use should be made of this possibility. For the time being, it does not look as if we are moving toward such rosy times. But so what? We are not concerned with our 'subjective opinion.' It is the *truth* that is to have its day, nothing more and nothing less. In a couple of years we should already be able to see more clearly. At any rate, I would like to make peace with you in this matter, if at all possible. This does not mean that you should espouse my way of thinking. But it does mean that you should agree that my way of thinking is Catholic."

In brief, the unpretentious proposal which I ask the Congregation to consider with benevolence is this: Without further discussion or other consequences, stop the proceedings which for years have been in progress against me and from which nothing good can come for either side. In this case, the questions raised in part one and two of this letter will no longer require an answer, not as far as I am concerned.

In the hope that your Congregation will examine this proposal, I greet you with singlular esteem.

Most devotedly yours,
(signed) Hans Küng

cc.

Cardinal Julius Döpfner, President of the Conference of German Bishops
Cardinal Dr. Hermann Volk, Bishop of Mainz
Dr. Carl-Joseph Leiprecht, Bishop of Rottenburg
Professor Dr. H. -J. Vogt, Dean of the Theological Faculty of the University of Tübingen

enclosures:

1. The "Declaration for the Freedom of Theology" in German, Italian, French, English, and Spanish
2. H. Küng-K. Rahner, Versöhnliches "Schlusswort unter einer Debatte" *Publik-Forum* (June 1, 1973)
3. *Fehlbar ? Eine Bilanz* ed. Hans Küng (Zürich/Einsiedeln/Köln) — under separate cover

Enclosure 31

LETTER OF THE CONGREGATION FOR THE DOCTRINE OF THE FAITH TO PROFESSOR KÜNG, March 30, 1974

399/57/i

Rome, March 30, 1974
Palazzo del S. Uffizio 11

Professor Hans Küng
Walshäuserstrasse 23
D-74 Tübingen
GERMANY

Dear Professor Küng:

The Congregation for the Doctrine of the Faith has received your letter of September 22, 1973. As we mentioned when we acknowledged receipt of your letter on October 22, 1973, the Congregation intended to send you a comprehensive reply. This reply we convey to you at this time.

In a letter to you on July 4, 1973, the Congregation for the Doctrine of the Faith explained its position with regard to the doctrines dealt with in the Declaration *Mysterium Ecclesiae.* Should you subscribe to the doctrine of this Declaration, which has the approval of the Pope, the Congregation would regard as terminated the proceedings pending against your doctrines. We cannot understand why it should be "cynical" on the part of the Congregation to make this statement or why it should be "a shame" or a "condemnation" for a Catholic theologian to be urged to subscribe to the doctrine of the Church. Should you not want to subscribe to the doctrine of the Declaration *Mysterium Ecclesiae,* the Congregation has offered you the possibility of a discussion.

In your long letter you address many questions under the following headings:

1. Protest against the procedural norms of the Congregation, against the particular proceedings instituted against you and a request for information about what sense a discussion might make.
2. Remarks on the theological problematic.
3. Your own personal proposal.

The Congregation responds to the main contents of your questions as follows:

I. THE PROCEEDINGS

Your letters to the Congregation are a constant attempt at shifting the burden of the discussion toward procedural questions and away from the problem of your doctrines. Besides, we are of the opinion that our procedure is equitable, loyal, even if it allows for improvements.

1. The Norms of Procedure

Apparently, the basic mistake (and it is not yours alone) consists in looking upon the proceedings instituted by the Congregation as on a prosecution in a criminal case. What is involved is rather an attempt at investigating a theological opinion in order to ascertain "whether it coincides with divine revelation and the teaching office of the Church" (Art. 3). We are not dealing here with a private opinion, known only to the author, but with a doctrine publicly disseminated in the ecclesial community. This investigation and ascertainment unfolds in two phases. In the first phase, which unfolds within the Congregation, the Congregation, after examining the writing under investigation, arrives through its collegial organs at a judgment as to whether or not the doctrines of the writing under investigation contrast with the norm of faith. This investigation unfolds in a serious and collegial manner with the special assistance of an expert. The task of this expert is always to draw attention to the positive side of the arguments and concerns of the author. This expert is called "relator pro auctore" and should not be confused with the counsel for the defense in judicial proceedings. All the documents involved in this phase are only relative to the investigation performed by individual experts. This whole examination can lead to the conclusion that the doctrine under investigation does contrast with the doctrine of the Church. In this case, the second phase of the proceedings begins, and this is no longer confined to the Congregation alone.

The first action undertaken by the Congregation as such, which brings into play the authority proper to it, does not consist in the Congregation's making available opinions previously submitted by experts, but rather in the Congregation's formulating an opinion through the vote of the cardinals and the approval of that opinion by the Pope. The outcome of this official act is imparted in writing to the local ordinary and to the author. This letter contains the statements which, in the conviction of the Congregation, are incompatible with revelation and the doctrine of the teaching office. In this phase, after the Congregation has already precisely stated its objections, the author is invited to explain himself. The author himself, then, takes over the "defense" (since the "relator pro auctore" has already terminated his task in the investigative phase within the Congregation itself). The author gives his explanations in writing. If necessary, provisions are made for a discussion. After the explanations of the author have been examined, and in keeping with the outcome of this examination, the Congregation decides collegially what to do next. This decision is then imparted to the author and the local ordinary.

The norms of procedure do not deal with eventual further steps, nor do they speak of the possibility of an appeal, since this possibility is covered by general norms.

2. The Proceedings and the Investigation of Some of Your Writings

a. The Congregation for the Doctrine of the Faith maintains that it has observed the provisions of *Integrae servandae* and the "norms of procedure." The Congregation acknowledges that the investigative proceedings relative to your two books have been protracted too long. However, in no small measure, this delay was forced upon the Congregation by your own conduct. When you were invited to a discussion on your book, *Die Kirche,* you answered: ". . . an unplanned journey to Rome is out of the question as long as the semester at the University of Tübingen is in progress." You requested, in addition, that "the conditions . . . be agreed upon before my departure," and you listed five "essential" conditions. The Congregation responded to this request. On July 27, 1968, you made a new request. You wished to have "the Order of procedure of your Congregation worked out on the basis of *Intergrae servandae.*" In order to accede to your wish, we waited for the publication of this order of procedure, which had already been used in the praxis of the Congregation prior to publication. This order of procedure provides that the first step should be not a discussion, but the author's written reply to the objections raised. This is why you were asked to provide a written explanation as to the individual objections. Naturally, the points to be explained would be the same as the topics of a discussion, should one be held. To the letter of the Congregation dated July 12, 1971, you replied on January 24, 1972. On September 22, 1973, you answered our letter of July 4, 1972. It is true that in both cases the Congregation requested you to answer within thirty days, which accords with procedural norms applicable to all similar cases. But it is also true that the Congregation has waited for your replies even after the deadline was past and without taking any further steps.

I hope that these short and incomplete remarks will persuade you to tone down your complaints over delays and unilateral deadlines.

b. What has been said above concerning the order of procedure answers, by implication, your questions about "conditions."

The "complete access and free perusal of your dossier" at the Congregation (cf. your letter of May 30, 1968 and September 22, 1973) is not provided for by the procedural norms because the investigative proceedings are not a judicial act, or a prosecution and because the records of the pertinent dossier do not have the status of trial records. The published writings of the author, and not the eventual charge or the documents in the dossier, constitute the document that counts when it comes to determining what the author teaches. The position of the Congregation results only from the decision approved by the Pope after the termination of the investigation. This result was communicated to you in two letters of May 6, 1961 and July 12, 1971. Hence, letters, opinions of individual experts, consultants, or members of the Congregation can be looked upon only as provisional internal working instruments.

With regard to the "relator pro auctore" (who is not to be confused with legal counsel in a trial), the procedural norms provide that he should be appointed by the Congregation itself. His task is to help the Congregation in a dialectical way during that phase of the investigation in which the Congregation alone is involved, so that it may arrive at as objective an assessment of the author's doctrine as possible.

Sometimes the investigation of the Congregation may also come to the conclusion that the doctrines under investigation do conform with the doctrine of the Magisterium or that they are to be numbered among the opinions open to free theological discussion. In this case, the proceedings are terminated without the author being told or unnecessarily disquieted.

The author is entitled to defend himself. He is urged by letter to explain himself. If necessary, he is invited to a discussion.

Should the author believe that irregularities have occurred, he has the right to appeal. This right is guaranteed by the general norms of the Code.

3. The Discussion

You ask what sense there is to hold a discussion between the Congregation and yourself. You ask this question especially because of the publication of the Declaration *Mysterium Ecclesiae*, which you name "Lex Küng" and which, in your view, is prejudicial to the outcome of the discussion. In connection with what has been mentioned at the beginning, it must be clearly stated here that, should a discussion be held, the Congregation obviously would not change the doctrine of the two Vatican Councils or that of the Declaration *Mysterium Ecclesiae*. How can a Catholic theologian call this doctrine a "dictatorial act" ["Diktat"]?

A further clarification: This discussion is not to be equated with a free academic discussion among theologians or with an exchange of views, as is the case at a convention of scholars. What would be involved instead is a discussion at the scholarly level which the author conducts with the theologians appointed by the Congregation, the purpose being to ascertain most precisely the author's doctrine and to compare it with the statements of the Magisterium. The Congregation would do this in virtue of the authority delegated to it by the Magisterium of the Pope of Rome. The purpose of the discussion would be, then, once more to give you the opportunity to explain the reasons why you maintain that your opinions may be discussed without adversely affecting doctrines which are mandatory and normative for Catholics. Basically, then, the discussion is a new opportunity for the clarification of the opinion of the author, and, in this sense, for his "defense."

The Congregation cannot accept your objection that it proceeds disloyally against you on the ground that it has published the Declaration on your doctrines prior to a discussion. To begin with, the Declaration deals not only with your personal views, but also with the opinions of many other theologians.

As far as your writings are concerned, it must be said that, according to the procedural norms, a discussion with the author is optional, not obligatory. The Congregation is only obligated to request from the author a written explanation on the points that raise questions. This has been done. The publication of the Declaration *Mysterium Ecclesiae* also became necessary because, in your writings in many languages, in your lectures in various parts of the world, you have continued to disseminate opinions which have deeply confused the faith of the Christian community. Even though proceedings were pending against you, you have done this against the explicit invitation of the Congregation in December 1967, and in disregard of the valid law which prescribes the *Imprimatur* (Cf. the letter of the Congregation to you, February 12, 1971, and your answer on February 26, 1971). The competent authority of the Church was duty-bound to take measures in the defense of the faith and to intervene by way of providing a clarification to which the faithful are entitled.

You complain that "the situation has worsened . . . because of the way the Congregation has conducted itself publicly." The Congregation is amazed that you should voice such a reproach. Long ago you published the letters of this Congregation, you released statements to the press, you gave interviews on your "case," and you disseminated your doctrines while the investigative proceedings were in progress. The Congregation has kept silent even when you painted before the public a very black picture of it.

II. THE THEOLOGICAL PROBLEMATIC

1. You request of the Congregation "an argumentation that would prove the possibility of infallible propositions . . ." You want to know "how the corresponding texts from Vatican I and II are to be theologically grounded and responsibly substantiated." Actually, this is the fundamental question, not to say, the fundamental doubt in your book *Unfehlbar ? Eine Anfrage.*

The Catholic theologian is certainly permitted to raise a question which touches on a truth of faith and then, to seek an explanation. But, even if he should not promptly find a rational justification of this truth, the Catholic theologian may not call in question the truth of faith itself or deny it. As long as he is a Catholic, no Catholic theologian maintains that, in the name of theology, the denial or the doubting of a dogma of faith is admissible.

With regard to related theological problems, many competent authors have already responded to your inquiry.

2. Your distinction between infallibility and "infallible propositions" is interesting. It could be one of the topics for discussion. Thus, it could be asked: How can anyone uphold infallibility as dogmatically defined in Vatican I and II and still deny the possibility of infallible propositions?

3. "Why wouldn't 'historical condition' in particular cases entail even the possibility of error, as history seems to show in many ways?"

As a theologian, you do know which are the presuppositions on which infallibility rests. You also know the answer to the question: The Catholic Church believes (see Vatican I) that, due to the assistance of the Holy Spirit, these presuppositions exclude the possibility of any error in a dogmatic definition (cf. *Mysterium Ecclesiae,* 5). The question you raise at this point in your letter shows with sufficient clarity that these are located at the level of dogma and not at the level of free theological discussion. Do you believe that your statements accord with the doctrine of the two Vatican Councils?

4. You maintain that the Declaration *Mysterium Ecclesiae* fails to take adequately into account the international debate on infallibility. You lament the fact that the Congregation failed to send its experts to the graduate seminar on infallibility in Tübingen. You hold that the concern that comes to expression in your book is not "to the undoing but to the edification of the Church."

As you know, the competence of the Congregation extends to the doctrine of the faith. It does not extend to doctrines that may be freely debated, though these too are known to the Congregation in their international dimensions. But the Congregation is not a theological faculty. It is an organ in the service of the teaching office of the Pope.

Whether or not your doctrines are "to the edification of the Church" does not depend on your intentions. It is a question of fact. It would not be "to the edification of the Church" to contradict defined doctrines of the Church.

III. PERSONAL WORD

1. You appeal to the freedom of the theologians. However, the Congregation must remind you of the highest principle that presides over the exercise of this freedom: Both the teaching office and the theologians are *in the service* of revealed truth. Therefore, a believing Catholic is not free to deny a revealed truth

in the name of theological freedom. Besides, theologians are *accountable* also to the ecclesial community and to ecclesiastical authority to which Christ himself has entrusted the task to teach and protect revealed truth (*Lumen Gentium,* 25; Abbott, 47-50; *Dei Verbum,* 10; Abbott, 117-118).

For the good of the community of believers, who are entitled to receive sound doctrine, the Congregation has published the Declaration *Mysterium Ecclesiae,* not as a kind of theological essay, but in compliance with the directives of the Pope and with his approval. When you advocate positions which conflict with this Declaration, you must ask youself whether you still acknowledge that there is in the Church a doctrinal authority superior to your own.

The question is, in fact, not an idle one. In all your answers, the level of dogma seems to be totally nonexistent. It all goes as if the doctrines you advocate were all material for free theological discussion and did not touch upon any truth binding on a believing Catholic. Hence the question: What value do you credit to dogmas and to the statements of the teaching office of the Church? Do you subscribe to the dogmatic character of Vatican I?

2. In the end, you propose as a solution that you yourself and the Congregation should keep silent. History would prove who is right.

The Congregation regrets that it is not in a position to accept the judgment of history as a criterion of faith. In the Church, there is a criterion other than the judgment of history. This is the authority of the living Magisterium which is instituted to serve revealed truth. With regard to the infallibility of the Church and of the Pope, the Declaration *Mysterium Ecclesiae* rests on a defined dogma. It is difficult to see how such a defined doctrine could be left to the judgment of history.

If, then, your proposal to keep silent is likely to veil or conceal the unambiguousness and clarity of the doctrine of faith, the Congregation cannot accept it.

But, if that silence should be understood and clearly interpreted as an act of respect on your part toward the Magisterium, and as a time for reflection so that you could examine your doctrines and conform them to the Magisterium, your proposal might perhaps make sense.

The Congregation, then, stands by its offer of a discussion that would give you the additional opportunity to defend and better explain yourself. As already mentioned, this discussion would deal with the questions which the Congregation put to you in the letters of May 6, 1971 and July 12, 1971.

The Congregation's only concern is that the Catholic doctrine should be proclaimed in its purity and in fidelity to Christ. It has no intention of persecuting anybody. It wants only to make sure that the Catholic community receives the spiritual nourishment to which it is entitled. In view of the fact that both the Congregation and you, each in their own way, are responsible for the proclamation and profession of the doctrine of the Church, personal considerations and prestige are matters of secondary importance. In humble service to God's Word, we, all of us together, must hold on to the rule of faith. This entails two things: fidelity to tradition and a dynamic orientation toward the future. What matters is that we serve the truth of Christ. Because we have so much confidence in your spirit as a priest, we trust that you will act in genuine fidelity to that truth.

Would you please let the Congregation know whether you intend to make use of this opportunity to defend yourself and when you can come to Rome. The date and the participants in the discussion will be arranged immediately after you confirm your acceptance. The Congregation would like to dispose of this matter as soon as possible.

With cordial greetings,

Franc. Cardinal Seper, Prefect
+ Fr. Jérome Hamer, O.P., Secretary

Enclosure 32

LETTER OF PROFESSOR KÜNG TO THE CONGREGATION FOR THE DOCTRINE OF THE FAITH, Septebmer 4, 1974

74 Tübingen
September 4, 1974

His Eminence
Cardinal Fanjo Seper
Prefect of the Congregation for the
Doctrine of the Faith
Vatican City

Your Eminence:

The answer of your Congregation to my letter of September 22, 1973, dated March 30, 1974, came into my hands on April 6, 1974 via the Apostolic Nuncio in Germany. I, herewith, kindly acknowledge receipt of this letter. I, too, needed many months to consider my reply. The latest initiative of the Congregation and the complications that ensued forced me once again to wait even longer before replying.

I do appreciate the fact that for the first time in the course of these negotiations which have been in progress over seven years about the books, *Die Kirche* and *Unfehlbar ?,* the Congregation comprehensively addresses most of my questions, and attempts to give reasons for its own position. I am especially grateful for the instructions concerning the legal situation, inasmuch as this cannot be ascertained from the norms of procedure of the Congregation. Unless I am mistaken, this is the first time that these instructions have been given me. The considerations on the theological problematic, too, help me to see the whole affair in a clearer light.

Unfortunately, the expectations voiced in my last letter concerning a termination of the proceedings have not been fulfilled. On the contrary and to my chagrin, at the time when my letter was being answered, the Secretary of the Congregation addressed himself to the public in an interview of many pages in the *Herder-Korrespondenz* to defend and justify the self-understanding and methods of the Congregation as they are applied to the proceedings against me. Because of this unexpected escalation, the Congregation is responsible for continued press discussion of the various Roman proceedings and for considerable unrest in large segments of the Catholic clergy and laity. It is easy to understand why the disturbance has erupted most visibly in my own country, Switzerland, where the Pfürtner case has left behind persistent bitterness and indignation against the methods of the Congregation. This commotion has not only produced individual statements, petitions, and press reports, but it has also been noted in the synod of my own diocese, Basel, together with many cantonal synods and numerous other Church bodies. All these groups have serious reservations about the way the Congregation operates and request that the proceedings against me be terminated.

The most important theological reactions to the interview of the Secretary most radically question both, on the theological and juridical grounds, the self-understanding and the methods of the Congregation. They suggest that the Congregation should undertake a general revision of its procedure. I take the liberty of enclosing the particularly well-balanced and objectively grounded statements of Professor Dr. Johannes Neumann, "Es ginge anders besser," *Herder-Korrespondenz,* June, 1974, and of Professor Dr. Josef Blank, "Macht und/oder Wahrheit ? Zur Problematik der römischen Glaubens-Kongregation als einer Wahrheitsverordnungsbehörde," *Publik-Forum,* No. 13, 1974. There is no doubt that the competent articles of these renowned experts entail clear consequences also for the proceedings against me.

Against the background of the very grave and fundamental questions which have now been addressed to the Congregation by others, it does not seem expedient at this time to address again all the individual points; to strengthen my objections against the proceedings as a whole, especially against the "coordinated initiative" against me on July 7 of last year; and to ward off the objections of the Congregation relative, for instance, to the fact that the proceedings have been delayed for years, and to other things as well. When one reads the letter of the Congregation, especially the Secretary's justification of its methods, as it appeared simultaneously in the *Herder-Korrespondenz,* the procedure of the Congregation seems, at first, to be correct. But even in Rome, it will perhaps be understood that these methods seem less correct to me, the person concerned, — and indeed to some theologians who in the last decades have been disciplined or even dismissed from their chairs through such proceedings, which are not supposed to be punitive, according to your letter. Understandably, your Congregation would gladly get rid of the smell of the Inquisition. In the eyes of the public, however, apologetics makes the desired impression only if the Congregation should decisively revise its procedural norms, as requested. These norms still carry the marks of the Inquisition. In the long letter of the Congregation and in the even longer interview of its Secretary, not a word is said about the reasons why the Congregation refuses to adopt the proposals of the 1360 theology professors the world over (Declaration "For the Freedom of Theology"). In my letter, I have again insistently requested that these proposals be adopted. Should the Congregation adopt them, there would be no need to engage in any kind of apologetics. No one doubts their legality, fairness, and practicality. They can only contribute to the prestige of the Congregation and of the Roman Church. The Congregation could also address itself to the "Promotion of the Faith" in keeping with the mandate of Pope Paul VI in 1965. I would like, therefore, again to request the Congregation to take to heart the wishes of the 1360 theologians, which I enclosed in many languages in my last letter.

Now, right at the beginning of your answer, I am being told reproachfully that my letters to the Congregation are "a constant attempt at shifting the burden of the discussion toward procedural questions and away from the problem of your (my) doctrine." Since the Congregation is conducting two "proceedings" against me at the same time (with possible disciplinary consequences), I am forced to direct my attention to these "procedural norms" and time and again beg of your Congregation at least to take a stand with regard to these "procedural questions." This repeated request has been honored at last. But never did I intend to shift the discussion away from my doctrine. On the contrary, I have over and over again drawn attention to my "inquiry." I have not managed for the first time to have the Congregation address the theological problematic. Of course, the Congregation has not answered my "inquiry" as to infallible propositions. If my understanding is correct, the Congregation looks upon it as an inquiry to which a response has already been made. But I cannot take this to be a grounded response to my inquiry, a response which I would be entirely prepared to accept with respect.

I still have other numerous and important individual questions concerning the legality of the proceedings, for example:

— about the two-phase theory and especially the secretive phase within the Congregation itself;

— about the non-punitive nature of proceedings which do, however, have punitive consequences;

— about the relator pro auctore, who "assists the Congregation in a dialectical way," and whom the author himself is not permitted to know;

— about "the documents relative to the investigation," produced by the Congregation ("letters and opinions of individual experts, consultants, or members of the Congregation"), which, for reasons I do not understand, the person concerned is not allowed to see;

— about the access to the records, which is again being denied me in such a general way and the incomprehensible reasons behind this denial;

— about my exclusion from the decisive first phase of the proceedings on the "charge" and also from the last phase which is decisive in terms of judgment or condemnation;

— about the "eventual further steps" which are not dealt with in the procedural norms, but are mentioned in your letter;

— about the possibilities of appeal, on the basis of the Apostolic Constitution *Regimini Ecclesiae,* possibilities which are still unclear to me;

— about the discussion, which is conducted "at a scholarly level" and yet is not supposed to be "a free academic discussion" in which, apparently, it is not anticipated that the Congregation, too, could be theologically mistaken;

— about the fact that the publication of the Declaration *Mysterium Ecclesiae,* which goes beyond Vatican I and II in various respects, prejudices the proceedings as a whole; etc.

All these questions show only too well how justified is the request that the procedure of the Congregation be subjected to a wholesale revision. Before I address the theological problematic, I would like to refer briefly to an objection which, in this context, cannot go unchallenged. The Congregation objects to the fact that I have in various ways addressed myself to the public, whereas, "the Congregation has kept silent." Apparently, it is not remembered in the Vatican that the very biased indiscretions published in the Italian press on June 12, 1968, and later also in the press elsewhere, originated in Vatican circles. According to these reports, in the first meeting of the Cardinals of the Curia, the "Council of Ministers" newly constituted by the Pope, measures were decreed against the author because he had "offended the Pope." Since no dementi could be secured from the Vatican and your Congregation kept stubbornly silent about all the rumors, never coming to the defense of my Catholic sentiment, I was forced to release a correction to the press and still later to inform the public objectively. I cannot be expected to leave the concerned public uninformed when, in secret proceedings and without my being heard, your Congregation decrees that the further dissemination and translations of my book, *Die Kirche*, are forbidden, as it happened in the "explicit invitation of the Congregation in December 1967." Since that time, a biased piece of public-relations work from the organs of the Vatican could be observed unfolding against me from Germany to Korea and New Zealand. Against this background, the "silence" of the Congregation, as much as my public reactions, do take on a different look.

In the meantime, the Congregation has broken into the proceedings still pending with a Declaration that goes beyond Vatican I. Since the concerns of both sides had been clarified at this time, I made an offer to the Congregation orally and in writing in the fall of 1973 that I would no longer speak publicly about the infallibility question unless the Congregation itself should force me to do so. This was a way of bringing to an end an unprofitable public confrontation about difficult theological problems. I have adhered strictly to this voluntary pledge. But now it is the Congregation that takes it upon itself once again to direct the attention of the press to this affair. It challenges me to defend myself against a procedure which still does not seem to me to be either just or appropriate.

Among the misleading pieces of information given out to the public is the communique about the inquiries which the Swiss bishops addressed to your Congregation. For years, I have been denied access to my dossier 399/57/i, and especially to the acts of the proceedings against my books, *Die Kirche* and *Unfehlbar ? Eine Anfrage*. I have been denied the assistance of counsel, yet the Swiss bishops were given to understand that both these things had been granted me. Unfortunately, this public statement, which was at least open to misunderstanding, had to be challenged likewise by means of another public statement.

These new complications have emerged from the way the Congregation has proceeded. Other complications can only too easily follow. This shows once more that it would have been better immediately to have adopted my proposal, and for the time being hand over the whole affair to the theologians and let them discuss it. They would ascertain (this is what my "doctrine" is all about) what is the "revealed truth" about the point which is being addressed in my inquiry. You, too, are of the opinion that not only the theologians, but also the "Magisterium of the Church" must be in the "service" of that revealed truth.

That "theologians are accountable to the ecclesial community and to the ecclesiastical authority" and above all to the Lord of the Church is a truth which I hold in high respect. True, no one in the Church has "the freedom to deny revealed truth." To the extent to which the teaching office of the Church is "in the service of revealed truth," I, too, have always acknowledged "a teaching authority in the Church." In fact, I have often wished that, when it comes to the decisive statements of the Christian message, the "Magisterium" would advocate "sound doctrine" with more intensity, more concentration, and more conviction.

My whole inquiry seeks precisely to ascertain what are those truths which are "located at the level of dogma" and "are binding on Catholics." That this is not so easily done is evidenced by many of Rome's doctrinal decisions from the Galileo case through the *Syllabus errorum* and all the way to the encyclicals *Humani generis* and *Humanae vitae.* Even in Rome, the problematic character of these decisions is being perceived. The same is evidenced by the diverging interpretations of the definition of Vatican I. In my theological publications, I have concerned myself intensively with this definition. I would not have done so if I had not credited a "dogmatic character" to it.

It is generally admitted that my inquiry concerning infallibility has touched on an obscure point in the doctrine of the Church. In the Catholic Church and in Catholic theology, there is no unanimity as to the response to be made to this inquiry. This much is certainly known even in Rome. It has been shown in the book I edited in 1973 under the title, *Fehlbar ? Eine Bilanz.* The Congregation, too, admits that we are dealing here "not only with your (my) personal views, but also with the opinions of many other theologians." It is this admission on the part of the Congregation that corroborates the fundamental objection against the appropriateness of these proceedings. I cannot understand why the Congregation has instituted these proceedings just against me. Nor can I understand why, of all the theologians in the world, I should be the one to whom the Declaration *Mysterium Ecclesiae* was delivered officially at home, and who was required to formally "accept" it. In view of this, the surmise that this Declaration of the Congregation is a "Lex Küng" is not without foundation.

Finally, I would like to correct an important theological misunderstanding on the part of the Congregation. The Congregation assumes that for me "the judgment of history" is the "criterion of faith." The assumption is false. For me, as for the Congregation, the "criterion of faith" is "revealed truth." But, obviously, it is only in the course of history that it becomes clear to the teaching office of the Church what is revealed truth on a particular point. "The authority of the living Magisterium which is instituted to serve revealed truth" must hold this truth just as much as the theologians. In its Declaration *Mysterium Ecclesiae,* the Congregation admits in a particularly clear way that the articulations of the faith on the part of the Magisterium are contingent on the situation, that they are imperfect, perfectible, open to additions, and replaceable. Which seems to show that, when it comes to "revealed truth" no one should count himself among the "*beati possidentes.*"

I made the proposal that, since both sides had made public their positions, the affair should be put to rest, and time should be allowed for a clarifying discussion among theologians. The purpose of this proposal was not exactly "to veil or conceal the lucidity and clarity of faith," but rather to expose this fully to the light. To date, I have hardly added anything to what had been said. I, therefore, reiterate the personal proposal I submitted in my last letter. Besides, it is difficult to say what decisive things the Congregation could add to what it has said in its Declaration. If this Declaration actually has revealed truth on its side, lucidly and clearly, it will certainly prevail in the Church without any help from disciplinary coercive measures.

I will never lack "respect toward the Magisterium" any time it bears witness to revealed truth. It goes without saying that I do not by any means exclude that, in the course of time, I will get to know revealed truth better, more clearly, and unequivocally. On the contrary, I take pains every day to achieve this clearer understanding, always prepared to accept any correction demanded of me for reasons. In this sense, I gladly accept the "time for reflection" allowed me by the Congregation "to examine 'my' doctrines," as is the duty of each and every scholar and especially of a serious theologian. Thus, I certainly do not exclude that, in the course of time, my doctrine could "fall in line" with that of the Magisterium. Likewise, the Congregation remains no doubt open to new developments and insights. As I explained at the outset with reference to voices that count, a fundamental reflection on the self-understanding and the methods of the Congregation suggests itself as particularly desirable. I too, would like to reconsider the whole thing in a broader theological and ecclesial context in order to clarify, for my benefit and the benefit of others, what is actually the "revealed truth," and thus, what is the "doctrine of the Church," and ultimately what is the content of our faith.

With the assurance that it will always be my concern to be of service to the Christian community and its faith, I remain, with particular esteem.

Devotedly yours,
(signed) Hans Küng

cc.

Cardinal Dr. Julius Döpfner, President of the Conference of German Bishops
Cardinal Dr. Hermann Volk, Bishop of Mainz
Bishop Dr. Anton Hänggi, Bishop of Basel
Vicar General and Suffragan Anton Herre, Rottenburg
Professor Dr. Wilhelm Korff, Dean of the Department of Catholic Theology, University of Tübingen

enclosures:

The aforementioned statements of Professor Josef Blank and Professor Johannes Neumann.

Enclosure 33

LETTER OF CARDINAL HÖFFNER TO PROFESSOR KÜNG, December 23, 1974

December 23, 1974

Professor Dr. Hans Küng
74 Tübingen
Waldhäuserstr. 23

Dear Professor:

When I returned from the Synod of Bishops in Rome, I found your friendly letter of October 17, 1974 and your new book, *Christ sein.* I thank you kindly for both.

In my interview with the newspaper of the Diocese of Cologne on October 11, 1974, I did not concern myself ultimately either with the discipline of theology as we learned it at the Gregorian or with the position of the Roman Congregation for the Doctrine of the Faith, but I concerned myself with the faith of the Church as proclaimed by Vatican I and confirmed by Vatican II. It is with this faith of the Church that I cannot reconcile your view of the infallibility of the Pope and of the councils.

Do the latest developments in theology and society have the authority required to change the faith of the Church? Besides, today there is no such thing as the doctrine of theology. Some do profess with the faith of the Church that the Pope is infallible when he speaks *ex cathedra* and issues definitive decisions about the faith. Others say that neither the Pope nor the Councils nor the Apostles could proclaim faith propositions which would be infallible.

Some profess that God has created not only the visible world, but also the angels. Others say that there are no angels and that, when Holy Scripture mentions angels, it refers only to God's tender and loving care for us.

Some profess the existence of evil spirits, that is, of evil beings who had been created by God good in their nature, but fell away from God through their own fault. Others say goodbye to the devil and explain that the belief in the devil is a dubious heritage of time-conditioned biblical conceptions.

Some profess that the Virgin Mary gave birth "to the Son of God on earth without having known a man, overshadowed by the Holy Spirit." Others say that Mary conceived her Son through intercourse with a man.

Some profess that Jesus Christ arose from the dead and appeared to his own. Others say that, after Jesus died, his memory was so powerful in the disciples that they dared to say, figuratively, that he was dead no longer, but had been raised from the dead.

Some profess that the Eucharist sacrifice can only be offered validly by an ordained priest. Others say that all the faithful are empowered to consecrate the Eucharist.

Some profess that a sacramental marriage which has been consummated is indissoluble because God wills it to be so. Others say that the indissolubility of marriage is only a commandment one ought to strive to observe, so that remarriage is to be allowed during the lifetime of the other spouse, if the earlier marriage is hopelessly wrecked, that is, "dead."

Some profess that Jesus gave the mandate to make disciples of all nations and to baptize them in his name. Others say that the purpose of missionary work is to make sure that a Hindu becomes a better Hindu.

Obviously, there is no such a thing as *the* doctrine of the theology professors. A few of them not only say it differently; they say different things. Who decides who is right? The stronger arguments? Both sides claim to have the stronger arguments.

The question I am asking is this: By what authority do you profess your opinions?

Your new book, *Christ sein,* has been sitting on my desk for quite a while. I haven't found yet the time to read it. Your dedication "In the Service of the Common Christian Cause" has pleased me.

Sincere good wishes for Christmas and the New Year.

Yours,
(signed) + Joseph Card. Höffner

Enclosure 34

LETTER OF PROFESSOR KÜNG TO CARDINAL HÖFFNER, January 10, 1975

January 10, 1975

His Eminence
Cardinal Dr. Joseph Höffner
Archbishop of Cologne
5 Cologne 1
Eintrachtstr. 164

My dear Brother:

I have read your letter attentively. Totally contradictory statements cannot, of course, be true at the same time. The question is, then, who is correct about the particular points. It is, however, too simple a solution to appeal to the "doctrine of the Church," since even the "Magisterium" is being asked how it understands that doctrine. Even according to Vatican II, the Magisterium does not stand above the Word of God; it must serve that Word. Whether it does this in all the points is at least a question. You asked me: By what authority do you profess your opinions? My reply would have to be: By the authority of the Word of God which I, as a theologian, must serve.

Whether I do this correctly, is, of course, an open question. However, the representatives of the Magisterium should in turn argue on the basis of the Word of God, instead of merely decreeing again what has been handed down. I have given reasons for the questions raised and for the views I set forth, for all of them. With regard to the question you have raised, I have disclosed my mind, particularly in the volume of essays entitled *Fehlbar ?* To-date, no one has refuted me.

In my opinion, a discussion in which both sides always appeal formally to an authority is not likely to take us far. One ought to speak about the thing itself. I would, therefore, be very pleased if you, as bishop, would find the time to read this book. So many are reading it at this time.

I sincerely wish you God's blessings for the year already begun and send you cordial greetings.

Yours,
(signed) Hans Küng

Enclosure 35

DECLARATION OF THE CONGREGATION FOR THE DOCTRINE OF THE FAITH, February 15, 1975

In fulfillment of its mandate to promote and defend doctrine concerning faith and morals in the whole Church, the Congregation for the Doctrine of the Faith has examined two books of Professor Hans Küng, *Die Kirche* and *Unfehlbar ? Eine Anfrage,* which have been published in many languages. In two different letters, dated May 6, 1971 and July 12, 1971, the Congregation informed Professor Küng about the difficulties it had found in his views and requested him to explain in writing how these views were to be reconciled with Catholic doctrine. In a letter of July 4, 1973, the Congregation offered Professor Küng the further opportunity to explain his opinion by taking part in a discussion. In his letter of September 4, 1974, Professor Küng declined to make use of this opportunity. In his answers, he failed to prove that some of his views on the Church do not contradict Catholic doctrine. He rather persisted in them, even after the publication of the Declaration *Mysterium Ecclesiae.*

In order to eliminate any doubts about the doctrine which the Catholic Church holds and in order that the faith of Christians should in no way be obscured, the Congregation recalls the doctrine of the Magisterium, as set forth in the Declaration *Mysterium Ecclesiae,* and declares:

In the two aforementioned books of Professor Küng, there are views which, in various measures, contrast with the doctrine of the Church which is held by all the faithful. Because of their particular importance, we mention only the points to follow, while abstaining from passing judgment on other views which Professor Küng advocates.

The view which at least doubts the dogma of the infallibility of the Chruch or reduces it to the Church's fundamental indefectibility in the truth, with the possibility of error in propositions which the Magisterium of the Church teaches definitively as propositions to be held, does contradict the doctrine defined by Vatican I and confirmed by Vatican II.

Another error which heavily burdens the teaching of Professor Küng relates to his view of the Magisterium of the Church. He does not apply the genuine notion of authentic Magisterium. According to this notion, "[the bishops] are authentic teachers, that is, teachers endowed with the authority of Christ, who preach to the people committed to them the faith which they must believe and put into practice" (Vatican II; Dogmatic Constitution *Lumen Gentium*, 25 [Abbott, 47]) for "the task of authentically interpreting the Word of God, whether written or handed down, has been entrusted exclusively to the living teaching office of the Church" (Vatican II; Dogmatic Constitution *Dei Verbum*, 10 [Abbott, 117-118]).

Further, the view already suggested by Professor Küng in his book, *Die Kirche*, namely, that, at least in case of necessity, the Eucharist can be validly consecrated by a non-ordained baptized person, is not compatible with the doctrine of the Fourth Lateran Council and with Vatican II.

In his letter of September 4, 1974, Professor Küng does not at all exclude that, given adequate time for thorough study, he could bring his views in line with the authentic doctrine of the Magisterium of the Church. In view of this and in spite of the importance of these doctrines, the Congregation, so directed by Pope Paul VI, *for the time being* imparts to Professor Küng the admonition not to advocate these doctrines any longer. It reminds him that the ecclesiastical authority has authorized him to teach theology in the spirit of Christian doctrine, but not to advocate views which distort that doctrine or call it in doubt.

The bishops in Germany and in other places where the situation requires it, especially where the aforementioned doctrines are advocated in theological faculties, seminaries and other institutions dedicated to Catholic or priestly education, are to see to it that the faithful are appropriately instructed about the doctrine of the Church, about the Declaration *Mysterium Ecclesiae*, as well as this declaration.

Priests who, by virtue of their office, are proclaimers of the Gospel, teachers of the Catholic faith, and catechists are under obligation to profess faithfully and to set forth the doctrine of the Church concerning the questions at issue here.

Finally, theologians are again requested to investigate the mystery of the Church and the other mysteries of the faith in the obedience of faith and to the true edification of the Church.

With this declaration, the proceedings of the Congregation for the Doctrine of the Faith in this matter are *for the time being* terminated. In the audience granted to the Prefect of this Congregation on February 14, 1975, Paul VI has approved this declaration and ordered its publication.

Given in Rome, at the Congregation for the Doctrine of the Faith, February 15, 1975.

(signed) Franc. Cardinal Šeper, Prefect

(signed) + Fr. Hamer, O.P., Secretary

DECLARATION OF THE CONFERENCE OF THE GERMAN BISHOPS, February 17, 1975

Declaration of the Conference of German Bishops at the termination of the doctrinal proceedings of the Congregation for the Doctrine of the Faith relative to Die Kirche *and* Unfehlbar ? Eine Anfrage *by Professor Hans Küng.*

I

Upon the termination of the doctrinal proceedings relative to the books *Die Kirche* and *Unfehlbar ? Eine Anfrage* by Professor Hans Küng, the Conference of German Bishops thanks the Congregation for the Doctrine of the Faith in Rome for the decision it has reached. The fact that severe disciplinary measures have been administered should not dispense from an unequivocal clarification as regards the question of truth. The Declaration of the Congregation on February 15, 1975 states this very clearly and in detail. After the Declaration *Mysterium Ecclesiae* of July 5, 1973 and after the present decision, the Conference of German Bishops does not need to comment on Professor Küng's book, *Unfehlbar ?* It stands without change by the position it took in this matter on February 4, 1971 and reaffirms that position.

The decision just reached by the Congregation and approved by Pope Paul VI renounces the use of other measures. In so doing, it assumes with the cooperation of Professor Küng. The Conference of German Bishops concurs, therefore, with the admonition of the Congregation for the Doctrine of the Faith and expects that Professor Küng will no longer advocate the positions which the Magisterium of the Church has repeatedly disavowed. To the extent to which they may possibly have adopted these positions and declared them to be compatible with the understanding which the Church has of herself, this applies also to all those who, by virtue of a mandate of the Church, preach and teach.

II

In this connection, the Conference of German Bishops calls to mind principles which pertain to the basic understanding of what Catholic theology is and which are not sufficiently taken into account in individual works of Professor Küng, especially in *Die Kirche, Unfehlbar ?, Fehlbar ?, Wozu Priester ?,* and *Christ sein.* All these principles relate to the fundamental stance of the theologian and of every Christian toward tradition and ultimately toward the understanding of what the Church herself is.

1. Normative Significance of the Tradition of the Church

It is rightly demanded today that Christian life and the theologian's work be brought in line with the witness of Holy Scripture. It is part and parcel of this that the proclamation of the faith and theology should time and again ask themselves whether they conform to the spirit and contents of Holy Scripture, and whether they are unremittingly prepared to learn from it. Historic-critical exegesis is a valuable help here; today, it is an indispensable help. And yet, within the Church, historic-critical exegesis can in no way be the sum total of what constitutes a legitimate interaction with the Scriptures. Catholic faith lives out of the whole of Scripture. In the interpretation of the Scriptures and in the theological use of them, faith does not permit a onesided or even an exclusive preference for some, mostly "earlier" layers, nor does it permit discrimination against later stages of development. The fact that different scriptural assertions are connections as to their contents and that there is development of doctrine within the New Testament is recognized in the act of accepting the writings into the scriptural canon.

In post-biblical times, the interpretation of revelation at the hands of the Church reflects in its own way and with the historical means then available, the truth of revelation witnessed in Scripture. This unfolding of the Gospel of the Apostles is not merely a piece of historical theology. Because of the assistance of the Holy Spirit, it constitutes, especially in its normative decisions, a true and permanent history of the faith of the Church. This is why, in its function as interpreter of the origins, this binding transmission of the faith has, even today, the significance of a norm.

This normative significance of the ecclesial unfolding of the faith plays too slight a role not only in the writings of Professor Küng which the Congregation has examined, but also in the writings mentioned above. In his theological thinking, Professor Küng often leaps from the New Testament to the present, without retrieving or sufficiently appreciating the rich history of the faith of the Church with its manifold experiences and insights. At the level of execution, this unhistorical confrontation between Scripture and the present is fraught with problems, because no account is taken of the changed situation, especially the spiritual and theological situation. The result is the erection of questionable parallels. Only with the help of the whole of Scripture and the whole of tradition, and only by thus acknowledging that doctrine develops historically, is it possible to preach God's Gospel without doing injustice either to its contents or to the situation and to prevent surrender to momentary and short-lived fads to which even theology is exposed.

2. *The Relationship between the Teaching Office and Theology*

Given the way in which Catholic thought envisions the relation between revelation and reason, every claim of faith must be accounted for; today especially, it must be subjected to disciplined analysis and reflection. And yet, from the beginning, theology is irrevocably dependent on the witness of Scripture and on the normative interpretation of God's Word that comes to fruition through the teaching of the Church. Theology shows whether and how a truth of faith or a theological proposition is grounded in Scripture and in the tradition of the Church. Thus, theology also performs a thoroughly critical function. It ascertains whether there is agreement with the Bible, the earliest witness, and with the normative tradition of the Church. Theology deepens understanding; it brings out hidden presuppositions or connections hitherto undiscovered, and these it discusses and clarifies. And yet, even when all the scientific methods are used, there is no place outside Scripture and the living tradition of the Church where with regard to the whole tradition one can stand and play the part of a detached and neutral umpire, *and* no place from which to construct at the same time a theology that would be valid enough within the ambit of the Church. Just as Scripture did not originate outside the early Church; so too there is no Catholic theology outside its own concrete community of faith. In all his efforts at disciplined illumination of the faith, the theologian stands squarely upon the faith-conviction of the Church. By his own resources, he seeks to ground that conviction and appropriate its meaning. In the course of this work, tensions may indeed be engendered, as for instance when new questions are asked. Yet, because of Christ's own promise, the Catholic theologian has an implicit faith in the tradition of the Church. He seeks to set forth convincingly and also for the benefit of the present, the spiritual power of that tradition.

Professor Küng has neglected his structure of Catholic theology several times, but especially in his book, *Unfehlbar ? Eine Anfrage.* He seems to argue his points from a position outside the community of faith. He places the "burden of proof" for dogmatic decisions only on the shoulders of the Magisterium of the Church and withholds a clear-cut assent to the normative truth of faith until these proofs are delivered. Professor Küng demands from the Magisterium of the Church "proofs" which the *theologian,* precisely as theologian, is himself supposed to provide, and not only through a historical-critical investigation of the Scriptures. The threat here is a reversal in the relationship between the Catholic theologian and the faith tradition of the Church.

True, the claims of this tradition need to be theologically grounded, but even greater is the need to give reasons for contradicting the faith of the Church. With regard to Sacred Scripture and its interpretation and with regard to the whole reality of faith in general, no scientific method can give us such a certainty as would be adequate for us to ground upon it our life and our death in the Christian hope, unless, by virtue of the Spirit sent to her, the Church tells us what the Bible is, which interpretation of the Bible is legitimate, and which development of doctrine may count as legitimate. Besides, the theologian can never make definitive judgments with regard to the tradition of the Church or else the unity of the faith would fall victim to subjective and discretionary decisions. This is all the more obvious if we pause to think that theological inquiry is almost inevitably exposed to constant change. In our time, it often labors also under a pluralism fraught with contradictions.

It is, then, a necessary component of theological method that the theologian should lean on the Magisterium of the Church. True, the theologian is entitled not to give ready-made answers to new questions. Hence, there has to be room in the Church for attempts at clarification. Yet, these attempts should not be made to pass for assured truth or even for Church doctrine. That such attempts are possible is evidenced by the history of the development of the faith of the Church. This development reveals the faith without depriving it of its identity.

3. Concrete Normativeness in the Faith

Anyone who grounds himself and his life in faith in God's self-disclosure in Jesus Christ must have the certainty that he is building upon the truth. In the service of this certainty the Catholic Church has always insisted that the contents of the Christian faith and of its developments be dependably and intelligibly asserted. The Christian faith, too, requires this certainty, for the

Christian message, based as it is on the eschatological Christ-event, is decisive and irrevocable. As God actually casts His lot with man in his own concrete history, He also claims us decisively for Himself. This claim comes to fruition through the Church which is commissioned and empowered for this in the Holy Spirit. The Church's speaking with fullness of power and her performance of sacramental actions are part and parcel of the decisiveness with which God claims man in his concrete historical situation. Thus, for all the influence of historical circumstances upon linguistic formulations and despite the time-conditioned manner in which problems are raised, an absolutely valid and unalterable truth lives on in the dogma of the Church. For this very reason, that truth is binding upon us concretely and in all seriousness, and regardless of the situation in which it first emerged and was put into words. To the Church, and more precisely to the Pope and the bishops as the successors of Peter and the other Apostles, the Lord of the Church has given the mandate and promised the grace of listening attentively to revelation and so of interpreting the word of God with authority and, therefore, normatively. The "infallibility" of the whole Church, of the college of bishops, and of the Pope, is meant to serve no other purpose. It is grounded on no other foundation than the promise of Jesus Christ and the influence of his Spirit.

Professor Küng does not deny the possibility of binding propositions, but he does seem to restrict their necessity and the historical range of their validity to cases of necessity, for which he himself discloses no substantive criteria. His theology fails to guarantee a determinate and permanent normativeness to the doctrinal decisions of the Church.

III

The Conference of German Bishops is aware of the fact that, in the methodical pursuit of theology, various models and emphasis can be adapted today without prejudice to the unity of the faith. For instance. theology can be more or less biblical, more or less speculative in its orientation. Yet the principles enunciated above, which are not at all exhaustive, are binding and non-negotiable across the board for any Catholic theology.

When Professor Küng fails to observe, as a basis for his theological work, the norms of the Christian faith that come to expression in these principles, conflicts with the Magisterium of the Church are bound to emerge. Hence, even Professor Küng's "declarations," necessary as they may be, will not do. Thus, even in Professor Küng's new book, *Christ sein* (München, 1974), whose theological concern and pastoral purpose we recognize, there is a series of assertions which do not exhibit conformity with the principles mentioned above (cf. especially the Christology, the doctrine of the Trinity, the theology of the Church and of the Sacraments, the place of Mary in the history of salvation).

Closely connected with this basic stance are frequently repeated summonses to take it upon oneself to change Church discipline through so called "demands for reform" contrary to the responsible declarations of competent bodies. See, for example, once more in *Christ sein,* pp. 481 ff.; 515-517, concerning the recognition of offices, intercommunion, etc. . . .

In conclusion, the Conference of German Bishops addresses an urgent appeal to Professor Küng to reexamine, in light of the principles set forth here, the method and the objectionable assertions of his theology.

Bad-Honnef, February 17, 1975

Enclosure 37

LETTER OF CARDINAL DÖPFNER TO PROFESSOR KÜNG, February 17, 1975

Bad-Honnef
February 17, 1975

Professor Dr. Hans Küng
7400 Tübingen
Waldhäuserstr. 23

Dear Professor Küng:

In a Declaration of Feburary 15, 1975, the Congregation for the Doctrine of the Faith in Rome informed you that the proceedings of this Congregation relative to certain doctrines in your publications, *Die Kirche* and *Unfehlbar ? Eine Anfrage,* have been terminated. At the same time, the Congregation stated that some views in the above publications contradict the doctrine of the Church. The Congregation appended the admonition not to advocate such doctrines any more.

In a Declaration which I enclose, the Conference of German Bishops has applauded the way in which the proceedings were ended and expressed the hope that you will take seriously the admonition of the Congregation.

In its Declaration at the conclusion of the proceedings, the Conference of German Bishops felt obliged to refer to principles which, in its view, pertain to the understanding of what Catholic theology is, and which, in the opinion of the German bishops, are not always sufficiently honored in some of your publications. The bishops persistently beg of you to consider and observe these principles in your further work. These principles are not unknown to you, since they have been pointed out to you in many a discussion. However, it does make good sense that they are now being articulated in writing.

As you know, for a long time, the German bishops have taken pains to make sure that the proceedings should be conducted with fairness, and that, if possible, they should be brought to a favorable conclusion. This is also the reason why they are grateful to the Roman Congregation for the Doctrine of the Faith for the decision it has now taken. They do, however, recognize their own obligation to care for the complete and uncurtailed truth of the Gospel of Jesus Christ and to promote that truth. The manner in which the Congregation for the Doctrine of the Faith has terminated the proceedings also has the advantage of settling the conflict arising from the fact that both the Magisterium and theology uphold and value their respective tasks in a manner that could represent a significant step forward.

If this business is to be settled once and for all, we fervently hope that you will in turn be willing to make the contribution which is now required on your part. We would be very grateful if this Declaration should signal the end of an era of confrontations, an era which, in the eyes of the world, has not done much good to our Church and our common task as theologians and bishops.

I would like to note explicitly that neither the Congregation for the Doctrine of the Faith nor the Conference of German Bishops ever intended to question your integrity as a Christian and as a priest or to assess negatively your theology as a whole. If you read both Declarations carefully and without prejudice, you will notice how, in spite of all the firmness which they exhibit, all the proper delimitations and restrictions have been precisely and carefully included. The German bishops will endeavor also to interpret the Declarations in this sense for the benefit of the public. You will also notice, no doubt, that we recognize and appreciate your zealous theological efforts and particulalry the pastoral orientation of your theological work. It would be all the more regrettable if new differences should emerge.

In conclusion, may I mention that the enclosed Declaration will not be released to the public until next Thursday, February 20, 1975 at 2:00 o'clock P.M. (release time).

I very much hope that next Wednesday, Febraury 19, 1975, we shall be able to have a good conversation, as agreed last Friday in München.

With cordial greetings, I remain,

Yours,

(signed) + Julius Card. Döpfner

enclosure:

Declaration of the Conference of German Bishops at the Termination of the Proceedings of the Congregation for the Doctrine of the Faith relative to *Die Kirche* and *Unfehlbar ? Eine Anfrage,* by Professor Hans Küng (February 17, 1975).

I may be reached by telephone in Bad-Honnef, at the Secretariat of the Conference of German Bishops, numbers 02224-2815 and 02224-2680.

Enclosure 38

DECLARATION OF PROFESSOR KÜNG AT THE TERMINATION OF THE DOCTRINAL PROCEEDINGS, February 20, 1975

AN ACT OF RECONCILIATION?

My concern is not that I should be proved right against Rome and the bishops in the controversy about infallibility and Church order. The question is not who is right, but what is right. The truth will prevail, no matter on whose side it be.

As a theologian and pastor, my concern is to give a Christian answer to the urgent questions people ask. Numberless responses bear me out in this.

Now Rome and the bishops have returned their answers. These Declarations have not disproved anything which I had to say on theological grounds. The Declaration of the Roman authorities is rather the public admission that the secret proceedings against me have proved unworkable and have now been stopped. Also such inquisitional proceedings do contradict the Gospel, human rights, and the spirit of the "Holy Year of Reconciliation."

Since 1968, I have time and again requested to be given access to the records and to have legal counsel. All in vain. In the latest Declaration, this is, of course, concealed by the Congregation which now shifts onto the accused the burden of proving his own innocence. I have never refused to participate in a discussion in Rome, but I have insisted on just and humane preconditions. I could not submit to inquisitional proceedings. The Congregation has never agreed to the standstill I have repeatedly proposed. True, under pressure from the German bishops, the Roman ex-Holy Office has abstained in praiseworthy fashion from disciplinary measures. Yet, because of the renewed attack against my Catholic orthodoxy, an attack that adds nothing new to the Declaration *Mysterium Ecclesiae* (1973), I am also forced to respond before the public.

Under the prevailing circumstances, I welcome the fact that the German Declaration now addresses the controversial points with more precision than hitherto and recognizes that there ought to be "room in the Church for attempts at clarification." Now positions can be compared and one can form one's own judgment. In the Declaration of the Conference of German Bishops, it is suggested that I have done theology "from outside the community of faith." This I have never done. Neither will I be restrained from ministering to the people as a theologian in an ecumenical spirit, nor from teaching what, on the basis of the New Testament and of the great Christian tradition, can be advocated as Catholic doctrine.

As I go about this task, I will certainly continue to reflect upon the method and contents of my theology in a spirit of theological accountability. Hopefully, the Roman Curia will also take to heart the theological principles of the Conference of German Bishops, even if the consequences for the method and contents of Roman theology are bound not to be slight.

February 20, 1975

Enclosure 39

LETTER OF PROFESSOR KÜNG TO CARDINAL DÖPFNER, February 26, 1975

Tübingen
February 26, 1975

His Eminence
Dr. Julius Döpfner
8 München 2
Kardinal-Faulhaber-Strasse 7

Dear Brother:

Eight days have now passed since I received the two Declarations. With the benefit of a little distance, I can now look back upon the past events which have happened in such quick succession. This time, I would like to write you a personal letter, since, unless I hear differently from you, the two Declarations do not necessarily require that I respond officially. In this way, I need not return to the unpleasant shortcomings in the proceedings or to the theological questions which the two documents fail to answer.

Even from this distance, I am still of the opinion that it would have been better for all concerned if the proceedings had been terminated silently, or if my questions had been addressed in a more positive way. On the other hand, I can also understand that, in Rome, no more than this could be achieved and that the situation was very difficult for the authorities there.

Thus, after all the heavy confrontations which, most unfortunately, had to take place even between you and me, I can limit myself to conveying to you a genuine and cordial word of gratitude. I am fully aware how much trouble you have taken in Rome, and no doubt also in Germany, to achieve such a solution, a solution in which both sides were able to save face. I am immensely grateful that you have mustered the patience and endurance that have made all this possible. The impending wholesale confrontation could have brought about the unforeseeable, not only for our Church, but also for me personally. More than anyone concerned, I am in a position to appreciate the fact that I was spared all this.

I was likewise aware that my public statement could not have pleased you at the moment. For me, that statement represented the least that seemed necessary for me to say in view of the abortive proceedings and the unanswered theological questions. This is why I have nothing but admiration at the fact that, in the press conference which I was able to follow in the Tübingen radio station "LIFE," you explained the position of the Episcopal Conference in a way that was fair and friendly from beginning to end and without offending me in any way whatever.

Your defense before so great an audience has very decisively influenced my reaction, which, on the whole, is still very mild. In press interviews, on radio and television, as has been rather generally recognized, I was able to adopt for precisely that reason a moderate attitude, and to abstain from counterattacks, especially with regard to the doctrinal point under discussion. Your attitude in the press conference is also responsible for the fact that I have called off all the initiatives that had already been started to show solidarity on my behalf. Finally, I have also abstained from writing a lengthy article in the *Frankfurter Allgemeine Zeitung* for which plans had already been made eight days ago. There I was supposed to present my own theological position in a way that would differ from the way in which this has been done in the Declaration of the bishops, and to raise very pointed counter-questions. Of course, with this, as you yourself hint, I do not intend to say that at some later time I will not define my theological position on the Declarations. For the time being, however, I have no plans in this respect. In any case, I would not want to aggravate the discussion unnecessarily. Should nothing much happen after these Declarations; no statement on my side would be needed.

As you have publicly stated, an unpleasant time, unpleasant for all concerned, has now been brought to an end. If very often I had to take a "hard" line and could not be disengaged from certain juridical demands and theological positions, all this did happen — and I beg of you to believe this — not because of stubborness and willfulness on my part, but because of an obligation of conscience grounded on Christian faith. This obligation impelled me to sustain these demands in and out of season. All the same, this is, on the whole, a happy ending. Rome has even been given some credit for "wisdom" and you personally have won much sympathy even in circles which are otherwise inclined to be critical. This makes me hope also that the Congregation will thoroughly revise its order of procedure and that in other proceedings it will not let things go that far. I would like to voice once more my personal thanks. It would please me much if, in the future, you and I could stand up together for what is by far the more important thing for both of us: the common Christian cause.

With all good wishes for your heavy pastoral ministry, I am, with cordial greetings,

yours,
(signed) Hans Küng

Enclosure 40

LETTER OF CARDINAL DÖPFNER TO PROFESSOR KÜNG, May 6, 1975

München
May 6, 1975

Professor Dr. Hans Küng
7400 Tübingen
Waldhäuserstr. 23

Dear Brother:

Many thanks for your letter of February 26 and for your writing of March 20, 1975. Next I want to thank you that, when the termination of the proceedings was announced, you did your part — at least as far as the substance of your statement was concerned — to bring the affair to an end in the eyes of the public in a reasonable way. The reaction of the public has indeed shown that the direction taken in the resolution of this issue is being appreciated.

There is certainly no need for me to reiterate my public declaration of February 20 concerning the decision of the Congregation for the Doctrine of the Faith. It goes without saying that I stand by what I said there. With satisfaction, I have taken cognizance of the appreciation you have shown and of the thanks you have expressed for the efforts of the German bishops.

For the sake of honesty, I would not want to conceal my disappointment at the fact that not only couldn't you find a single word of thanks for the Congregation for the Doctrine of the Faith, but that you chose instead to engage only in harsh accusations and in attacks objectively unjust ("public admission," "secret proceedings," "inquisitional proceedings," "ex-Holy Office"). Unless responsible circles within the Congregation for the Doctrine of the Faith had not shown considerable good will toward the decision taken, the solution adopted would not have been possible. You may have noticed that commentators in the liberal press, otherwise well disposed in your regard, have pointed out this time — albeit in subordinate clauses — that your response was limited. I was relieved that, compared to your declaration, your televised response in the evening of February 20, 1975 was, a few passages excepted, well balanced.

The unsigned article "How Often Still Mr. Küng?" in the German edition of *L'Osservatore Romano* of February 28, 1975 was published without my knowledge, let alone by previous arrangement. It would have been better if many things had not been said in this way. But articles of this kind carry no weight in the Episcopal Conference. And yet, you should not be too surprised at the tone and style of this response. If you go over your Declaration of February 20, 1975 once more, you will recognize without trouble that in many respects the article was a not particularly skillful and yet perhaps an inevitable response to your attacks.

I have heard about a statement of the Archbishop of Freiburg concerning *Christ sein*, but I do not know the exact text. Such individual statements by bishops about which I myself am not informed ahead of time come under the judgment and discretion of the individual brothers. You will no doubt understand that I can in no way "steer" these writings and that, on principle, I do not intend to.

[eight lines of text are blanked out in the original]

What concerns me most is what lies behind your more theologically oriented comments, both in the declaration to the press on February 20, 1975, and in your letter of February 26, 1975. I find indefensible the way in which you continue to reduce the question of faith, addressed in the proceedings, largely to the level of Church politics (in the broader sense). You reduce everything to a pragmatic-tactical issue. This begins with the catchword "standstill proposal" ["Stillhalteangebot"], and permeates also the tenor of your letter. Cf. for example, ". . . in Rome no more than this could be achieved . . . the situation was difficult for the authorities there." I do not intend to deny that such factors as these do exist and that they do make some difference. But this is not how we are going to solve the problem. When all is said and done, what is very much at stake is the question of the truth of our faith and the preservation or loss of the identity of our Church — *in principle.* To deflect the whole problematic into the domain of so-called "Church reform" and to make of it a tactical game is something I regard as entirely inadmissible.

In the same connection, I have another concern. In your declaration of February 20, 1975, and in your letter of February 26, 1975, you contend that the Declarations of the Congregation for the Doctrine of the Faith and of the Conference of German Bishops had disproved nothing of what you had to say on theological grounds. It is difficult for me not to see an extreme obstinacy in these utterances, an obstinacy that could easily have compromised the outcome of the whole affair. Even after *Fehlbar ?,* you cannot possibly overlook the important objections of a large number of theologians to the core propositions of *Unfehlbar?* Even after the Declaration of the Conference of German Bishops, time and again you keep confusing the two different levels: the Church's Magisterium on the one side and theology on the other. Otherwise, a whole string of propositions and assertions could not surface in your statements in the form in which they do. But as long as you efface the difference that distinguishes the discourse of the Magisterium from that of theology regarding legitimation, function, and consequently mode of argumentation, and as long as you allow the "Magisterium" only a very limited "pastoral" task, the conflict, I fear, is bound to flare up again when you define your position on questions relative to Church doctrine. In this connection, I will not deny that there is a need to reflect upon the Magisterium of the Church as regards its functions and that it could be even more specific than it is in its own statements. But here we are concerned with fundamentals.

These points distress me, as I reflect again and reread your letter and Declaration. I, therefore, beg of you once more to consider how matters precisely stand and to do this deeply and seriously. If we had to quarrel anew over these difficulties, and no rapprochement were in sight, I would be at my wit's end.

Hoping to work together with you fruitfully in the service of the common mandate of your Lord, I wish you God's blessings on your work. With cordial greetings, I am,

Yours,
(signed) + Julius Cardinal Döpfner

Enclosure 41

LETTER OF PROFESSOR KÜNG TO CARDINAL DÖPFNER, April 27, 1975

Tübingen
April 27, 1975

To the President of the Conference of German Bishops
Cardinal Julius Döpfner
Kardinal-Faulhaber-Strasse 7
8 München 2

Your Eminence:

A visit to Rome and private conversations with Cardinal Seper and Archbishop Hamer, as well as two longer conferences with the Bishop of Rottenburg, Dr. Georg Moser, induce me to send you a short report which could presumably be of interest to the members of the Episcopal Conference.

The visit to Rome was occasioned by the publication of the *Italian edition of Christ sein.* I was convinced that a press conference in the place itself, with a prepared statement on the Catholicity of the book (see enclosure), was the best method for avoiding right at the beginning of the discussion biased and false reports in Italy (as happened in *Spiegel* when the German edition was published). As the reporting in the press shows, we were largely successful. There was no unpleasant sensationalism concerning individual points after I clearly expressed my loyalty to the Catholic Church and her doctrine. The only shrill sound was heard in the Italian press, and then in the international press because of a statement by Father Galot, S. J. on the same day on Vatican Radio. The statement disparaged me personally and was crammed with misunderstandings and allegations. I did not let this Vatican provocation lead me into responding in kind. I also managed to ward off the penetrating questions of journalists concerning the Vatican document on sexual ethics, divorce, abortion, and domestic politics in Italy, etc. . . .

In spite of Galot's and similar distortions inflicted on my book in isolated church sheets, I hope that the majority of Italian Catholics will receive and understand the book in the way it has been understood in Germany, that is, as a help offered to people within and without the Church in their Christian faith and life. Since complaints and denunciations about my book will no doubt reach Rome and the bishops, I would like to take this opportunity to point out that none of my books has yet been as widely acclaimed as *Christ sein* alike by Catholic pastors, religion teachers, sisters, and men and women involved in Church work. I often wonder whether it might not be useful to publish some striking expressions of the "sense of the faithful."

The private conversations behind closed doors first with *Cardinal Seper,* then with *Archbishop Hamer,* lasted about five hours. They were conducted with habitual openness and cordiality and touched upon almost all the questions that are important at this time. It was recognized that I have loyally observed the "admonitions" of the Congregation for the Doctrine of the Faith of February

15, 1975. It also became clear that no new Roman proceedings, not even against *Christ sein,* are being planned. On the other hand, neither was there any willingness to give me any kind of assurance that proceedings would not be initiated in the near future. Of course, in both conferences, I most emphatically pointed out that the Declaration of the Congregation for the Doctrine of the Faith and the additional Declaration of the Conference of German Bishops, which have already taken a stand with regard to *Christ sein*, have been interpreted by the international public, and also by me, as meaning that everything that was pending had been cleared away, and that in the future a whole "new style" would be adopted in similar disputes in matters of doctrine. In Germany, Switzerland and far beyond, people would not understand why new proceedings would again be initiated, and precisely against a book which is so very helpful to so many. Besides, given their particular mechanics, such proceedings would again lead to the same hopeless situation as all the others thus far. The credibility of the Catholic Church and of her theology would certainly be hurt. Be that as it may, my partners in the conversation seemed to realize that a new conflict would entail quite incalculable risks for both sides.

I shifted the conversation toward von Balthasar and the volume *Diskussion um Hans Küngs Christ sein,* which, against my intention, is provoking a public confrontation. I was told that this was a "quarrel among theologians" which did not concern Rome. I acknowledged that progress has certainly been made when controversial theological questions can be discussed in a scholarly way by theologians, instead of being settled magisterially through disciplinary measures. Of course, I cannot understand why — in view of the onesided choice of contributors — the author being discussed was not allowed to have his say in the same volume as a partner in the discussion. This is customary in a volume of discussions and is the only way in which the reader can form an objective judgment about truth and error. I was told that I could certainly reply to this volume in an article.

Given the importance of the authors and the ripple effect of a book, I thought that my reply should appear not in a scholarly journal but in a serious newspaper of wider circulation. This article will appear shortly. I hope that the German bishops, too, will understand, that, if a newspaper article on highly complex questions in defense of my Catholic integrity is to be understood at all, it must be written differently from a scholarly theological article. I have taken the greatest trouble not only to study the volume exactly and in detail, but also to discuss it with colleagues and, finally, in a symposium of many days. All the same, this article is not supposed to be my last word in the matter. I hope to find time in the near future to address anew in scholarly fashion the exegetical, historical, systematic and hermeneutical questions raised in the volume and elsewhere. It goes without saying that a theological reconsideration of the subject matter includes clarifications and corrections, completions and deepenings of my own position, too. As already stated in the book itself, I am convinced that a postiive updating is quite possible, and indeed desirable, with regard to various doctrinal points — also and especially with regard to those which the Conference of German Bishops finds objectionable.

I do have the impression that critics overlook or fail to take seriously enough, important assertions of *Christ sein,* as for example my clear agreement with what represents the basic aims of the Council of Nicaea against Arius: "In Jesus the one true God is present, not a second God, or demi-God. Our whole redemption depends on the fact that in Jesus we are concerned with the God who is really God" (p. 438; ET by E. Quinn, Hans Küng, *On Being a Christian* [New York: Pocket Books, 1976], p. 448). Or the interpretation of the formula "true God" ["*vere Deus*"] in the Council of Chalcedon: "The whole point of what happened in and with Jesus depends on the fact that, for believers, *God himself* as man's friend was present, at work, speaking, acting and definitively revealing himself *in* this *Jesus* who came among men as advocate and deputy, representative and delegate, and was confirmed by God as the Crucified raised to life" (p. 439; ET, 449). Or about the Incarnation: "As became clear through all the previous chapters, it was in Jesus' *whole* life, in His *whole* proclamation, behavior and fate, that God's word and will took a human form. In His whole speech, action and suffering, in His whole person, Jesus *proclaimed, manifested, revealed* God's word and will. Indeed, it can be said that He, in whom word and deed, teaching and life, being and action, completely coincide, *is the embodiment of God's word and will. . .* He might almost be called the *visage* or *face of God* or — as in the New Testament itself — the *image* or *likeness of God.* The same thing is expressed also in other terms: when Jesus is called the *Word of God* or even the *Son of God*" (p. 434; ET, 443; 444). According to all this, it is obvious that I have never thought of denying the divine Sonship of Jesus (or the Trinity)!

Whether or not these interpretations, which I do not advocate alone, do suffice, is open to debate also in my case — just as in the case of the other Catholic theologians of our time. Today, the difficulties entailed in Christological interpretation, deriving from the exegesis of the New Testament, the history of dogmas, and modern consciousness, are considerable for every Catholic theologian; but also for every preacher and proclaimer of the Christian message. I am certainly aware that my book, or more often biased press reports or reviews of my book, can at first disquiet traditional Catholics, especially when they have not been appropriately instructed through religious education and preaching and when they read only parts of my book or none of it. In any case, I would like to stress this: my expositions are not at all meant to curtail, conceal, disquiet, trouble, but to help the disquieted, to afford clarity to these who are at a loss, to overcome polarizations, to strengthen the Christian faith. For this help, numberless people are grateful to me.

I was glad, and have said so publicly, that in the press conference in February 1975, Your Eminence, as President of the Conference of German Bishops, explicitly acknowledged my "strong commitment and pastoral concern," as well as my "integrity as a priest and as a Christian." Many — not all — contributors to the volume of discussions and a few other theologians (some of them are members of the German Doctrinal-Commission), have again descended below the level to which the discussion has risen. I would like, therefore, to explicitly beg of the German bishops to keep on upholding this my "integrity." They should urge their theological advisers "to stress in the future what we have in common more than what makes us different," which is what you hoped in that press conference and what the authors in the volume do not do.

Even during the most difficult phases of the infallibility debate, I have consistently affirmed that it is beneficial to have in our Church a pastoral office of teaching or proclamation of which the Pope and the bishops are in charge. Yet, even in Rome, I have recently tried with all possible emphasis to make the point that this office can serve its purpose in our time only if it is not one-sided, but truly Catholic and does not attempt to disregard distinctive representative directions in today's Catholic theology. The Declaration of the bishops on the Council of Nicaea would have elicited a larger and more positive response if the Catholic theologians who were quoted verbatim (perhaps without many bishops knowing it) had been invited to dicuss and cooperate. This is the only way in which to avoid the much lamented polarizations and the unfavorable pastoral consequences. It is only for this reason that I have abstained from taking a public stand with regard to this document. I would rather take advantage of the opportunity to reaffirm my willingness to engage in every possible kind of constructive cooperation with the bishops "for the edification of the Church."

To summarize: as far as *Christ sein* is concerned, after the official Declaration of the German bishops on *Christ sein,* after the Declaration on Nicaea, and especially after the aforementioned volume, I am of the opinion that the time has come to let peace enter. Official and semi-official criticisms have been heard, and I have responded to the extent to which it was necessary to do so in my defense at this particular point in time. I would be grateful to Your Eminence and to the German bishops if I should be permitted to do my theological work in peace and quiet. I hope that, by my restraint and also by means of this letter, I may have said something that will bring us closer to a proper resolution of the present situation. May I convey to you, together with my best wishes, my cordial greetings.

Very devotedly yours,
(signed) Hans Küng

c.

Dr. Georg Moser, Bishop of Rottenburg

enclosure:

Statement for the press conference in Rome

Enclosure 42

LETTER OF CARDINAL DÖPFNER TO PROFESSOR KÜNG, June 24, 1976

München
June 24, 1976

Professor Dr. Hans Küng
Waldhäuser Str. 23
7400 Tübingen 1

Dear Professor Küng:

Because of my three-week journey to Africa, I am only now able to acknowledge receipt of your letter of April 27, 1976, and to thank you for it.

With interest, I have taken cognizance of your conversations with Cardinal Seper and Archbishop Hamer and of your statement as to how you view the criticism published to-date on your book, *Christ sein.*

Because I, too, am of the opinion that your letter is of interest to the members of the Episcopal Conference, I have forwarded that letter to the chairman of the Doctrinal Commission with the request that the Commission should discuss the questions which have resurfaced in the debate.

I must confess that your "Reply to My Critics" in the *Frankfurter Allgemeine Zeitung* of May 22 has been a rather great disappointment for me. After the letter in which you reported being engaged in a comprehensive study of the essays in the volume *Diskussion um Hans Küngs Christ sein,* I would have expected the reply to be to the point.

You do indeed say in your letter that you intend to take up in scholarly fashion the questions and concerns of your critics. You expressly stress that "clarifications and corrections, completions and deepenings" of your position are entirely possible. My dear Professor Küng, I have been waiting for these clarifications now for a long time. In recent years, you have made such a promise time and again in different connections. Your reply to the "critics" would have offered you an extremely favorable opportunity to make good on that promise. I must, therefore, remind you of the urgent appeal which the Conference of German Bishops addressed to you at the end of their Declaration of February 17, 1975, a Declaration you know, "to reexamine in the light of the principles presented above the method and objectionable assertions of his theology."

But when your respect for your "critics" is as slight as it appears to be in your reply in the *Frankfurter Allgemeine Zeitung,* it is hard to make anyone believe that, well over one year later, this reexamination has been started at all.

I have always looked upon such serious reexamination as a non-negotiable component of the "new style" in the clarification of doctrines which can be misunderstood or are to be described as false. This much I am entitled to expect from you.

Repeatedly, you have stated publicly and in your letter to me that you were, of course, prepared to reflect upon the statements against which objections have been raised. I am sorry to say that up to this moment, this has not in fact happened. On the contrary, your statements in the *Frankfurter Allgemeine Zeitung* article convey the impression that, as far as you are concerned, such a reexamination of your own position is, ultimately, out of the question. In your letter of April 27, you merely express the hope to find time, in the foreseeable future, to readdress the questions that have been raised.

Through all this, you create a new situation for the bishops. No need to emphasize that I regret this very much.

I, therefore, insistently urge you again to reflect seriously and reexamine the method objected to in the Declaration of the Conference of German Bishops, and the substantive assertions being called in question.

With cordial greetings,

Yours,
(signed) + Julius Card. Döpfner

Enclosure 43

LETTER OF CARDINAL HÖFFNER TO PROFESSOR KÜNG, August 31, 1976

Cologne
August 31, 1976

Professor Dr. Hans Küng
Waldhäuserstr. 23
7400 Tübingen 1

Dear Professor Küng:

On the last day before his untimely death, Cardinal Döpfner had drafted the letter below. The letter was to be written the next day, July 24, and mailed, but it never came to that.

The text of the letter was as follows:

Dear Professor Küng:

Many thanks for your letter of June 28, 1976, which you sent also to Cardinal Volk and Bishop Moser of Rottenburg.

In the meantime, the Doctrinal-Commission of the Conference of German Bishops, in compliance with my request, has discussed the situation which has now emerged. On the basis of the suggestions I have received, I propose a discussion aimed at clarifying some key questions relative to *Christ sein.* I hope that this discussion will lead to a clear agreement for the sake of our common faith and eliminate some confusions which have arisen in connection with your book.

If you wish, I am agreed that you ask one of your colleagues to take part in this discussion. On my side, I would like Cardinal Volk, Bishop Moser, as well as Professors Lehmann and Ratzinger, to join as participants.

Today, I would like to ask of you to agree in principle to take part in this discussion. The place could be the Catholic Academy of the Diocese of Rottenburg in Stuttgart-Hohenheim.

After I receive your answer, I will ask Dr. Homeyer, who comes back from vacation on August 8, 1976, to fix together with you the exact date of the discussion. I have in mind the second part of September or a date in October of this year.

With cordial greetings,

Yours,
(Julius Card. Döpfner)

After speaking with Cardinal Volk, I propose that the discussion be held, as suggested by Cardinal Döpfner. I have asked Dr. Homeyer to get in touch with you about the precise date.

Probably, it will not be possible to hold the discussion before October. By that time, the new President of the Conference of German Bishops will have been elected. If need be, he will be able to take part in the discussion.

With cordial greetings,

Yours,
+ Joseph Card. Höffner
President pro tem of the
Conference of German Bishops

Enclosure 44

LETTER OF BISHOP MOSER TO PROFESSOR KÜNG, January 28 1977

Rottenburg am Neckar
January 28, 1977

Professor Dr. Hans Küng
Waldhäuserstrasse 23
7400 Tübingen 1

Dear Professor Küng:

After our talk last Saturday, I have been asking myself over and over again what our next step should be in this affair. Although I am satisfied with the course of the discussion, which you yourself described as "constructive," I still do regret that, for many reasons, you did not think that before long you would be in a position to clarify some key Christological questions, as mentioned in the discussion and to make these clarifications public in whatever form. One thing is obvious to me: it will not be easy for the bishops who took part in the discussion to convey to the Episcopal Conference as a whole an impression that will be convincing in every respect, unless in the long run we can show them results which have been produced by you or which you at least helped to produce.

I was all the more pleased that, after the discussion, you assured me that before the spring meeting of the Conference of German Bishops (February 28-March 3),you would write a letter to the President of the Conference. We were agreed that, in addition to your introductory observations (8 points), your letter would contain most of all substantive statements from or on our discussion. In my view, dealing with the questions we discussed together is even more important and effective than rehearsing the introductory remarks, whose significance I do not at all underestimate. I understand very well that, in that letter, you cannot engage in a detailed theological discussion. And yet, when I check my notes — the transcription of the tapes will take a little longer — I encounter some remarkable statements on your part which should not be ignored in that letter.

Permit me to draw your attention, in outline form, to some important points. It would be important to note that you yourself see that certain assertions not only might be complemented, should one choose to do so, but must be. You no doubt agree with Karl Barth who in his Preface to the second edition of his Commentary on Romans wrote: "Every piece of work man does is only preliminary; a theology book is more so than any other work."

According to our discussion, these are the points that need complementing:

- the normativeness of the classical Christological definitions of the Councils;
- the relation to the two-nature doctrine;
- a more precise qualification of functional Christology (the character of it, and how it relates to essentialist Christology);
- more attention to be paid to Johannine Christology;
- relation between a Christology "from above" and a Christology "from below";
- the underivability and unsurpassability of the person of Jesus Christ (not only of his claims!);
- closer description of the way in which Jesus is one with the Father (for example, the indissoluble structure of this unity).

Indeed, other themes were also addressed, but, obviously, you will not be able to address everything in one letter. I would, however, very much welcome clarifying remarks on the theme of Soteriology which Cardinal Volk addressed. In preparing this letter, you might succeed in articulating many points with more precision than was possible on Saturday in a relatively spontaneous discussion.

I have once more written a special letter to you because I believe that the letter you are to write is very important. It could go a long way toward resolving the tensions of the moment. Even if you feel, at present, that it is not possible for you to write a comprehensive answer to the questions addressed in the discussion, a letter personally from you can be an effective signal. In the interest of the issue at hand, I would be grateful to you, if you would devote to this letter enough time to produce a comprehensive presentation.

I am still prepared to talk about this matter with you in case you should find it necessary.

With cordial greetings and best wishes, I remain,

Yours,
(signed) + Georg Moser

Enclosure 45

LETTER OF PROFESSOR KÜNG TO CARDINAL HÖFFNER, February 21, 1977

Tübingen
February 21, 1977

His Eminence
Cardinal Dr. Joseph Höffner
President of The Conference of German Bishops
Eintrachtstrasse 164
5000 Cologne

Your Eminence:

On January 22, 1977, in the Catholic Academy in Stuttgart-Hohenheim, the discussion on *Christ sein* took place with Your Eminence, Cardinal Volk, and Bishop Moser. You had invited Professors Lehmann, Semmelroth and Prelate Homeyer to join, and I had invited Professor Neumann. I am grateful to the bishops that, this time, a personal discussion with me was preferred to a new public declaration and that the discussion was conducted in an open and friendly atmosphere. All participants did no doubt realize that, in this way, many important points could be clarified. As suggested to me, I would like to consign to writing some of these points for the attention of the German bishops.

1. My book, *Christ sein*, as well as my earlier books, can only be understood if one perceives that the objective they pursue is pastoral. Although I do substantiate my views in scholarly fashion, I am never interested in a purely academic, ivory-tower scholarship, but in positive answers to the questions people ask today, in the light of the Christian message. Among all the questions discussed in connection with *Christ sein*, there isn't a single one which I have myself fabricated. Everywhere I have addressed questions that beset people within and without our Church. Anyone who has read this book, can recognize that I have gone to great lengths to provide constructive answers to these questions.

2. One does justice to the book only if one sees it as a whole, and refrains from taking into consideration in a 675-page book only the 50-page chapter entitled "Interpretations" which deals mainly with the history of dogma. The extraordinary success of the book among pastors and religious educators, a success the bishops often mentioned, can only be traced to the fact that there the Christian message of the earthly, crucified, and risen Jesus has been elaborated

in a manner that is convincing to them and helpful in their pastoral activity. No other book of mine has yet met with such wide acclaim among Catholic pastors, religion teachers, sisters, and men and women engaged in Church work. I often wonder whether it might not be useful to publish some impressive expressions of the "sense of the faithful." Above and beyond, this book has appealed to circles outside the Church which are hardly ever reached by theological literature or by the Christian proclamation. Thus it has already proved to be a new basis for the difficult dialogue with Jews about Jesus Christ. This is connected with the points to follow.

3. One does not do justice to the book unless one perceives that, from beginning to end, something like the perspective of the first disciples of Jesus is being consistently adopted, which is the perspective of the questioning person of today, the historical difference, of course, being taken into account. This is the way in which to construct on solid historical foundations a Christology "from below," as suggested by the whole historical research of the last 200 years. The Christology "from above" is known to me from my seven years of study in Rome, as well as from the new Catholic and Protestant interpretations of our time. From *Rechtfertigung* (1957) to *Menschwerdung Gottes* (1970), I myself have tried to elucidate this Christology through research in the history of dogmas, philosophically, theologically, and systematically. I still regard it as a legitimate Christology. Yet I have already explained in *Menschwerdung Gottes* why today it seems to me to be objectively right and pastorally appropriate to approach Christology "from below."

Every Christology is dependent, to be sure, on the witness of the New Testament, the witness of the Church of the Apostles, but this is not what is meant by the expression "from below." In every Christology "an element of a theology from above" does play a role insofar as *God*, the Kingdom of God, the will and action of God are already involved in the proclamation, the conduct, the claims of the Jesus of history, and not only in his resurrection. But even if this figure of speech be regarded as unimportant, it makes a decisive difference all the same, methodologically, whether, in dealing with the interpretation of the New Testament witness, as well as with the traditional Christology from the Fathers to Karl Barth, a doctrine of the Trinity and of The Incarnation is the premise from which we start, and then move deductively from God ("from above") to the man Jesus of Nazareth; or whether I, as well as various other Catholic and Protestant theologians, begin by taking stock of modern exegetical discussions, and, placing ourselves time and again in the perspective of the first disciples of Jesus, as it were ("from below"), we systematically think our way to God, inductively and interpretatively. When one attempts an exact definition of the concepts, one cannot think with methodological consistency "from above" and "from below" at the same time. From a methodological point of view, we have here a genuine either/or! An illustration: If you want to climb a mountain step by step from below, you cannot at the same time keep on calling down from the top. Obviously, we are dealing here with two different interpretative models (paradigms) of the Christian message. Both have their advantages and disadvantages. By competing with each other in a honorable theological contest, they both can prove what service they can render to the Gosepl and to the people of today.

4. I have no doubts that, when we engage in our critical inquiry into exegesis

and the history of dogma, we must adhere if not to the letter, then certainly to the broad objectives and substance of the ecumenical councils and especially of the councils of Nicaea and Chalcedon, which are of fundamental importance in classic Christology. Even in the book *Unfehlbar ? Eine Anfrage,* I have shown something to which too little attention is being paid: the Church is dependent both on short recapitulative propositions of the faith (professions and symbols of faith), and, in extreme cases, on propositions of the faith which are defensive and defining (definitions and dogmas of faith; cf. pp. 116-120 [ET, pp. 143-150]). Thus, practically for the past twenty years I have tried over and over again to achieve a positive understanding of the great and even of the little known conciliar tradition, from the Christological councils of Nicaea and Chalcedon to the late Byzantine councils (cf. *Menschwerdung Gottes*), from the medieval papal synods, the councils of Constance and Basel (cf. *Strukturen der Kirche*), and Trent (cf. *Rechtfertigung; Wozu Priester ? Eine Hilfe*) to Vatican I and II (cf. *Strukturen der Kirche; Die Kirche; Unfehlbar ? Eine Anfrage; Fehlbar ? Eine Bilanz*). With regard to the elaboration of the Christological tradition, the explicit "prolegomena" to *Christ sein* are constituted by *Menschwerdung Gottes,* a fact which has also been too little noted. From the beginning and always since, it seemed indispensable to me that the ecclesial and also the conciliar tradition should be measured against the Christian message as originally witnessed to in Holy Scripture, in fact against Jesus Himself, as the primary criterion of every theology.

5. Although time and again, I am being publicly compared with the "case Lefebvre," I must for the reasons already indicated absolutely refuse to let my position be equated with that of Archbishop Lefebvre.

a. It has never occurred to me to pose as infallible in my own right or to contest the orthodoxy of the Roman authorities, as Mgr. Lefebvre has repeatedly done. In my confrontation with Rome I have criticized, asked questions, made proposals, urged discussion and reform, but all the while I have acknowledged that there was also another Catholic opinion and that I am fallible.

b. In all the criticisms, I directed at the halfheartedness of many conciliar documents, I certainly had no cause to discredit Vatican II globally as a neo-modernistic, neo-Protestant, and an heretical council. I have rather shown clearly how much the "novelties" of Vatican II — relative, say, to the reform of the liturgy and the adoption of the vernacular — have on their side not only the New Testament but also the old Catholic tradition, a tradition of which Mgr. Lefebvre seems to be ignorant.

c. I have founded no ("progressive") group of my own. I have deliberately recoiled from all sectarian endeavors. I have never intended to be more Catholic than the Catholic Church. To the best of my ability, I have spoken and worked everywhere for the unity of our Church, last but not least in connection with the Lefebvre case.

d. Nor have I ever tried, in exclusive and doctrinaire fashion, to impose my views precisely on priests in formation or even in a seminary of my own. In a regular church-affiliated or state-run school — and also among us here in Tübingen — the students are exposed from the first to the most diverse influences (more conservative or more progressive), and this I have always welcomed.

In short, I have never made a secret of the fact that, in spite of all the difficulties which have been created for me in this my Church, almost since I received my doctorate in theology, I remain loyal to this my Church and I stand up passionately on her behalf. I am happy to say that numberless Catholics, clerics as well as lay, at home and abroad, have time and again given me strength along this path.

6. With regard to the Christological dogmas which presuppose the doctrine of the two natures, I have taken considerable trouble to safeguard the great objectives and the substance which have the authority of the New Testament and to show their relevance. In keeping with the well-known word of John XXIII, the conceptual and representational framework need not be adopted as if it were normative. The "substance" of the faith must be safeguarded; the formulation, which is the "garb," can change. This applies also to the dogmatic assertions concerning pre-existence, incarnation, redemption, and Mary, all questions on which I have much to say in *Menschwerdung Gottes* and *Christ sein.*

I do have the impression that critics overlook or fail to take seriously enough, important assertions of *Christ sein,* as for example my clear agreement with what represents the basic aims of the Council of Nicaea against Arius: "In Jesus the one true God is present, not a second God, or demi-God. Our whole redemption depends on the fact that in Jesus we are concerned with the God who is really God" (p. 438; ET by E. Quinn, Hans Küng, *On Being a Christian* [New York; Pocket Books, 1976], p. 448). Or the interpretation of the formula "true God" ["*vere Deus*"] in the Council of Chalcedon: "The whole point of what happened in and with Jesus depends on the fact that, for believers, *God himself* as man's friend was present, at work, speaking, acting and definitively revealing Himself *in* this *Jesus* who came among men as advocate and deputy, representative and delegate, and was confirmed by God as the Crucified raised to life" (p. 439; ET, 449). Or about the Incarnation: "As became clear through all the previous chapters, it was in Jesus' *whole* life, in His *whole* proclamation, behavior and fate, that God's word and will took a human form. In His whole speech, action and suffering, in His whole person, Jesus *proclaimed, manifested, revealed* God's word and will. Indeed, it can be said that He in whom word and deed, teaching and life, being and action, completely coincide *is the embodiment of God's word and will* . . . He might almost be called the *visage* or *face of God* or — as in the New Testament itself — the *image* or *likeness of God.* The same thing is expressed also in other terms: when Jesus is called the *Word of God* or even the *Son of God*" (p. 434; ET, 443; 444. According to all this, it is obvious that I have never thought of denying the divine Sonship of Jesus (or the Trinity)!

7. Whether or not these interpretations, which I do not alone advocate, do suffice, is open to debate also in my case — just as in the case of other Catholic theologians of our time. Today, the difficulties entailed in Christological interpretation, deriving from the exegesis of the New Testament, the history of dogmas, and modern consciousness, are considerable for every Catholic theologian, but also for every preacher and proclaimer of the Christian message. I am certainly aware that my book, or more often biased press reports or reviews of my book, can at first disquiet traditional Catholics, especially when they have not been appropriately instructed through religious education and preaching and when they read only parts of my book or none of it. In any case, I would like to stress this: my expositions are not at all meant to curtail,

conceal, disquiet, trouble, but to help the disquieted, to afford clarity to those who are at a loss, to overcome polarizations, to strengthen the Christian faith. For this help, numberless people are grateful to me.

In this connection, I was glad, and have said so publicly, that the late Cardinal Julius Döpfner, as President of the Conference of German Bishops, in his press conference in February 1975, explicitly acknowledged my "strong commitment and pastoral concern," as well as my "integrity as a priest and as a Christian." A few theologians (some of them members of the German Doctrinal-Commission) have descended again below the level to which the discussion has risen. I would like, therefore, explicitly to beg you and the German bishops to keep on upholding this my "integrity." They should urge their theological advisers "to stress in the future what we have in common more than what makes us different."

8. As far as the discussion on *Christ sein* is concerned, I have tried since the publication of the book to clarify, reexamine and deepen those controverted dogmatic questions which are in need of further theological investigation, as I myself had already declared in the book. This is not just an empty "promise," as the following facts prove:

— A three-day discussion among doctoral students on the comparison between *Jesus der Christus* of Walter Kasper and *Christ sein;*

— A further three-day discussion among doctoral students on the volume of discussions entitled, *Diskussion um Hans Küngs Christ sein;*

— Many hours long discussions with well-known experts on the questions at issue, especially Christological questions;

— A seminar on the aforementioned volume which ended with a discussion between Walter Kasper and myself;

— I have conducted discussion or exchanged letters on problems still pending with most of the authors who contributed to the aforementioned volume.

9. While trying conscientiously to come to grips with the points at issue, I have also been waiting for a long time for constructive contributions from my colleagues, contributions, namely, that would be truly helpful and take seriously the present state of exegetical, historical, and systematic research. In this respect, the volume co-edited by various advisers of the Doctrinal-Commission of the Conference of German Bishops was a major disappointment for me. Hence, some remarks on my reply in the *Frankfurter Allgemeine Zeitung* of May 22, 1976, a reply which the bishops have found objectionable.

Last spring, in my conversations with Cardinal Seper and Archbishop Hamer, I acknowledged that, without a doubt, progress has been made when controversial questions in theology are discussed by theologians in scholarly fashion, instead of being settled magisterially through disciplinary measures. Of course, I could not understand then, and still cannot understand, why — considering the onesided choice of contributors — the author being discussed was not allowed to have his say in the same volume as a partner in the discussion. This is customary in a volume of discussions and is the only way in which the reader can form an objective judgment about truth and error. I was told in Rome that I could certainly reply to this volume in an article. Given the importance of the authors and the ripple effect of a book and of the attacks on my Catholic orthodoxy, I thought that my reply should appear, not in a scholarly journal, but in a serious newspaper of wider circulation. I hope that the German bishops, too, will understand that, if a newspaper article on highly complex questions in defense of my Catholic integrity was to be understood at all, it had to be written differently than a technical article. A totally different reaction would have been possible on my side,

a. If the articles by von Balthasar, Grillmeier, Rahner, and Ratzinger had shown the same constructive willingness to dialogue as the articles by Deissler, Kasper, Kremer, Lehmann and Schneider;

b. If a firm defense of my Catholic orthodoxy had not, to my chagrin, been called for because of general allegations and accusations of heresy;

c. If in the same volume I should have been permitted to answer the questions of my colleagues.

This "discussion," as unpleasant as it is even for me, has not been provoked in this form by me, since, on my side, I have never started a personal polemic. I am still not interested in a further escalation and would be grateful if I could be spared such escalation. The articles of the authors who contributed to the volume have made it all too clear how difficult it is, even for the theologians who criticize me, to answer these questions. The most important thing now is constructive cooperation on all sides. At any rate, one thing is clear: I alone cannot be saddled with the burden of clarifying questions shared by all.

I may also remark that, as has been the case before in the infallibility debate, this "theological rage," complete with hateful personal attacks from fellow theologians, has only been the case in German-speaking countries. These polemics — spread about in all kinds of leaflets and pamphlets — have contributed to the unsettling of the Christian people more than my book has. Before my critics began to engage in polemics, the book had been received by the public in an entirely positive way. Upon my return from Ireland and England, I was able to report in the discussion in Stuttgart how positively my book had been received there. The same is true of the United States, where I was in November, and in Italy, where the book was published already last year and caused none of that excitement, and later also in Brazil. In all these countries — soon this will no doubt be the case also in Spain and France — people seem to have understood the book for what it wants to be. It aims to help people in their Christian life and faith within and without the Catholic Church.

10. It goes without saying that the article I wrote for the *Frankfurter Allgemeine Zeitung* is not my last word in the matter. As I already mentioned in a letter to Cardinal Döpfner, I hope to find time in the near future to address anew in scholarly fashion the exegetical, historical, systematic and hermeneutical questions raised in the volume and elsewhere. It goes without saying that a theological reconsideration of the subject matter includes clarifications and corrections, completions and deepenings of my own position too. As already stated in the book itself, I am convinced that a positive updating is quite possible, and indeed desirable with regard to the various doctrinal points — also and especially with regard to those which the Conference of German Bishops finds objectionable.

In our discussion in Stuttgart, we came to agree that some Christological expositions need to be complemented. In keeping with the basic attitude I have already often explained, I have declared that I am prepared to contribute in an appropriate way to the clarification of the debated questions. For the time being, this will happen especially in my book, *Existiert Gott ?* to be published next year, which is a complement to *Christ sein.* In this volume, I will extensively address the basic problematic many critics have addressed, namely, the relationship between reason and faith, as well as the understanding of God which is at the root of all the questions. I will also touch upon the question of Jesus' relation to God, the Father. In connection with this question, one could for example clarify something that came to expression our discussion, namely:

— That "functional" Christological assertions should not be regarded as "unreal" assertions, so to speak (Jesus *is* really Son of God);

— That in Jesus Christ acting and being cannot be separated;

— That uniqueness and underivability apply not only to the origins of Jesus Christ, but also to His person;

— That the Johannine Christology which had to be dealt with with relative brevity in *Christ sein* (although very emphatically, and in considerably more places than many critics have noted in their superficial reading of the book) can be brought out more extensively, etc. . .

11. Even during the most difficult phases of the infallibility debate, I have consistently affirmed that it is beneficial to have in our Church a pastoral office of teaching or proclamation of which the Pope and the bishops are in charge. Yet, even in Rome I have recently tried with all possible emphasis to make the point that this office can serve its purpose in our time only if it is not one-sided but truly Catholic, and does not attempt to exclude out of hand distinctive representative directions in today's Catholic theology. This is the only way in which to avoid much lamented polarizations and unfavorable pastoral consequences.

12. I, therefore, take the liberty of reiterating here the proposals I made in the discussion in Stuttgart for the purpose of attaining to a common clarification of the issues pending for all theologians:

a. Study-projects relative to individual important issues (as example, the preexistence of Jesus Christ, divine Sonship, Soteriology) should be promoted and funded with the participation of the best qualified experts from pertinent disciplines;

b. Symposia should be promoted and funded in which individual important issues would likewise be discussed by specialists with openness and collegially;

c. For the sake of its own credibility, the German Doctrinal Commission should be so composed as to represent all important currents of today's Catholic theology, in order to preclude the impression that some theologians pass judgment on other theologians who are just as competent as they are. In the selection of advisers competence should be the criterion, not good conduct.

d. The Doctrinal-Commission, whose statements to the public have been hitherto almost exclusively negative, in the manner of the Roman Congregation for the Doctrine of the Faith, should address more positive tasks in the service of proclamation.

In conclusion, I may repeat what I have written in the past to Cardinal Döpfner: As far as *Christ sein* is concerned, after the official Declaration of the German bishops on *Christ sein,* after the Declaration on Nicaea, and especially after the aforementioned volume, I am of the opinion that the time has come to let peace enter. Official and semi-official criticisms have been heard and I have responded to the extent to which it was necessary to do so in my own defense at this particular point in time.

I would be grateful to Your Eminence and to the German bishops if I should be permitted to do my theological work in peace and quiet. I hope that, by means of this letter, too, I may have said something that will contribute to a proper resolution of the present situation.

I would like to ask you to send this letter to all the members of the Conference before the next meeting of the Episcopal Conference.

With best wishes and cordial greetings, I am,

Devotedly yours,
(signed) Hans Küng

c.
Dr. Georg Moser, Bishop of Rottenburg

Enclosure 46/1

LETTER OF CARDINAL HÖFFNER TO PROFESSOR KÜNG, March 4, 1977

Bonn
March 4, 1977

Professor Dr. Hans Küng
Waldhäuserstr. 23
7400 Tübingen

Dear Professor Küng:

Many thanks for your letter of February 21, 1977 which, in accordance with your wish, I forwarded immediately to the members of the Conference of German Bishops.

I regret very much that the Conference of German Bishops, whose conviction I share, could not rest satisfied with the results of our discussion of January 22, 1977, nor with the contents of your letter mentioned above.

The Episcopal Conference felt it should release a declaration to the press on the discussion of January 22, 1977. This declaration has already been sent to you. I enclose another copy.

The Episcopal Conference has directed me to impart to you the questions which emerge about *Christ sein,* and out of the Declaration of February 17, 1975, with which you are acquainted. Unfortunately, in the next two weeks I will either be away from Cologne or so burdened with appointments, that I will not be able to write that letter until later. I must, therefore, ask you to have a little patience.

With cordial greetings,

Yours,
(signed) + Joseph Cardinal Höffner

DECLARATION OF THE CONFERENCE OF GERMAN BISHOPS, March 3, 1977

SPRING MEETING OF THE CONFERENCE OF GERMAN BISHOPS February 28 to March 3, 1977

DECLARATION OF THE CONFERENCE OF GERMAN BISHOPS TO THE PRESS CONCERNING THE DISCUSSION WITH PROFESSOR KÜNG

The Conference of German Bishops has examined the results of the discussion with Professor Küng arranged by the Episcopal Conference and held in Stuttgart on January 22, 1977, Cardinal Höffner presiding. As it appears from the communiqué released to the press by the Secretariate of the Conference of German Bishops, the main theme of the discussion was constituted by the assertions of Professor Küng concerning the person and saving action of Jesus Christ in his book *Christ sein.* In this discussion, Professor Küng recognized that some Christological explanations in his book need to be complemented. The bishops felt that the amendments were urgently needed, since they concern assertions which are central to the Catholic faith. Professor Küng declared that he was ready to contribute "in an appropriate way" to the clarification of the questions at issue. What he has presented thus far will not do.

In spite of initial moves towards agreement, the Conference of German Bishops regards the inadequate and ambiguous assertions of Professor Küng as so momentous that it must again request Professor Küng to provide the necessary precisions and emendations.

The German Bishops once more reinforce what they said in their Declaration on the Creed of Nicaea on September 24, 1975: Jesus is not only an exemplary man, not only God's spokesman and advocate ["Sachverwalter"]; He is rather the eternal Son of God. "God from God, light from light, true God from true God, begotten, not made, of one substance with the Father," as the Church teaches in her profession of faith. Only if Jesus Christ is presented unequivocally and witnessed to in accordance with this profession of faith as true God and true man, can the Christian message of Redemption and Salvation remain uncurtailed and unadulterated. Because the book *Christ sein* fails to do justice to this central truth of faith, the Conference of German Bishops insists on a prompt correction or supplementing of the pertinent assertions of Professor Küng in keeping with normative Church doctrine, so that readers may not be mislead and confused. On February 17, 1975, the Conference of German Bishops drew attention not only to the Christology but also to the doctrine of the Trinity, the theology of the Church, and of the sacraments, and to the place of Mary in the history of Salvation.

This declaration of the Conference of German Bishops has been imparted to Professor Küng. The assembly would welcome it if Professor Küng should do what is required for a clarification.

Essen-Heidhausen
March 3, 1977

Enclosure 47

LETTER OF CARDINAL HÖFFNER TO PROFESSOR KÜNG, April 22, 1977

Bonn
April 22, 1977

Professor Dr. Hans Küng
Waldhäuserstr. 23
7400 Tübingen

OBJECT: *Your book,* Christ sein;
Here: *Answers to specific questions*

REFERENCE: *Discussion between representatives of the Conference of German Bishops and you, January 22, 1977 in Stuttgart-Hohenheim; your letter of February 21, 1977; my answer of March 4, 1977*

Dear Professor Küng:

On March 4, 1977, I informed you that the Conference of German Bishops was not satisfied with the outcome of the discussion of January 22, 1977, and with the contents of your letter of February 21, 1977, and that I had been directed to impart to you some questions relative to *Christ sein.*

Today, I would like to attend to this task. I deliberately limit myself to a few questions, although the compass of the controversial themes is not thereby exhausted.

1. In your letter of February 21, 1977 (No. 6), you declare that it had never been your intention to doubt the divine Sonship of Jesus or the Trinity. We acknowledge this helpful statement and a few others. And yet your statements in this matter, both in your book and in your letter of February 21, 1977, remain ambiguous. The long quotation from *Christ sein* (p. 434 [ET, 443]) at the bottom of page 4 of your letter, goes only as far as to assert that *"in His whole person, Jesus proclaimed, manifested, revealed God's word and will,"* and that He *"is the embodiment of God's word and will."* You do not go beyond the formula: in Jesus we are concerned with the God who is really God" (p. 438 [ET, 448]). You thereby admit a functional unity of manifestation and action between the Son and the Father, but obviously you do not want to go on to raise and answer the question that necessarily must be asked next, namely, about the relation that exists between the Father and the Son *at the level of being,* as the faith of the Church teaches. In this way, however, you do not do justice to the whole of Scripture. One cannot decide on the basis of your statements whether Jesus is Son of God because He is God's indispensable agent, or whether He is this agent because He is the Son of God. As a result, the divine Sonship, too, emerges as *one* of many possible *constructions* which is, at bottom, replaceable (cf. also p. 433 f.; p. 436 [ET, 442 f.; 445]). You avoid, deliberately it seems, clarifying statements such as Holy Scripture and the statements of the Councils

of Nicaea and Chalcedon demand as constitutive elements of the Catholic profession of faith.

You may of course refer to the fact that in your letter of February 21, 1977 (No. 10) you declare: "Jesus *is* really the Son of God." Unfortunately, this is an incidental statement which strains against almost all the others in your book or even stands in contradiction to them. The difficulty of a discussion consists in the fact that, time and again, you use statements with more than one meaning, and soteriological expressions to which you can refer when question are asked. In so doing, however, you dodge, in key Christological statements, a categorical profession cast in a language that allows for no equivocation.

In conclusion, then, I would ask you the following first question: *Is Jesus Christ the Son of God, eternal, not made, one in being with the Father?*

2. On page 434 ff. [ET, 444 ff] of *Christ sein,* you deal with the God-man formula, "true God and true man." There is no way of finding in your book a firm profession in this connection. For you, "true God" means obviously "nothing more" than *"the UNIQUENESS, UNDERIVABILITY AND UNSURPASSABILITY of the CALL, OFFER* and *CLAIM made known in and with Jesus ultimately not of human but divine origin and therefore absolutely reliable, requiring men's unconditional involvement"* (p. 440; [ET, 449]). With this you give a new interpretation to the normative profession of faith "true God and true man," ultimately to the effect "that God and man are truly involved in the story of Jesus Christ" (p. 439 [ET, 449]). This unequivocally bespeaks a curtailment and undercutting of the dogma of Nicaea and Chalcedon. You did declare in your letter of February 21, 1977, that you adhere to the faith of Christological dogmas, and that you would like to show their relevance (cf. No. 4 and 6).

In this context, a key Soteriological element is also contained which I cannot unfold in this letter, but the consequences of which I would like to mention. If it were not *God Himself* who offered Himself up for man, the core of Christian revelation is undone. The same applies to the emphasis on the humaneness or the humanity of Jesus. All assertions about Jesus' humanity have any relevance at all for the faith only if they are intrinsically connected with the "true God." This fundamental ambiguity accounts for the deficiency that has been repeatedly noted in the Trinitarian doctrine of *Christ sein.*

In conclusion, then, here is my *second question:* Taking for granted that explanations and deepenings are, ultimately, always necessary, *do you concur without reservations with the profession of the Church that Jesus Christ is true man and true God?* Since you always appeal to the Scriptures, and rightly so, precisely in this context I may remind you of the Johannine Christology (cf., for example, Jn 1:1 and 20:28; 31).

3. For the moment, I will overlook further Christological themes. I will, however, mention a key methodological problem closely connected with the questions above. You often say that you would like to sketch a Christology "from the perspective of the first disciples of Jesus" (No. 3). To the extent to which you refer to the normativeness of the original witness of the Apostles, what you are staying is essential. However, you declare at the same time that "the ecclesial and also the conciliar tradition (should) be measured against the Christian message as originally witnessed to in Holy scripture, in fact against Jesus Himself, as the primary criterion of every theology" (No. 4). You seem, then, to be of the opinion that, by the means available to historical reason, the

theologian can transpose himself directly into the perspective of the first disciples (and of Jesus Himself), and *thus* reconstruct the mystery of the person of Jesus Christ and His work, and from this position, the position of a detached observer, assess the Church's profession of the Christ, and eventually raise questions about "discrepancies" within that profession.

I may, therefore, ask you the *third question*, which I would like to unfold in two parts (while bracketing out the hermeneutical-historical problems):

a. *Doesn't the return to the "perspective of the first disciples" require* — at least in a theological sense — *a mediation on the part of the living faith-consciousness of the Church?*

b. *Isn't the Church's confession* (for example, of the divine Sonship of Jesus) *the pre-given which a theologian must explicate with the help of all his methodological tools? Or do you maintain that a hypothetical historical reconstruction is per se sufficient to give us access to the theological understanding of Jesus Christ?*

This question has already been put to you with all possible clarity in the Declaration of the Conference of German Bishops on February 17, 1975 (cf. II, No. 1). You were asked to consider it. To this day, you have not adequately responded.

I will not discuss here many important problems, for example, the Christology "from above" and "from below," even though I cannot at all subscribe to the positions you take in your letter of February 21, 1977 (No. 3). I would, however, comment on at least two sets of problems from your letter (No. 12).

1. *Study-Projects and Workshops*

The Conference of German Bishops is not disinclined to examine more closely your proposals, which, incidentally, are not at all new. Workshops of a similar kind are conducted regularly within the full assemblies of the Conference of German Bishops. All the same, your proposal does raise some fundamental questions. Such study-projects should not obscure the fact that certain faith-assertions are entirely clear as to their basic meaning. Therefore, they are already normative at the outset of any such project (which is, of course, concerned with the quest for a deeper understanding). In no case should any such symposium, which is always conceivable as a project within theological circles, obscure the difference between the function of theology and that of the Magisterium, and make of discussion among theologians the only criterion for decisions about doctrine.

2. *Composition of the Doctrine-Commission*

In the name of the Conference of German Bishops, I most decisively disavow your contention that advisers to the Doctrinal-Commission are chosen on the basis of "good conduct" and not of the technical expertise of the gentlemen in question (cf. No. 12). I regard it as a particularly regrettable blunder on your part that you should have used your letter to me to denigrate your colleagues who are highly reputed even internationally. As I can personally testify, it is precisely your case that, for many years, has been taken under advisement by the Doctrinal-Commission with the utmost objectivity, circumspection, and patience.

Dear Professor Küng, I beg you for an answer especially to the three substantive theological questions mentioned above. As you answer, please abstain from a great many references to your books, since, in our opinion, these do not answer these questions, not with an adequate measure of clarity.

Nor can the bishops go along with you when you believe that you can respond to these questions by making declarations of intention as to projects you intend to undertake. Your answers can be very brief and pointed since, in the first and second questions, we are dealing above all with formulations taken from the Creed. This is also the reason why the bishops cannot let the fundamental answer to these questions be contingent on study-projects and workshops.

In the discussion of January 22, 1977, you had the opportunity of convincing the representatives of the Conference of German Bishops that, in fundamental Christological questions, you agree with the faith of the Church. In spite of some important contributions to the discussion on your part, the overall outcome will not do. Unfortunately, you did not take advantage of your letter of February 21, 1977, to clarify anew the questions and answers addressed in Stuttgart-Hohenheim, even though the Bishop of Rottenburg, in a letter of January 28, 1977, had especially drawn your attention to this opportunity and to the importance of the matter. You will, therefore, realize that, in the name of the Conference of German Bishops, I must again insist on a clarification of the questions at issue.

I urge you, then, in spite of the many and sundry tasks of a semester in progress, to answer these questions in writing by June 15, 1977. Understand that your answer is of utmost importance for the Conference of German Bishops.

In the hope of receiving a satisfactory answer from you, and with cordial greetings, I remain,

Yours,
(signed) + Joseph Cardinal Höffner

Enclosure 48/1

LETTER OF PROFESSOR KÜNG TO CARDINAL HÖFFNER, June 13, 1977

Tübingen
June 13, 1977

His Eminence
Cardinal Dr. Joseph Höffner
President of the Conference of German Bishops
Eintrachtstrasse 164
5000 Cologne

Your Eminence:

I acknowledge receipt of your letter of April 4, 1977. Since you expect an answer from me by June 15, I will not delay my answer any further. The answer is, of course, provisional.

I have just returned from a rather long stay in the United States of America and from a theological congress. I now find myself back in the middle of the summer semester in Tübingen. Much effort is required to fulfill the ordinary obligations of a university professor. In the discussion in Stuttgart on January 22, whose minutes have come to me with considerable delay on April 12, 1977, I already exhaustively explained that, in these months, it is physically impossible for me to devote still more time to this discussion which has already demanded from me an enormous amount of time. The many formal as well as substantive questions which arise here cannot be answered in a hurry.

In the discussion in Stuttgart, and especially in my long letter of February 21, 1977, I have already done more than could equitably be expected of me. Many experts share this view. I have been really surprised that, contrary to the impression you gave me at least after our discussion in Stuttgart, you are still not satisfied with my oral as well as my written reply.

At any rate, I must ask Your Eminence again to understand that I cannot answer your letter appropriately before my book on the God question is finished, and before I have given the official address at the five-hundreth anniversary celebration of the University of Tübingen.

With cordial greetings,

Very devotedly yours,
(signed) Hans Küng

c.
Dr. Georg Moser, Bishop of Rottenburg

Enclosure 48/2

LETTER OF CARDINAL HÖFFNER TO PROFESSOR KÜNG, July 8, 1977

Bonn,
July 8, 1977

Professor Dr. Hans Küng
Waldhäuserstr. 23
7400 Tübingen

OBJECT: *Your book,* Christ sein
Here: Request to answer questions forwarded to you on April 22, 1977

REFERENCE: *Your letter of June 13, 1977*

Dear Professor Küng:

With some surprise, I have taken cognizance of your letter of June 13, 1977. You will easily understand that I cannot in any way regard your letter as an answer.

The questions to which I had requested an answer had already been put to you in the discussion with the representatives of the Conference of German Bishops on January 22, 1977 in Stuttgart-Hohenheim. These were known to you also from the discussion which professional theologians have conducted about your book *Christ sein.* Do then try to see my request in the context of the clarification of these important substantive questions and of the concern which the Magisterium of the Church has been expressing for almost ten years about the many theological assertions contained in your books. Perhaps you will then perceive the seriousness of the situation. For two and a half years, the bishops have been waiting in vain for the clarification of some urgent and fundamental questions, especially concerning also *Christ sein* (cf. the Declaration of February 17, 1975). Despite the obscurities and deficiencies you are acquainted with, *Christ sein* is being disseminated at home and abroad without emendations. The regard so often exhibited toward you is, therefore, just about exhausted.

In its meeting of February 28, to March 3, 1977, the Conference of German Bishops directed me to report at the fall meeting concerning the answers to the questions put to you. I must therefore ask you to convey to me by *September 10, 1977,* at the latest, your answer to my letter of April 22, 1977. The meeting of the Conference of German Bishops begins on September 19.

You have, then, two more months at your disposal, two months in which you are unburdened by academic obligations. Given the situation, other priorities should not be allowed to interfere.

In spite of your disppointing answer of June 13, 1977, I still hope for a statement on your part that will make for substantive progress.

With cordial greetings, I am,

Yours,
(signed) + Joseph Cardinal Höffner

Enclosure 48/3

LETTER OF PROFESSOR KÜNG TO CARDINAL HÖFFNER, September 12, 1977

Sursee
September 12, 1977

His Eminence
Cardinal Dr. Joseph Höffner
President of the Conference of German Bishops
5000 Cologne

Your Eminence:

I would have been glad to answer your letter of July 8, 1977 in the way you wanted it answered, but, as I tried to explain in my letter of June 13, 1977, I am extremely busy at this time. The completion of my book on the God question and the speech at the celebration of the fifth centenary of the University of Tübingen must be given absolute priority. Many personalities in public life, including the Federal President, will take part in this celebration.

I have nevertheless tried to add precision and concreteness to the terms of the very complex questions you have raised, and especially to those which relate to Christology. In my opinion, these are questions that cannot be given a catechism answer. After having already exhaustively answered your questions for hours in Stuttgart, after addressing a long explanatory letter to the Conference of German Bishops, after many thorough discussions with the Bishop of Rottenburg, I have once again reflected radically about the whole problematic in connection with the God question, and the foundational question of faith and knowledge, and have consigned my reflections to writing in a 900-page book. I am of the opinion that, by locating your questions in a broader theological context, one makes a more helpful contribution to the clarification of the situation. I will take the liberty of sending to Your Eminence a copy of this book as soon as it is published, which is soon. I hope that the Conference of German Bishops will know how to appreciate not only the pastoral intentions which preside over this book, but also the importance of the substantive theological statements which are broadly set forth in this my "Answer to the God Question of Our Time."

With cordial greetings,

Devotedly yours,
(signed) Hans Küng

Enclosure 48/4

LETTER OF CARDINAL HÖFFNER TO PROFESSOR KÜNG, September 21, 1977

Bonn
September 21, 1977

Professor Dr. Hans Küng
Waldhäuser Str. 23
7400 Tübingen

Dear Professor Küng:

I acknowledge receipt of your letter of September 12, 1977. In this letter you again refuse to answer questions with regard to your book *Christ sein.* You have been asked questions about the fundamental truths of the Christian faith. These questions could have been answered merely by making a profession of this faith. I am sorry that you failed to do this. You have thereby made it obvious that, from within the theology advocated in your book, an unequivocal yes to fundamental assertions of the Catholic faith is not possible.

Cordial greetings.

Yours,
(signed) + Joseph Cardinal Höffner

Enclosure 48/5

LETTER OF PROFESSOR KÜNG TO CARDINAL HÖFFNER, November 7, 1977

Tübingen
November 7, 1977

His Eminence
Cardinal Dr. Joseph Höffner
President of the Conference of German Bishops
Kaiserstrasse 163
5300 Bonn

Your Eminence:

With amazement, I have taken cognizance of your letter of September 21, 1977. I regret having to state that this letter shows hardly any appreciation for the difficult theological problematic or for my own personal burdens at this time, which I have repeatedly mentioned. Under these circumstances, I would like to say here briefly what I regard as decisively important.

I emphatically reject your allegation that I have again refused to answer questions in connection with my book, *Christ sein.* On the contrary, on January 22, 1977, in Stuttgart, I participated in a four-hour discussion with you and other bishops and theologians in which you had the opportunity to ask all the questions that beset you. Above and beyond that, on February 21, 1977, I addressed to the Conference of German Bishops a long explanatory letter which, among other things, also contains a clear profession of the divine Sonship of Jesus. Finally, in two further letters, June 13 and September 12, 1977, I explained that I would answer your questions in the context of my next book, *Existiert Gott ? Antwort auf die Gottesfrage der Neuzeit,* which will appear in February 1978. In view of all this, how can you maintain that I am refusing to answer questions relative to *Christ sein?*

You further maintain that the questions you have raised could have been answered merely by making a profession of Catholic faith. I am outraged that a profession of faith should be demanded of me, a full professor of Catholic theology, as if I had denied that faith. In this connection, I emphatically reject the allegation, already made against me in the Declaration of the Episcopal Conference on March 3, that I regard Jesus Christ only as a "spokesman and advocate" (sic ! [Sachverwalter]) of God and that I deny assertions of the Council of Nicaea. To these allegations, which defame my Catholic orthodoxy at home and abroad, I will come back in terms of a public retraction on your part. Here I will say only one thing: It has never occurred to me to deny the essential tenets of our faith, nor do I see any basic contradiction between the statements of my book, *Christ sein,* and the statements of the first ecumenical councils. Naturally, I regard it as indispensable that an interpretation be provided for the people of our time. I would like emphatically to request of you that, in the future, you should always start by taking for granted that you and I stand on the ground of a common Catholic faith.

Finally, you maintain that an unequivocal yes to the basic assertions of the Catholic faith is not possible from within the theology advocated in *Christ sein.* As it appears from foregoing, this, too, is an indefensible allegation. Of course, I do not let anybody force upon me the way in which I should answer these questions. As it appears also from other Christological publications of recent years, we are dealing here with extremely subtle and complex problems, which face all theologians, and which, also in the opinion of other Catholic theologians, cannot be coped with by means of catechism answers. In my book, I hope to contribute to the clarification of the situation, which is what can be equitably expected of me.

I would be grateful to Your Eminence if you would at least take cognizance of the fact which, to no avail, I have tried to explain to you in two letters. At present, my work load is excessive. This year I have not been able yet to take one day off, and I am once again fully immersed in academic work. I had mentioned to you that I would give the address at the celebration of the fifth centenary of the University of Tübingen. I have given this address on "Science and the God Question." The reaction tells me that the address has been looked upon far and wide as a great service to the cause of the Christian faith. It will appear in print in the next few days together with the address of the Federal President Walter Scheel. I take the liberty of enclosing a copy of the manuscript. As I also promised you, I will also send you a copy of the new book as soon as it is published. I still hope that the Conference of German Bishops will appreciate not only the pastoral intentions that preside over these books, but also the importance of the substantive theological assertions they contain.

With cordial greetings,

Devotedly yours,
(signed) Hans Küng

Enclosure:

Address given at the celebration of the fifth centenary of the University of Tübingen on "Science and the God Question"

cc.

Dr. Georg Moser, Bishop of Rottenburg
Dr. Anton Hänggi, Bishop of Basel

Enclosure 49/1

LETTER OF CARDINAL HÖFFNER TO PROFESSOR KÜNG, November 17, 1977

Bonn
November 17, 1977

Professor Dr. Hans Küng
Waldhäuserstr. 23
7400 Tübingen

Dear Professor Küng:

In your letter of November 7, 1977, whose receipt I acknowledge, you stress that it has never occurred to you to deny the essential tenets of our faith, and that you and I stand on the ground of the same Catholic faith. I respect this personal profession of faith without reservations and gratefully.

However, the bishops are not worried about your personal faith — we have stressed this repeatedly — but about the fact that apparently you have not managed to adequately express in your book *Christ sein* the common faith-conviction you have emphasized.

In the discussion of January 22, 1977 in Stuttgart, the bishops placed their concern before you and urged you to correct and qualify the vague assertions mentioned in the discussion. You have refused to do this and made reference to an overcrowded schedule and a book to be published. The bishops strongly intimated to you then that they could not accept this.

Neither could your letter of February 21, 1977 convince the bishops. Thereupon, in my letter of April 22, 1977, I put to you some unequivocal questions. Your answer would have gone a long way toward clarifying the statements to which we object.

Please, take it for granted that the bishops, too, are acquainted with the difficult theological problematic. They also thoroughly appreciate the true help which theologians give for the deepening of the Christian faith in our time. This effort should not, however, lead anyone to misinterpret essential tenets of the faith or to formulate them in such a way that they leave the impression they are being contested. Even today, the faithful are entitled to a complete and unequivocal presentation of the essential truths of faith.

As shown in the discussion of January 22, 1977, and as I stated more precisely in my letter of April 22, 1977, your book, *Christ sein,* contains statements on essential tenets of our faith which, in the opinion of the bishops, fail to do justice to the traditional doctrine of the faith.

Since you refuse to produce a more precise version of these statements, the bishops feel that they must provide these necessary clarifications in a letter to all the faithful.

I emphatically remind you of the Declaration of the Conference of German Bishops of February 17, 1975, and of the request made of you at that time to reexamine your theological method in keeping with the principles set forth in that Declaration.

With cordial greetings,
(signed) + Joseph Cardinal Höffner

P.S.
Enclosed is the text of the "Message of the German Bishops" concerning your book, *Christ sein,* and the text of letters exchanged between you and the Conference of German Bishops, also concerning your book, *Christ sein*. These texts are to be published tomorrow.

Enclosure 49/2

DECLARATION OF THE CONFERENCE OF GERMAN BISHOPS ON THE BOOK, *CHRIST SEIN,* November 17, 1977

MESSAGE OF THE GERMAN BISHOPS TO THE FAITHFUL

In the Declaration of the Conference of German Bishops of February 17, 1975, at the termination of the doctrinal proceedings of the Congregation for the Doctrine of the Faith relative to Professor Küng's books, *Die Kirche* and *Unfehlbar ? Eine Anfrage,* the Conference of German Bishops defined its position also with regard to the book, *Christ sein,* published a short time earlier (*Nachkonziliare Dokumentation,* Vol. 43; Trier, 1975, p. 206; cf. also all the other entries until 1975). With reference to the normative significance of the Christian tradition, the Declaration states: "When Professor Küng fails to observe, as basis for his theological work, the norms of the Christian faith that come to expression in these principles, conflicts with the Magisterium of the Church are bound to emerge. Hence, even Professor Küng's 'declarations' necessary as they may be, will not do. Thus, even in the new book of Professor Küng, *Christ sein* (München, 1974), whose theological concern and pastoral purpose we recognize, there is a series of assertions which do not exhibit conformity with the principles mentioned above (cf. especially its Christology, the doctrine of the Trinity, the theology of the Church and of the Sacraments, the place of Mary in the history of salvation)." A theological discussion among experts ensued (cf. many individual articles, and the volume *Diskussion über Hans Küngs Christ sein,* Mainz, 1976). Until the last hours before his untimely death, Cardinal Julius Döpfner, then President of the Conference of German Bishops, pressed for a clarification of these misgivings, especially with regard to the person and work of Jesus Christ. In a discussion with representatives of the Conference of German Bishops, Professor Küng was urgently requested to make necessary emendations and additions to the aforementioned book. He has never complied with this request; he merely promised possible clarifications in a forthcoming book.

In a very extensive letter to Professor Küng dated April 22, 1977, the President of the Conference of German Bishops raised specific questions regarding various assertions in *Christ sein.* Even after repeated urgent exhortations in subsequent letters, Professor Küng has failed to answer these questions.

The book *Christ sein* is being disseminated without emendations and translated in other languages. Since this book presents itself as a kind of "small 'Summa' " (p. 14 [ET, p. 20]) of the Christian faith, and is also being understood and used by many as a text in teaching Catholic faith, the Conference of German Bishops feels impelled to define again its position with regard to this book. It would not do this if it did not feel that it is its duty to do so for the sake of the faith of believers. As we are often told, Küng's *Christ sein* has contributed considerably to a distressing undermining of the faith.

In this Declaration we do not intend to make a judgment as to what Professor Küng personally believes or does not believe. Nor are we dealing here with what Professor Küng has written in earlier books, or will write in books to come. Here we are concerned rather with the book, *Christ sein*, although this book is premised on a way of thinking and doing theology set forth in earlier books. With regard to this theological method, the German Bishops have already defined their position in the aforementioned Declaration. Although *Christ sein* thinks of itself as of a "small 'Summa'," it does not deal with everything that pertains constitutively to the Catholic faith, for example, the seven sacraments and their significance for Christian life. We must ask, however, whether what is treated in the book is treated in accord with the Christian faith. Here, we do not propose to mention in detail everything that is inadequately set forth, for example, the doctrine of the Trinity, the doctrine of the Church, of the sacraments, and of Mary. Consistently applied, the theological method used by Professor Küng, the shortcomings of which have already been mentioned in the Declaration of February 17, 1975, brings about by way of consequence a breach with traditional faith and doctrine in matters of importance. The dissociation of theological method from the previous tradition of the Church and a prejudiced and selective use of Scriptural texts lead to a diminishing of the faith. We do not thereby question the positive concern of Professor Küng. Yet, he does fail to present to the reader the whole Christ and His saving action in all its fullness. It is not enough to proclaim in a general way one's fidelity to the constitutive articles of the faith. These must be unequivocally affirmed and their contents unfolded.

1. JESUS CHRIST, TRUE GOD AND TRUE MAN

Prescinding from the theological method and the truths of faith just mentioned, we need to advert here to the shortcomings inherent to a onesided and inadequate Christology. The doctrine of the Christ is the foundation of the Christian faith. It needs to be especially stressed. (With regard to the doctrine of the Church, cf. the Declaration of Congregation for the Doctrine of the Faith, *Mysterium Ecclesiae* of July 24, 1973, and the Declaration of the Conference of German Bishops of February 25, 1975). In the book, the divinity of Jesus is slighted. Jesus of Nazareth is true man and true God. These two assertions may not be abridged; the one is not to be collapsed into the other. For Jesus Christ cannot do what He does, if He is not what He is. In the Incarnation, the eternal, not made, Son of God, divine as the Father is divine, one in being with the Father, is bound in personal unity with the man Jesus. This is indeed a great mystery, but it must be held and also affirmed; otherwise the doctrine of salvation, as the fruit of the redemptive deed of Jesus of Nazareth, will be seriously impaired, and the Gospel, the good news of our salvation in Jesus Christ, in whom God Himself has ultimately bound Himself to our humanity, can no longer be asserted as to its constitutive contents, or proclaimed. The casual statement that Jesus was the Son of God does not suffice as a description of the Christ, since even the gracious deed of redemption, for instance, does afford us the status of children and sons, as it is said in Gal 3:26: "Each one of you is a son of God because of your faith in Jesus Christ." According to the word of the Lord, we, too, can and should call God our Father.

Our Creeds clearly and unequivocally assert who Jesus is. In the Solemn Formula of Faith it is said: "[We believe] . . . in one Lord, Jesus Christ, the only Son of God, eternally begotten of the Father, God from God, Light from Light, true God from true God, begotten, not made, one in Being with the Father. Through Him all things were made. For us men and for our salvation He came down from heaven: by the power of the Holy Spirit He was born of the Virgin Mary and became man." In the Formula of the Apostles we confess: "[We believe] . . . in Jesus Christ, His only begotten Son, our Lord." This, too, is an unequivocal profession of the divinity of Jesus Christ, for the words "only begotten" profess the oneness in being, as asserted in the doctrine of the Most Blessed Trinity. Besides, Jesus as the Christ, could not be our Lord, as He is, if the man Jesus were not so much one with the divine Son that, in Him, God himself and His saving Lordship are present and operative.

In *Christ sein* we find a whole string of titles of office and designations which are to apply to Jesus the Christ in a unique way. Thus, Jesus is often called God's agent ["Sachwalter"]. But, even if this title should apply to Jesus Christ in a unique way, it is not enough as an adequate description of what Jesus Christ really is. There have been many agents of God: before Christ, Moses and the Prophets; after Christ, the Apostles and the envoys of the Church. But all these agents point above and beyond themselvs to the Messiah to come, or to the Messiah who has come. Jesus, on the contrary, points directly to His own self. Thus Paul can write: "It is not ourselves we preach but Christ Jesus as Lord, and ourselves as your servants for Jesus' sake" (2 Cor 4:5). In the Gospel of John, Jesus says about Himself: "I am the way, and the truth, and the life; no one comes to the Father but through me" (Jn 14:6). In the discourse about the bread of life, which refers to the Eucharist, we read:

"I myself am the living bread
come down from heaven.
If anyone eats this bread
he shall live forever;
the bread I will give
is my flesh, for the life of the world. . .
He who feeds on my flesh
and drinks my blood
has life eternal
and I will raise him up on the last day.
. . . Just as the Father who has life sent me
and I have life because of the Father,
so the man who feeds on me

will have life because of me."
(Jn 6:51; 54; 57)

Words such as these would be totally unintelligible, if Jesus, unlike all the other agents of God, were not Himself God, the eternal, not made, Son of God. Because of this unique claim on the part of Jesus, it is said, in connection with the passage quoted above: "From this time on, many of His disciples broke away and would not remain in His company any longer" (Jn 6:66). Jesus is not the Son insofar as, and because, He is God's agent; rather He is God's agent because He is God's Son. We do not understand in what sense Jesus is and how He claims to be the agent of God, unless He be also the eternal, not made, Son of God.

2. GOD'S SELF-SURRENDER FOR US IN JESUS OF NAZARETH

It is a mistake to consider all this a quarrel about words. What is at stake here is rather that Jesus is not only our teacher and model, but also the redeemer and life eternal, if we unite ourselves to Him with a total faith. Numberless are the witnesses who, by their lives and deaths, have borne witness to their faith in God. The Letter to the Hebrews speaks of a "cloud of witnesses," and says that "the world was not worthy of them" (Heb 12:1; 11:38). But these witnesses could not redeem us, not even through their lives and deaths. Jesus, however, did redeem us through his life and death, because He was not only true man, but also God's divine Son, sent by the heavenly Father to effect our redemption. In the First Epistle of Peter, it is said: "Realize that you were delivered from the futile way of life your fathers handed on to you, not by a diminishable sum of silver or gold, but by Christ's blood beyond all price: the blood of a spotless, unblemished lamb" (1 Pet 1:18 f.). Hence, we are right to pray: "We adore you, we bless you, because through the holy cross you have redeemed the world." For we have not been redeemed by just any sufferings; only the passion and death of the Son of God become man, who once and for all becomes one with all human beings, embody the power to redeem.

When the divinity of Jesus of Nazareth — true man and true God — is not asserted and held with unmistakable clarity, a distorting diminishing of the Gosepl follows as the inevitable consequence. For the core of the Gospel as the message of salvation is this: God Himself loves us, He loves every human being, even the sinner, even us as sinners.

"At the appointed time, when we were still powerless,
Christ died for us godless men. . . It is precisely in
this way that God proves His love for us: that while
we were still sinners, Christ died for us. Now that
we have been justified by His blood, it is all the more
certain that we shall be saved by Him from God's wrath.
For if, when we were God's enemies, we were reconciled
to Him by the death of His Son, it is all the more
certain that we who have been reconciled will be saved
by His life." (Rom 5:6; 8-10)

God's love for us is not just sentiment. God's love is not an inactive, but an active love. In His love, God not only does something for us; He goes all out for us, in that He sends His one and eternal Son to us and for us, in order that in Him we may have access to life eternal, which we had lost and missed.

"Yes, God so loved the world
that He gave His only Son
that whoever believes in Him may not die
but have eternal life.
God did not send the Son into the world
to condemn the world,
but that the world might be saved through him."
(Jn 3:16 f.)

Abraham, who was prepared to sacrifice his only son Isaac, is only a weak prefiguration of what the heavenly Father has done. The angel from heaven said: "Do not lay your hand on the boy . . . Do not do the least thing to him" (Gn 22:12). The heavenly Father on the contrary does not hold back. He gives up the only Son, His beloved, and thereby He gives Himself for us. It is not for us to ask whether God could have saved mankind in some other way. The Father did go out of His way for us without consideration for Himself, which is the reason why God's own self, as well as our own self, is involved in what is Christian and no substitute is possible. For what is actually involved is that in the Incarnation of the divine Son, God's covenant was sealed with our own selves once and for all. Hence, the covenant in Jesus Christ is the new, the final, the eternal covenant. This also means that, through Christ man not only achieves fulfillment in and for his own self. As he now relates to himself in the all-encompassing depth of his heart, he achieves fulfillment through and in Christ and, in Christ, also through the Father.

This self-surrender which the Father effects in the sending of the Son becomes embodied without curtailment or reservation in Jesus, the Son become man. Jesus prolongs that surrender. When, in the Garden of Gethsemani, Jesus in mortal dread begged to be spared, the cup of suffering did not pass away from Him. Jesus accepts suffering and death. Thus, in His surrender to the will of the heavenly Father, Jesus makes His own God's love for us without curtailment. "There is no greater love than this: to lay down one's life for one's friends" (Jn 15:13).

Note here that the unconditional surrender of Jesus Christ on the cross does not mean that He had failed or that He missed the purpose of His life. On the contrary, through His unconditional surrender to the design of the heavenly Father for sinners, He achieves fulfillment for His own self. His words on the cross, "Now it is finished" (Jn 19:30) mean not only that His life has come to an end, but also that He has carried out His mandate, that He has fulfilled it. In the Letter to the Hebrews we read: "Son though He was, He learned obedience from what He suffered; and when perfected, He became the source of eternal salvation for all who obey Him, designated by God, as high priest according to the order of Melchizedek" (5:8-10). The resurrection, then, is the incontrovertible sign that His self-surrender did not imply His own undoing. Rather, it paved the way to His glorification in eternity.

"Because of this
God exalted Him
and bestowed on Him the name
above every other name,

So that at Jesus' name
every knee must bend
in the heavens, on earth,
and under the earth,
and every tongue proclaim
to the glory of God the Father:
JESUS CHRIST IS LORD."
(Phil 2:9-11)

All this is of the greatest importance for our faith and for our understanding of our own Christian life and destiny. It makes it clear to us that Christian life hinges on love and that in love our own selves are at stake, our own disposition of ourselves, the surrender of our own selves to Jesus Christ and to the Father. Since God has loved us first and loves us unconditionally in Christ to the point of self-surrender, therefore love for God and neighbor is the chief commandment. "On these two commandments the whole law is based, and the prophets as well" (Mt 22:40). Hence "faith expresses itself in love" (Gal 5:6). The self-surrender of Christ in death is the sacrifice of the New Covenant, which becomes present in the holy Mass, so that inner participation in the holy Mass entails unconditioned self-surrender to God, in fulfillment of the chief commandment. As was the case for Jesus Christ, the Christian, too, achieves his own self and attains to fulfillment before God and in God through such surrender of his own self to Christ and, in Christ, to the Father.

Our love for God and for our neighbor must come to fruition in our conduct.

"He who obeys the commandments he has from me
is the man who loves Me;
and he who loves Me will be loved by my Father.
I too will love him
and reveal Myself to him."
(Jn 14:21)

Love, then, is not a substitute for deeds. Nor are deeds a substitute for love. Rather; love finds expression in deeds. Love does not cease when the deed is done; it outlasts the deed. "Love never fails" (1 Cor 13:8). We cannot, then, want to do good in order to escape the obligation to love. In this case, we would take shelter behind our deeds. We would do a deed in order not to make ourselves available to others in love, not to surrender our own selves. A deed of this kind would be compliance with law; it would not be love, nor a response to God's love, for God not only does something for us, but surrenders His own self for us in the Incarnation of His Son.

All this fails to come adequately to the fore in the book, *Christ sein.* True, Jesus of Nazareth is God's agent among us and for us, but it is not clear that in the sending of the Son, that God manifests Himself as love. The Scripture says: "God is love. God's love was revealed in our midst in this way: He sent His only Son to the world that we might have life through Him" (1 Jn 4:8 f.). In the last section of the book, some 100 pages long, entitled "Practice" the commandment of love is mentioned but not treated thematically. Like Peter, we are being asked: "Do you love me?" (Jn 21:15). This fact does not receive its due in a "small Summa" on being a Christian, such as we have in *Christ sein.* We cannot, then, regard this presentation as adequate. God's saving action in Jesus Christ is curtailed there in a fashion which we once again disavow.

3. CURTAILMENT OF THE REALITY OF REDEMPTION

Since the saving action of God in Jesus Christ is slighted in its presentation, it is inevitable that the fruits of the redemptive deed of Jesus Christ should also be defectively described. The fruits of redemption are a mystery. This does not mean that we do not know anything with any precision about the matter. Mystery means rather that the gracious deed of redemption joins us with Christ more closely than anyone ever could; so closely that our capacity and our notions are transcended. This union is affirmed in the simile of the vine and the branches, in the designation of Jesus Christ as the head and of the Church as His body, and of the individual as a member of His body. This is stated in over one hundred passages of the New Testament, which declare that we are in Christ and Christ in us. Only because of such an assimilation with Jesus Christ, which does not come about unless we become His members, do we call God Father. In the gracious deed of redemption, Jesus has made us His own brothers and sisters. "But when the designated time had come, God sent forth His Son born of a woman, born under the law, to deliver from the law these who were subjected to it, so that we might receive our status as adopted sons. The proof that you are sons is the fact that God has sent forth into our hearts the Spirit of His Son which cries out 'Abba' ('Father'). You are no longer a slave but a son! And the fact that you are a son makes you an heir, by God's design" (Gal 4:4-7). In the Second Epistle of Peter, we read: "By virtue of them [God's glory and power] He has bestowed on us the great and precious things He promised, so that through these you who have fled a world corrupted by lust might become sharers of the divine nature" (1:4).

Because of this union with Christ which God effects, we share His destiny, His death, which is indeed the consequence of sin, but can be transformed by us into a surrender of our life and, thereby, of our own selves. But we share with Him also the destiny of His resurrection. "Just as we resemble the man from earth, so shall we bear the likeness of the man from heaven. . . This corruptible body must be clothed with incorruptibility; this mortal body, with immortality" (1 Cor 15:49; 53). Thus this graced union with Christ becomes the ground of our hope. For nothing that may happen to us can curtail or dissolve this union with Jesus Christ. Only we ourselves can destroy it through mortal sin. The fact that nothing of a temporal nature can separate us from Christ (see Rom 8:38 f.), this fact is the supreme ground of our hope.

In the Mass, as we mix water with wine, we pray: "By the mystery of this water and wine may we come to share in the divinity of Christ who humbled Himself to share in our humanity." Professor Küng, on the contrary adopts this quote: "But does a reasonable man today want to become God?" (p. 433; [ET, p. 442]). One can read this only with regret. Does anyone think, or is it being taught anywhere, that, in the redemption, man ceases being a man because he has become God? In the Incarnation, the divine Son does not cease being God; in the redemption, man does not cease being man. He has not become God, but partakes of the eternal life given him, and thereby of the blessedness of God. The sign and content of that life is the resurrection from the dead, as assured participation in the eternal and blessed life of God. This too is a mystery; it surpasses our understanding. And yet, in the absence of a description of that mystery, the Christian faith is diminished. In the book *Christ sein* the description of the reality of salvation, of the fruit of God's saving action in Jesus Christ, is lessened, and this distorts the reality described.

The bishops must, therefore, stress that, in regard to the points indicated here by way of example, *Christ sein* cannot be regarded as an adequate presentation of the Catholic faith. The bishops issue this declaration because it is their duty to bear witness to the true faith and to defend that faith.

The required emendations and additions also call for the use of another theological method. The assertions of Sacred Scripture in their totality, and the normative doctrine of the Church must be incorporated without diminution. One is not entitled to look upon this demand as if it were away to make the faith in Christ unnecessarily complicated. Jesus Christ is true man and true God. This is the content of our faith in Christ. This double affirmation permits no alternative, that is, neither the choice of a Christology one-sidedly or even exclusively "from below" (centered, that is, on the humanity of Christ) nor that of a Christology only "from above" (centered, that is, on the divinity of Christ). Both affirmations can and must be made together; both must be given their due. In a presentation of the Christ and of what it is to be a Christian, this is indispensable, and the bishops insists that it is so.

This double affirmation, that Jesus of Nazareth is true God and true man, is the essential affirmation of the first ecumenical council of Nicaea in the year 325, which condemned as erroneous the doctrine of Arius, who maintained that the Son of God is the highest creature (cf. the Declaration of the German Bishops of September 24, 1975, on the occasion of the 1,650th anniversary of the Council). To identify with the faith as established at Nicaea does not detract from an ecumenical concern. The witness of the first ecumenical councils is shared by Catholic, Orthodox and Protestant Christians. This is precisely the basis for efforts to achieve unity among all Christians. If this basis is questioned or merely permitted to grow dim, the striving for unity is deprived of its foundation. If by chance a unity should emerge, it could not be regarded as standing in continuity with the origins of Christianity.

The bishops would not want anyone to think that they do not esteem the theologian's proper task or that they are not grateful to theologians for their genuine assistance in the deepening of the Christian faith in our time. All of us labor for a renewal of the Church stemming from her source, Jesus Christ. This is precisely the reason why we cannot dispense with the task of bearing witness to the mystery of His person and setting forth that mystery without curtailment.

With appreciation for the legitimate concern of Professor Küng, the bishops insist that faith in Christ must be witnessed to in its entirety and that this witness must extend to all the articles connected with that faith. They are convinced that an undiminished faith in Christ is more credible than a diminished one, even though an undiminished faith includes mysteries and the affirmation of the same. "The mysteries of God are more credible than human solutions."

Enclosure 50

DECLARATION OF PROFESSOR KÜNG TO THE PRESS, November 18, 1977

Reaction of Professor Küng as reported by the Deutsche Presse Agentur, November 18, 1977

In a first reaction to the Declaration of the Conference of German Bishops, Küng called that Declaration "a doctrinaire self-justification without self-criticism." He predicted that it would not achieve its purpose. In the difficult situation in which Church and society find themselves, people expect from the bishops not condemnations but "constructive answers to questions which are also theirs." The readers of the book being attacked by the bishops will make up their own minds.

Küng regretted that the bishops had not had enough patience and insight to wait for the clarification in his forthcoming book of the theological questions concerning in particular the divine Sonship of Jesus, which he has never denied. The bishops knew that this book would be published in 1978. The theologian also strongly objected to the fact that his personal letters to the President of the Conference of German Bishops had been published in a biased context, without his consent and without giving him the opportunity to define his own position. "When will the bishops let me work in peace?" asked Küng in the end, with reference to the fact that this is the third time the bishops have taken a stand on his book *Christ sein.*

Enclosure 51

EXCERPT FROM PROFESSOR KÜNG'S BOOK, *EXISTIERT GOTT?* (1978)

[Page 855, Footnote 11]

[11]Not so the Conference of German Bishops. In their second declaration to the press concerning *Christ sein* on March 3, 1977, the bishops alleged that, for the author, Jesus Christ is "only an exemplary man" and "only God's spokesman and advocate (sic! ["Sachverwalter"])." I reject this allegation as an incomprehensible distortion inflicted on my thinking. The same applies to the allegation that I have denied the Christological assertions of the Creed of Nicaea. On the contrary, it has been my purpose to make it possible for people today to understand that Creed. One must ask whether it makes any sense at all to be willing to discuss, to engage in clarifying discussions, to write letters to bishops. Apparently, the teaching office is unteachable. This being the situation, who is to blame for "readers being misled and confused"? To this context there belongs also the volume against *Christ sein,* which was launched, together with various measures, in 1976 by picked theologians, with the knowledge of the "Doctrinal-Commission" of the German Episcopate. It carries the misleading title *Diskussion um Hans Küngs Christ sein.* In various articles we are dealing

less with a discussion than with misunderstandings, misinterpretations, denigrations, allegations. No better proposals are offered. Just as in the infallibility debate earlier, the author is not even given the opportunity to add his reply in the same volume. A clear "Reply to My Critics" became thus a plain necessity for me. This reply was published in the *Frankfurter Allgemeine Zeitung* of March 22, 1976. People today expect the bishops to stand up in a credible way, not only for a dogmatic system and an institution, but also for the cause of God and of Christ in the society of today. They expect them to proclaim the message in understandable language and to undertake long overdue practical reforms. Then perhaps hasty public denunciations of theologians would not be necessary.

While the manuscript of *Existiert Gott?* was being printed, a third declaration against *Christ sein* appeared, together with a set of documents published by the Conference of German Bishops. I find it unbearable that the strongest protests which I, the person concerned, had to make against publicizing, without my consent, my personal letters to the President of the Conference of German Bishops were in vain. But even more unbearable do I find the fact that the Conference of German Bishops would not wait until the controversial questions were again addressed in this book, more deeply treated and hopefully resolved. In my many letters to the Conference of German Bishops, I had declared that it was my intention to do this. In consequence, I felt obliged to consent in turn to the publication of a documentation which will display the whole truth. It is entitled, *Um nichts als die Wahrheit. Deutsche Bischofskonferenz contra Hans Küng. Eine Dokumentation,* and edited by W. Jens (München, 1978). Cf. there my "Appell zur Verständigung." Further information about the theological and biographical background appears in a book likewise published in the spring of 1978, *Hans Küng: Weg und Werk,* ed. H. Haring and K. -Kuschel (München, 1978).

Enclosure 52/1

LETTER OF CARDINAL HÖFFNER TO PROFESSOR KÜNG, February 22, 1978

Bonn
February 22, 1978

Professor Dr. Hans Küng
Nauklerst. 37a
7400 Tübingen

Dear Professor Küng:

I have received your letter of February 10, 1978.

Not even with the best will in the world could I regard as helpful your comments on the documentation published by Walter Jens.

In the press conference at the spring meeting of the Conference of German Bishops, I was asked by reporters about my opinion concerning this documentation. I take the liberty of enclosing my reply.

Agreement cannot be achieved by appealing to the public. You need to address the questions repeatedly put to you and comply with the exhortations that have come to you from the Conference of German Bishops.

With cordial greetings,

Yours,
(signed) + Jos. Cardinal Höffner

enclosure
cc. Bishop Moser and Cardinal Volk

Enclosure 52/2

DECLARATION OF CARDINAL HÖFFNER TO THE PRESS, February 16, 1978

Declaration of the President of the Conference of German Bishops concerning the Documentation issued by Walter Jens, February 16, 1978

1. I regret that Professor Küng has made public the transcript of the discussion in Stuttgart. Confidentiality had been explicitly agreed upon.

2. On the other hand, this publication offers everyone the opportunity to make up his own mind. The question whether that discussion was a trial or a dialogue answers itself.

3. Walter Jens' Preface is not conducive to mutual understanding. It reinforces prejudices and stirs up emotions. Professor Küng's Epilogue uses high-handed langauge; the tone is pedantic. This makes it more effective for digging up new graves than for promoting mutual respect. In view of what comes before, the appeal to mutual understanding in the concluding section of the appeal sounds barely credible.

4. It is painful to notice how, in the Preface and in the Epilogue, an attempt is made to play against each other the attitudes of the Conference of German Bishops under Cardinal Döpfner and under Cardinal Höffner. Cardinal Döpfner was deeply disappointed that Professor Küng was not prepared to give an inch. See, in this context, the letters of June 26, 1974, and June 24, 1976, printed in the book, pp. 115 and 208.

5. The documentation displayed by Professor Jens is not complete. It begins in 1973, whereas an exchange of letters between Professor Küng and the Congregation for the Doctrine of the Faith had begun in previous years. Professor Jens has indeed included the 1968 Declaration of the theologians for the freedom of theology, but has omitted other documents of this time.

6. In this affair, the confrontation is not between theology and the bishops. Küng's book *Christ sein* has been severely criticized not only by the Conference of German Bishops, but by a large number of renowned theologians.

7. If one examines carefully the documentation presented by the Conference of German Bishops and by Walter Jens, one realizes that in the documentation of the Conference of German Bishops nothing is being distorted. After consulting with Professor Küng, letters were omitted which had been addressed to Cardinal Döpfner and not to the President of the Conference of German Bishops, and could, therefore, be regarded as personal, as well as letters in which third parties were concerned. The Conference of German Bishops has not claimed that it was offering a complete documentation.

The impression which the publishers tried to create when they announced the publication of the book — namely, that only in the documentation of Walter Jens one could secure comprehensive information — is therefore misleading.

Ludwigshafen
February 16, 1978

Enclosure 53

LETTER OF PROFESSOR KÜNG TO BISHOP MOSER, February 10, 1978

Tübingen
February 10, 1978

His Excellency
Dr. Georg Moser
Bischof-von-Keppler-Strasse 7
7507 Rottenburg

Your Excellency:

As I informed you at the last meeting of the Ordinariate and the Faculty, the Documentation on the controversy between the Conference of German Bishops and me, edited by Walter Jens, is being published today. The reasons which impelled me to take this step are set forth in the enclosed letter to Cardinal Höffner and in my "Appell zur Verständigung."

You know that I have not been able to understand the conduct of the bishops with regard to *Christ sein,* especially in the last phases. For theological and pastoral reasons, many people, even in our diocese, were also disappointed, together with me, by the course of action which the bishops have taken. You also know that I have always shown appreciation for your difficult situation within the Episcopal Conference and have responded constructively to your efforts at mediation. On my side, I, too, now ask you to understand that I had no choice but to take the course of action I have taken. My action was nothing more and nothing less than a reaction which I would gladly have avoided.

I have written my "Appell" in the spirit in which you closed your statement at the Conference of Deans on November 17, 1977. In spite of all the difficulties that beset me so often, I, too, pledge myself "to standing resolutely together for the sake of the living Church." For the sake of keeping the Diocese informed in an impartial manner, I now ask you kindly to convey my "Appell zur Verständigung" to those who have received the Declaration of the Episcopal Conference. I enclose a copy of my text for duplication.

With cordial greetings,

Yours,
(signed) Hans Küng

enclosure

Enclosure 54

LETTER OF BISHOP MOSER TO PROFESSOR KÜNG, April 3, 1978

Rottenburg am Neckar
April 3, 1978

Professor Dr. Hans Küng
Waldhäuserstrasse 23
7400 Tübingen 1

Dear Professor Küng:

For quite some time, since the Declaration of the German Bishops on your book *Christ sein* I have been wanting to write you a long letter with my impressions, questions and concerns. Unfortunately, a busy schedule has prevented me. I have also tried, but in vain, to speak to you on the telephone. You were away on a journey.

Because of my appointments, I shall not be able in the next few weeks to find the time and quiet I need for this letter. I would like, therefore, to at least confirm receipt of your letter of February 10, 1978.

Unfortunately, I am not in a position to comply with your request and disseminate the "Appell zur Verständigung" you have enclosed. In my view, Walter Jens' Documentation *Um nichts als die Wahrheit,* which closes with this "Appell," is anything but a documentation of mutual understanding. In the editor's Preface, there is no evidence of any willingness to promote mutual understanding. What comes through is a determination to engage in open confrontation. I cannot dissociate your own text from the whole context. However, I would not want to go into this any further.

For now, I would like to ask your indulgence for keeping you waiting so long for my response and now answering you so briefly. I do want to thank you sincerely for sending me your new book, *Existiert Gott ?,* and the *Festschrift* published on the occasion of your 50th birthday.

With cordial greetings and best wishes, I am,

Yours,
(initialed) G. M.

PROFESSOR KÜNG'S PREFACE TO A. B. HASLER'S BOOK, *Wie der Papst unfehlbar wurde,* 1979

PREFACE

THE NEW SITUATION IN THE INFALLIBILITY DEBATE

Can a large public question rest before it is answered? The old infallibility of rulers and kings, Emperors and Czars, has long since ceased being an issue. After the Second World War, after Auschwitz, after the advent of democracy in Spain, and the beginning of de-Maoizing in China, the more recent infallibility of self-appointed rulers, autocrats and dictators, Duces and Führers and Caudillos and Secretaries General has grown fragile. The question about the infallibility of political *parties* which "are always right" and of their representatives of the moment is being suppressed from Havana to Moscow with all kinds of oppressive and repressive measures. But what about the infallibility of the *churches* "which are always right"? What about the infallibility of their past and present representatives, who call on the Holy Spirit? All other differences aside, it has become obvious since Vatican II that the question about this infallibilty can no longer be squelched, not even in the Catholic Church.

By the time the first centenary of the definition of papal infallibility, at the First Vatican Council in 1870, was celebrated, the widely diffused and vague infallibility issue had taken the specific form of an "inquiry" in the book *Unfehlbar ? Eine Anfrage* (1970), an "inquiry" which is almost like an "interpellation" of the loyal opposition of His Majesty's Government in a free society. With the help of episcopal conferences, the Roman Congregation for the Doctrine of the Faith tried by decree to silence the issue suddenly come to life and to eliminate all discussion of it once and for all. But the question that was condemned to death remained alive, and the debate within the community of faith refused to be crushed.

Rome-watchers, even those among them who were free from prejudices, had certainly not expected that the infallibility issue could be put definitely to rest in this decade by rehearsing conciliar definitions whose infallibility was questionable to begin with and was now being questioned afresh. Earlier, kings and generals, fathers and teachers, and often professors too had tried to salvage their endangered infallibility in the same way: We are infallible, they would say, because we have said that we are!

But there was no way of escaping the next question: What right do you have, what right did your predecessors ever have, to claim infallibility, especially in the Church? What right do you have to claim the infallibility of God's Holy Spirit who breathes where and how He wills, you who are just human beings, not God? Is it not human to err, even in your case? Or has God somehow promised you His infallibility? If so, wouldn't this promise have to be certified beyond all doubt? People in the Bible, the New Testament included, and beginning with Peter, "the rock," do not exactly give the impression of infallibility. The cock crowed, but not only for Peter, whom Jesus once called "Satan," who denied the Lord three times, who even after the resurrection, in the quarrel with

Paul in Antioch, showed how fallible he was. Thus, for many centuries, the infallibility of the Bishop of Rome was not spoken of, nor at first the infallibility of the ecumenical councils. Hence, to the historian who would take a close look into the matter, infallibility was bound to appear as an innovation of the second millenium, of the last century, in fact. Where do we stand when it comes to the arguments for the infallibility of the Pope and of the councils in Scripture and in the old Catholic tradition?

Or is this a legitimate question in the first place? Is it already a sin to ask and a mortal sin to inquire? No. After the initial understandable shock, this cannot seriously be believed in Rome any more. This would betray anxiety, and we would certainly be provoked to ask the child's question about the emperor's new clothes. No, a Church which has nothing to fear from the truth, which has to fear nothing more than the untruth, a Church which claims to be the "pillar and bastion of the truth," this Church must be vitally concerned that the truth should not be "repressed" but "come to light" ever anew. In the long run, too much is at stake here to let silence prevail. For is it not precisely the problematical character of infallibility that, now as in the past, impedes far and wide renewal within the Church? Is it not the doctrine of infallibility that represents the gravest obstacle to the achievement of ecumenical understanding? Is it not the claim to infallibility that, again and again, causes the Church to be looked upon as unbelievable and to be ineffective, in spite of her undeniable achievements and her even greater opportunities in today's society? Poverty and underdevelopment in the Third World, the population explosion, birth control, the Encyclical *Humanae Vitae,* the infallibility of traditional Church doctrine, all these things are so closely bound up with each other, that precisely those who, with such a loud voice exhort the world outside, should be the ones who, instead of keeping silent on the issue, should raise their voices inside.

To be sure, the one who, loudly and clearly, has said what had to be said about the infallibility issue, does not need constantly to speak again. In an overheated atmosphere, this could impede rather than promote self-critical reflection and practical deliberation, and this on both sides! Constant readiness to engage in discussions was called for, as much as much thoughtfulness with regard to the people involved, without compromising on the thing itself. In this way, critical and self-critical reflection could always be expected to flourish. But a "stand-still agreement" can by no means be concluded, not in such fundamental questions, nor has it ever been concluded. And this, not only because the Roman Congregation for the Doctrine of the Faith has never yet embarked on such a cooperative venture, but also because, in the long run, those who ask questions would be put under obligation to observe a silence which would go against their conscience, against the freedom of scholarly inquiry, and also against the true interest of the Church and of Church leaders.

In fact, when the Catholic Church and her leaders are being asked questions and more questions in this matter, they should not take this to be an assault from without, but a help from within. After all, it is the Catholic Church and her leaders who stand to gain most if the dismantling of the absolutistic and authoritarian teaching authority, initiated by John XXIII and Vatican II, were to be brought to fruition so as to make room for a genuine spiritual authority. The Church would thus be freed from all insolences, coercions, nay, from the dishonesties of Curialistic theology and administration. Likewise, the Catholic

Church has everything to gain if the consequences entailed in the new departures of Vatican II were deliberately spelled out. Under the inspiration of John XXIII, Vatican II deliberately abstained from infallible definitions. It promoted in our time, and even practiced in part, a constructive mode of Christian proclamation which contrasts with traditional dogmatism. Finally, the Catholic Church has much to gain if the historical character of truth and of its expressions be again acknowledged in the Church. It would then be possible to make a better case for the Catholic faith and the timely renewal of the Catholic Church would go forward. Through it all, what Jesus Christ stands for, would be helped once more to break through an "ecclesiastical" system which often offsets the message of the very One to whom it appeals.

By this time, the latest phase in the infallibility debate has managed to make many things clear. A "balance-sheet" ["Bilanz"] drawn in 1973 and still unrefuted has already shown that it is so.

1. The Justification of the Inquiry.

The uncomfortable texts of Vatican I and II ought to be taken literally. (That they are uncomfortable is agreed upon by those who ask questions as well as by the Roman authorities). These texts are not to be minced and emptied of their own original meaning, as Catholic theologians have time and again tried to do until very recently and for only too obvious reasons. An opportunistic interpretation that goes as far as to contradict the text instead of appropriating its meaning — which is not unusual in authoritarian systems — conceals the nature of the problem, grates against intellectual honesty, and delays the overall solution. If the infallibility texts are understood in their original meaning as we can establish it according to the present state of our knowledge, they come to represent a challenge for every Catholic, a challenge even greater now than a hundred years ago. An "ostrich policy" is sure to lead nowhere. Theological enlightenment is as imperative as formerly in the Galileo issue. The Catholic faith should not be allowed to degenerate into the faith of the charcoal-burner who believes what he believes only because the parson says so. We do need to examine the ("extraordinary") infallibility of the Pope as he issues a definition ("How the Pope became infallible"); however, this is not the only question. There is another question, already so neglected by the anti-infallibility minority in Vatican I; it concerns the (likewise "extraordinary") infallibility of an ecumenical council as it issues definitions. A third question is particularly acute: The (day-in-and-day-out, usual, "ordinary") infallibility of the bishops scattered around the globe. According to Vatican II, when the bishops and the Pope are agreed to teach a certain doctrine of faith or morals (for instance, the immorality of "artificial" birth control), that doctrine is normatively binding. The question about the doctrinal consensus of Pope and bishops, a consensus which is decisive for *Humanae Vitae* and to which infallibility is assured even apart from a definition ("they can . . . proclaim Christ's doctrine infallible" Vatican II [*Lumen Gentium,* 25; Abbott, 48 — translator's note]), this question has proved and still proves to be an irritant which does not allow the infallibility issue to rest. Theologians of a traditional persuasion often see these connections even more clearly than so-called progressives. Thus, of course, the perplexity over the infallibility of precisely this "ordinary" Magisterium comes ever more clearly to the fore.

2. The Present Catholic Consensus.

A basic unanimity has emerged on three important points:

a. It is a fact that the teaching office is fallible. In Catholic theology today it is conceded, and with an openness which was formerly not the case, that even the organs of "infallible" doctrinal decisions can err at least basically (if not, perhaps, in determinate and defined situations), and have often erred. "No one who considers the history of the Church objectively can deny that, often enough in the course of history, the Church as a whole, and also those authorities in the Church which in her own understanding of herself the Church regards as organs of infallible doctrinal definitions, namely, the Pope and the ecumenical councils, as well as the college of the bishops, have erred in the ordinary exercise of the ministry of proclamation to the extent to which this proclamation happens uniformly" (O. Semmelroth).

b. Skepticism is in order with regard to the concept and practice of infallibility. Even conservative theologians admit that the concept of infallibility is subject to misunderstanding, nay, that it is unintelligible for people today. Since the latest debate, the word "infallible" has largely disappeared from theological and also from official-ecclesiastical vocabulary. Nobody today desires infallible definitions any more, neither for the promotion of piety nor for the solution of complex present-day problems. Had the infallibility of the Pope not been defined, it certainly would not be defined today! The plausibility structures, the political, social, cultural and theological presuppositions which favored the definitions of Vatican I in the 19th century no longer prevail today. As a result, Catholic people are left now with only the definition itself, a definition with which neither the ordinary faithful nor the theologians nor the Pope himself know what to do. The "exaggerations" and the "abuses" of the teaching office of the Pope in the last century are often being lamented. Of course, people are not as willing to concede that the negative developments are also grounded in the Vatican definitions themselves. The line from Pius IX and Vatican I to the anti-modernist campaign under Pius X to the *Humani Generis* purge under Pius XII no longer escapes notice. This era in the modern history of the Church came to an end with John XXIII.

c. In spite of all errors, the Church remains in the truth. Even the conservative defenders of infallible propositions consider the indestructibility (indefectibility) of the Church in the truth to be more fundamentally important than the infallibility of particular propositions. And since the errors of the teaching office of the Church cannot, in general, be contested, there is at least a basic and general agreement on the following proposition: The Church will persevere in the truth of the Gospel. How this should be understood, requires further consideration.

3. The Decisive Question.

But are there, perhaps, above and beyond this fundamental indefectibility, judgments, assertions, definitions, dogmas, *propositions of faith* which are not only true in fact (which is undisputed), but *infallibly true,* because, namely, determinate people (office holders or authorities) due to a special assistance from the Holy Spirit (!) cannot a priori, in a given situation, fall into error? After Vatican I, this is, in fact, the clear and specific way in which the question is asked. According to the Council, the authorities (Pope and bishops) are infallible only in very determinate judgments, assertions, sentences, definitions, "propositions." It is precisely such infallible propositions of faith which not only are not in fact false, but cannot be false because of the assistance of the Holy Spirit (example, the Marian dogmas), that have been until now at the center of the debate. And what has been the outcome? Briefly stated: not one theologian, not one official authority, has yet been able to produce an argument that would prove the possibility of such propositions (and of the authorities that stand behind them) guaranteed to be infallible by the assistance of the Holy Spirit. Judging by the very exhaustive investigations hitherto conducted on Holy Scripture and the great Catholic tradition, there are no solid grounds for admitting such infallibly true propositions or authorities. After all, counter-statements are not counter-arguments. Obviously, one begs the question when one argues on the basis of those doctrinal texts from Vatican I and II which are precisely what is at issue. What was not seen to be a problem either in Vatican I or in Vatican II has not been solved either by Vatican I or by Vatican II.

4. The Unexpected Confirmations.

The new (in fact, the older) Catholic position has received unexpected confirmations from the Catholic side:

a. Concerning *Peter.* In the latest exegetical investigations, even Catholics have again brought to light the genuine, yet fallible authority of Peter and the problems annexed to the "Petrine Office." Peter remained important in the Church as a symbolic figure even after the New Testament times. And yet there is scanty support in the New Testament and in the first three centuries for the infallibility of Peter (characteristically, the biblical witnesses always juxtapose positive *and* negative traits), let alone for the infallibility of the Bishop of Rome. In Vatican I, the main scriptural argument for papal infallibility is Lk 22:32 (". . . I have prayed for you that your faith may never fail"). This text is never used, not even by medieval canonists, as argument in support of a papal infallibility. What Peter is being promised is not freedom from error, but the grace of final perseverance in the faith. And not even this promise is applied by the medieval canonists to the Bishop of Rome, but to the faith of the Church as a whole. To apply Lk 22:32 to the infallibility of the Bishop of Rome is an innovation which has no basis in the text.

b. Concerning the *Ecumenical Councils.* The First Ecumenical Council of Nicaea in 325 A.D. got along without ever claiming infallibility. The latest historical investigations have brought to light how Athanasius, the leading figure in this council, and many Greek Church Fathers with him, as well as Augustine, envision the true, yet noninfallible authority of this council. The council tells the truth not because no canonical law had been violated in convening it, nor because the majority of the bishops of the world were assembled, nor because it was ratified by some human authorities or others, nor because it enjoyed an extraordinary assistance of the Holy Spirit, nor because a priori it could not fall into error. The reason was rather that, with new words, it says nothing new, because it hands down the old tradition in a new language, because it bears witness to the old tradition, because it breathes the Holy Scriptures, because it has the Gospel on its side. This classic Catholic conception of a council is to be distinguished in the East from the later mystical or juridical *byzantine* "revaluation of the councils." In the West, on the other hand, the classic conception is to be distinguished — especially in what concerns the authority of the papacy — from the *specific Roman* stamp which begins to appear with the popes of the fifth century, and later from the specifically *Roman Catholic* stamp that prevails with the Gregorian Reform and was raised to the status of a dogma in Vatican I.

c. Concerning *the Origin of the Roman Doctrine of Infallibility.* The latest historical investigations — perhaps the greatest surprise in the whole debate — have uncovered the unorthodox origin of the Roman doctrine of infallibility at the end of the 13th century. We owe this disclosure to the American historian Brian Tierney, who maintains that there was no slow "evolution" or "unfolding" of the doctrine of papal infallibility, but rather a sudden creation at the end of the 13th century. Papal infallibility and irreformability — the two belong together from the beginning! — were not "invented," as had hitherto been surmised, by the orthodox papalist theologians nor by the popes of the High Middle Ages who were also canon law experts, but by Petrus Olivi (died 1298), an eccentric Franciscan who was repeatedly accused of heresy. At first, Olivi's view was not taken seriously at all; it was condemned in 1324 by John XXII as the work of the devil, the father of deceit. During the Protestant Reformation, the popes were still unable to appeal to an infallibility universally recognized. Remarkably, the Council of Trent did not define the infallibility of the Pope. It was the ideologues of the Counter Revolution and Restoration, de Lammenais and especially de Maistre, who, from the standpoint of the history of ideas, were mainly responsible for the definition of infallibility in Vatican I. Essentially, infallibility is a "new idea of the 19th century" (C. Langlois). Not even the medieval canonists — the doctrine of the Church was at that time in the hands of canonists — had maintained that an infallible head is indispensable for the preservation of the faith of the Church. Rather they maintained that divine providence would see to it that the whole Church would not go astray, no matter how much the head of the Church might err.

On the basis of the exegetical, historical, and systematic investigations to date, this is incontrovertibly clear: The fundamental criticism leveled at the later Roman doctrine of infallibility has received more support than expected from Scripture and the great Catholic tradition. In many respects, this is now confirmed by a new book of an insider, a Catholic theologian and historian, and for many years a member of the Vatican Secretariat for the Unity of Christians, *August Bernhard Hasler.* He asked me for a word of introduction, a request which, coming from a fellow-countryman, I could hardly resist. What new things does this book contribute to the infallibility issue?

1. *Hasler's book tells the story of how the definition of the infallibility of the Pope came about.* Whoever has read the history of the First Vatican Council by Butler-Lang or the work of the Louvain historian Roger Aubert on Pius IX and Vatican I knows, in essence, what to expect. True, as far as the infallibility issue is concerned, Hasler tells the story more systematically, more in detail, more

vividly, and also more relentlessly. However, what counts is not the historian who tells the story but the story he tells. Without glossing over anything or appeasing anybody, Hasler unfolds what turns out to be a "chronique scandaleuse" about infallibility. He recounts how the infallibility debate was manipulated, how the definition was prepared for, engineered and made to prevail. Time and again, he reports on Pius IX. Here at last is a Catholic historian who takes seriously even those who were defeated at the time, and their arguments which, in the meantime, have repeatedly proved true. He makes exhaustive use of the notes taken by the episcopal opponents of infallibility (those which are accessible) and also of those taken by the most headstrong defenders of infallibility — often just as uncomfortable for harmonizing interpreters. He brings these to language without any mitigation, without playing down anything, and without any re-interpretation. Thus, through a one-sidedness of his own, with which we can sympathize, he corrects and balances, also on the basis of new sources, the one-sided historical presentation which had hitherto prevailed.

In places where the "inquiry" violates a taboo, Hasler seems to be digging into an open wound, which may well explain sporadic Catholic reactions to his earlier scholarly publications, reactions in which belittlement is preferred to argument. When it comes to the infallibility issue, all sorts of psychological defense mechanisms, barriers, repressions, anxieties, and vested interests make it difficult for rational arugments to be given rational consideration. In spite of all the attention given to theological forces previously at work and to developments and structures, it is especially the figure of Pius IX, as well as other historical personalities of international stature, which are being historically and psychologically probed. And this is quite in order in a history that was made to happen by this one man more than by any other. Without Pius IX, the dogma of infallibility would never have been defined. The story Hasler tells about Pius IX and Vatican I can be supported by historical sources. This appears more clearly in his earlier and more scholarly work which forms the basis of this new book. It is entitled: *Pius IX (1846-1878): Päpstliche Unfehlbarkeit und 1. Vatikanische Konzil. Dogmatisierung und Durchsetzung einer Ideologie.* In the presence of the copious testimonies of participants and observers, one is bound to ask whether all the questionable things reported there about the way the council originated and was conducted should not have a bearing on the question concerning the *truth* of this definition.

2. *Hasler's book sharpens the question whether the definition of infallibility rests on solid foundations.* The import of this book would be unduly minimized if it were looked upon as nothing more than a popular version of the story that tells how this strange late Roman development came to pass. No, fundamental questions are very specifically brought to the fore, questions which emerge from the history itself. Most of these had already been discussed during the council, or immediately afterwards, then drifted into the background, and now come explosively to the fore again against the backdrop of the latest infallibility debate. Historians may want to debate whether the import of individual sources has been correctly assessed, whether certain details have been arranged in the proper sequence, or other questions of this sort. But one would have to trot through history with dogmatic blinders on, not to raise questions in the face of

such an accumulation of critical data of such quality, questions like the following four:

a. *Was Vatican I a Truly Free Council?* Of course, in matters of history, freedom is a very relative notion. But suppose that it were shown that at that time a highly relevant number of participants in the council itself did not feel free, what then? To dismiss the question about the freedom of Vatican I by referring to the fact that freedom was lacking in other councils (for instance, Ephesus, in 431), merely serves to sharpen the question. Non-Catholic historiography unanimously disputes the freedom of Vatican I in the infallibility debate, which is the only thing we are here concerned about. But recent Catholic historians also concede that freedom was strongly curtailed. They do, however, minimize this fact by contending — on apologetic and dogmatic grounds rather than on historical ones — that the council enjoyed at least the necessary freedom for the decrees to be valid.

Now, the council was denied the necessary freedom by numerous prominent participants in and observers of the infallibility debate during the debate itself, so that today the question needs to be reexamined. Concretely: What are we to say of the freedom of a council whose discussions were entirely prejudiced in advance, whose procedural norms permitted only a limited freedom of speech and were largely ineffectual, and which stood from beginning to end under the overwhelming influence of a Pope whose claim to sovereignty and power was precisely what the discussion was about? The procedural norms and the way business was conducted were repressive. The choice of leading theological experts and the composition of the conciliar commissions, as well as of the presidency, were one-sided and partisan. The bishops of the anti-infallibility minority *and* of the pro-infallibility majority were both exposed to manifold pressures, moral and psychological pressures, political pressures from within the Church herself, police pressures, pressures from the press, economic pressures. The definition was carried through because of manifold manipulations instigated by the Pope himself before, during, and after the council. Is there any wonder that the old question about the freedom of the council, later pushed aside, resurfaces now under the impact of the recent infallibility debate? As embarrassing and as painful as it may be, this council did resemble the well organized and manipulated congress of a totalitarian party more than a free convocation of free Christians.

b. *Was Vatican I a Truly Ecumenical Council?* Historically, ecumenicity, too, is a relative notion. All the same, Church history does show that not every council which claimed to be ecumenical was accepted or, "received," as the expression goes, as such by the whole Church. The fact that lack of freedom in Vatican I calls in question the ecumenicity of the same should not be excluded from an objective reinvestigation.

What the French bishop Francois Lecourtier wrote at the time is confirmed by numerous similar testimonies from bishops and council observers: "Our weakness at this point in time comes neither from the Scriptures nor from the tradition of the Fathers, nor from the witness of the ecumenical councils, nor from history. It comes from our lack of freedom which is radical. An imposing minority which represents the faith of over one hundred million Catholics, that is, of almost one half of the entire Church, is crushed under the yoke of restrictive rules of procedure which violate conciliar traditions. It is crushed by commissions which are not really elected and which dare to insert into the text under discussion paragraphs previously not discussed. The postulatory commission is forced to comply with authority. There is an absolute lack of discussion, rebuttal, objections; there is no opportunity to ask for clarifications. Newspapers are urged to mount hunts on bishops and to instigate the clergy against them. When the newspapers are not up to par to do their job, nunciatures come in to lend a hand and to unleash wholesale confusion. They try to arouse priests to bear witness to the faith against the bishops. The bishops who are the truly divine witnesses are only allowed the role of delegates of the lower clergy. When they do not behave accordingly, they are taken to task. Most of all, the minority is crushed by the whole weight of the supreme authority which presses upon them the weight of the praises and encouragements it bestows on the priests in papal briefs. It is crushed by the manifestations in favor of Dom Guéranger and against M. de Montalambert and others."

The question that results from this situation cannot be evaded. Did the other "half" of the Catholic Church have adequate opportunity to be heard? Were not the representatives of this half from the first in a hopeless situation in the presence of the majority of Italian city-bishops, and the superior force of the Pope and of the Curial machinery? Did the numerical majority actually represent the entire Catholic Church, not to mention the entire Christian world? And was the definition of infallibility issued by this council freely accepted ("received"), at least subsequently, by the whole Catholic Church?

The drama of Bishop Lecourtier who, in desperation, finally threw the council documents into the Tiber and left Rome before the decisive vote was taken; after watering down the meaning of the dogma and without inner conviction, they later did subscribe to the dogma, but only under indescribable pressure from above and from below and often only for the sake of the unity of the Church; the banning of books, the depositions, the sanctions and the excommunications, all the methods of manipulation, repression, biased reporting, surveillance, and denunciation used by the Curia and the nuncios, and finally the schism of the Old Catholics, especially theologians and intellectuals, doesn't all this entitle one to ask whether the definition of infallibility issued by the council was freely accepted ("received") by the entire Church with any freedom at all?

c. *Was the Sacrifice Worth It?* The definition of infallibility crowned a Roman system which had been under construction especially since the Gregorian Reform in the 11th century. The dogma of infallibility had the function of a meta-dogma intended to mask and stabilize all other dogmas (and numberless doctrines and practices connected with them). With infallibility — and the aura of infallibility of the "ordinary" everyday teaching office is often more important than relatively rare definitions — it seemed as if the faithful were given a superhuman certainty and confidence which would make them forget all fear of human uncertainty, of freedom, and of the risk of faith. In this respect, the dogma of infallibility has certainly had integrative and psychologically beneficial results. It has most effectively promoted the unity, cohesion, and effectiveness of Roman Catholicism, which increasingly understood its position in the world to be that of a bulwark (Cardinal Ottaviani's "Il Baluardo"). Could anything legitimize and stabilize this system and immunize it against criticism more effectively than the dogma of the infallibility of its highest representative(s)? Only one question was left open: The dogma of infallibility itself. Is infallibility really legitimized, stabilized, and immunized against criticism? Is the *truth* of the dogma securely in possession?

Until Pius XII, the system seemed intact. Only under John XXIII, what had long been kept forcibly pent up and repressed broke loose. In a relatively short time, to the surprise of most, the Church developed a new attitude toward herself, toward the other Christian Churches, the Jews and world-religions, and toward modern society at large. What had been despised and condemned under Pius IX — religious freedom and tolerance, for instance, ecumenism and human rights — was now proclaimed to be Catholic doctrine. Already at the time of the council, the infallibility with the help of which traditional positions had been defended against all modern currents during an entire century seemed to have been dangerously shaken in the eyes of many in Rome and elsewhere.

Since John XXIII and Vatican II, people have come to realize again with what sacrifices the old authority, continuity, and infallibility had been paid for! Some of the theologians who had previously been condemned were appointed as official experts at the council by John XXIII, which gave some council Fathers food for thought. Even theologians of a more traditional persuasion asked themselves subsequently: Could it be that the definition of infallibility in Vatican I was, after all, a sort of "gigantic accident" (H. U. von Balthasar)? The schism of the Old Catholics, people, and especially intellectuals, inwardly forsaking the Church because they could no longer feel at home in this authoritarian and now often totalitarian Church, had all this been really necessary? Was it worthwhile to have bishops lowered to the rank of recipients of orders from Rome, and theologians purged under Pius IX, Pius X (Encyclical *Pascendi* and Anti-Modernism), and Pius XII (Encyclical *Humani Generis* and the priest-workers), and again under Paul VI (Encyclical *Humanae Vitae*)? And what about all the prohibitions to speak and to write, the pre-censorship and self-censorship, the condemnations and prohibitions of books, the excommunications and suspensions, the policy of restricted access to the archives, and the appointments of personnel to Curial positions and to the episcopacy only because they were committed to the party line, and on top of it all, the self-imposed isolation of the man who, in many ways, was "the prisoner of the Vatican"? Was Ignatius von Döllinger far from the truth when, in 1887, he wrote to the Archbishop of Munich that the papal dogmas had come about through coercion and force and must be paid for on and on with the coin of coercion and force?

There is no ignoring the fact that Catholic historiography, exegesis, dogmatics, moral theology and catechesis since Vatican I had to pay a high price because of this infallibility and irreformability which allowed for no genuine corrections and reforms, but at best only for "interpretations" and adaptations. A constant conflict must ensue with history and the modern world, a conflict which has shaken the credibility of the Church to its foundations. The Church had to be constantly defended against new knowledge and experiences, against criticism coming from the sciences, and against all sorts of genuine and alleged enemies. A gulf set in between Church and modern world, between theology and historical research, and increasingly also within theology itself, between history of dogma and dogmatics, and between exegesis and dogmatics.

For the sake of authority, continuity, and doctrinal infallibility, frightful sacrifices were exacted also from the "little people." The ban on birth control is only an especially glaring example of all the burdens imposed upon the consciences of people as actually defined doctrine in catechisms, guides for the examination of conscience, religious education and sermons. The exodus of numberless intellectuals, the inner estrangement of many faithful, the lack of creative people and initiatives in the Church, repressive trials, symptoms of rigidity and torpidity, psychological disorders, loss of sense of reality, and very often a spiritual power structure that functions only outwardly with no life within . . . With this lament we need not go any further, but the question forces itself upon us: Was all this necessary? Was it worth it?

d. *Should Pius IX Be Canonized?* In Rome, precisely at this time, strong forces bent on restoring the old order are engaged in an intensive effort to bring about the canonization of "the infallible teacher of the faith." Obviously, the reasons are ideological; they have to do with power politics: Pius IX and Vatican I being pitted against John XXIII and Vatican II, and so against any openness of the Catholic Church to Christianity and to the modern world. But the unfavorable utterances of so many bishops of that time and of other contemporaries concerning Pius IX are so weighty and numerous as to make it quite difficult to reconcile them with the required "heroic degree" of not only the theological virtues (faith, hope, and charity) but also of the four cardinal virtues (prudence, justice, fortitude, and temperance). A conceited sense of mission, double-dealing, a disturbed psyche, abuse of power, all these are negative marks which can hardly be turned into positive ones by appealing to an allegedly providential and especially ecclesial mission of this Pope. Next to the fact that the theological formation of the Pope was notoriously scanty, there is his anti-Jewish, anti-ecumenical, and entirely anti-democratic attitude. Is this a saint for the twentieth century? The investigation should focus less on hypothetical and speculative matters (after-effects of epilepsy, Cardinal Guidi as an illegitimate son of the Pope, and the like) than on the undeniable facts which militate against a canonization of the Mastai Pope. These would make it advisable to shelve the proceedings as soon as possible, lest the problematical character of such canonizations become even more obvious than it is — in particular, the canonization of papal predecessors at the hands of their papal successors.

Church historians have been anxious to have unrestricted access to the Vatican Archives. In view of the above, the opening of the Vatican Archives now becomes particularly urgent. What good is the solemn announcement that the secret Vatican Archives are being opened for the whole pontificate of Pius IX (and, very recently, for the pontificate of his successor, Leo XIII) if precisely the material relative to Vatican I and other documents important for research are withheld now as in the past? Only in a limited sense can we speak of a real opening of the Vatican Archives as long as there is no access precisely to the most important archives, namely, those of the Congregation for the Extraordinary Affairs of the Church and those of the Congregation for the Doctrine of the Faith, formerly the Congregation of the Holy Office, earlier still, the Congregation of the Holy Inquisition as well as the Congregation of the Index. If Leo XIII who opened the secret Vatican Archives for the first time claimed that the Church does not have to fear the truth, why still this repressive policy?

That the questions which emerge from Hasler's historical work are most uncomfortable, no one can deny. But even those who would answer these questions differently than Hasler does will admit that, without exceptions, these are questions one is entitled to ask. Nay, for the sake of the truth and of the credibility of the Church, they must be asked. Anyone who would choose to be scandalized here, should see the scandal where the scandal really is. He should not censure the one who tells the scandalous story, for he is entitled to have his findings discussed without prejudice, freely, and critically.

Of course, critical dismantling and historical reconstruction are only half of the theologian's business. The question that asks how the Pope became infallible is important, but more important still is the question: How can the Pope (once again) be pope without infallibility? A few thoughts about this were articulated in 1973 in connection with the infallibility debate.

How could the Pope "function" without infallible doctrinal definitions? In our time, we have known both possibilities. There was a Pope, Pius XII, who, almost a whole century after Vatican I, felt that he must at last claim the power credited to the Pope by the council, but never claimed, in order to proclaim to the whole world an infallible definition, a new Marian dogma. And yet, none of his doctrinal utterances were as controversial in the Christian world, and in the Catholic Church as well, as this "infallible" definition. Thirty years later, even the pastoral benefits which at the time were anticipated for the piety of the Christian people and the conversion of the world are being more than modestly assessed. Vatican II dissociated itself from extreme Marianism and this has rendered even more obvious the dubious quality of that definition.

The second example is the next Pope, John XXIII. He never conceived the ambition of issuing an infallible definition. On the contrary, time and again and in the most diverse ways, he stressed his own humanity and limitations. The halo of infallibility was wanting in him. And yet, none of the Popes in this century has made an impact on the course of the history of the Catholic Church and of Christianity generally equal to that of this Pope who did not set great store on infallibility. With him and Vatican II, a new era in the history of the Church has been ushered in. Without the help of any infallible proportions, he managed in many different ways to make the Gospel of Jesus Christ heard again in the Church. From the Gospel he derived an authority in and outside the Catholic Church that would have been totally unthinkable under the reign of his predecessor. With all his weaknesses and faults, he showed in outline — spontaneously rather than through deliberate planning, by gestures rather than programs — how the Pope could be pope apart from any claim to infallibility: no jealous insistence on powers and prerogatives, no exercise of authority, Ancien Régime style, but an authority of service in the spirit of the New Testament to the needs of today, brotherly partnership and cooperation, especially with the bishops and the theologians, cooperation and consultation, participation of the people concerned in the decision-making process, and summons to co-responsibility. In short, even in matters of proclamation and doctrine, the Pope should perceive his function as being entirely *in* the Church, *with* the Church, *for* the Church, not *above* and *outside* the Church.

However, this does not mean that a Pope cannot take a strong stand also *against* something or that he is not under obligation, under certain circumstances, to take such a stand. When Poland was attacked and when Jews were exterminated, no infallible definition was needed. A clear and understandable word of the "representative," spoken from the height of the Christian message, would have been entirely sufficient. Strange to say, in more recent times no infallible word was spoken precisely when numberless people would have expected it. Conversely, the Pope can serve the ecclesial community and its unity, in spite of all his fallibility, a fallibility the other bishops share with him. He can intensify his efforts on behalf of peace and justice, disarmament and human rights, the social freedom of nations and races, the commitment to the underprivileged of any kind. By his life and deeds, and without any recourse to infallibility, he can let the voice of the Good Shepherd be heard loud and clear in the Christian world, and far beyond. He would then be the one who inspires in the spirit of Jesus Christ and a leader in Christian renewal. Rome would become a place of meeting, of dialogue, and of honest and cordial cooperation.

It follows from all this that the Pope can also "function" without any infallible doctrinal definitions. In the condition in which Church and society find themselves today, he can fulfill his service even *better* without infallible doctrinal definitions. To question the Pope's authority to define propositions infallibility is not, then, to question the papacy as such. This must be said with all possible emphasis in the face of constant confusions, distortions and suspicions. Much has become questionable in the Petrine Office, especially the medieval and modern absolutistic ways which have persisted until our very time. A Petrine Office has a future, then, only if it be understood in keeping with the symbol which Peter is in the New Testament. The exegetical and historical proof of an *historical* succession of the Roman bishop has become problematical. Yet a Petrine Office does retain its meaning, if it is a service to the entire Church in the mode of a functional-practical succession, that is, if it is a *primacy of service* in the full biblical sense.

This primacy of service, such as could be observed, at least in outline, in the figure of John XXIII, embodies a true *opportunity* for the Church and the entire Christian world. A primacy of service would be more than "a primacy of honor." In a Church which is meant to serve, a primacy of honor cannot be bestowed. It is a passive structure which, for that very reason, is of no use to anyone. A primacy of service would also be more than a "primacy of jurisdiction." As sheer force and power, a primacy of jurisdiction would turn out to be a radical misunderstanding. Taken literally, it would ignore precisely what is of great importance, namely, the service. The Petrine Office, understood as it is in the Bible, can only be a "pastoral primacy," a ministry to the entire Church. So understood, it is *objectively* substantiated by the New Testament, in spite of all the unresolved and no doubt insoluble questions about apostolic succession. As such, it could be greatly beneficial for the entire Church of today.

All this also applies to the question Hasler raises concerning my own position: Yes, the ecclesial community was and is indeed possible again even "without strong authoritarian leadership, without a monopoly on the interpretation of Holy Writ and on the tradition of the Church's Magisterium." Free, unprejudiced, scientific inquiry does not lead to the "self-destruction" of the Church, but to her renewal. It goes without saying that this inquiry encompasses also the historical-critical interrogation of the New Testament witness (Cf. *Christ sein*), as well as critical reflection on the relationship between faith and understanding (cf. *Existiert Gott ?*). Within the framework of this Preface,

I would not want to address the theological issue relative to the indefectibility of the Church in the truth, which is admittedly a question of faith. Instead, there appears simultaneously a small Theological Meditation entitled "Kirche — gehalten in der Wahrheit?"

There remains in the end only the question whether a Catholic theologian who advocates such a critical position may *remain a Catholic.* Excommunication, suspension, the withdrawal of the authorization to teach are in fact still possible. Where they work, they are still applied. Even for theologians who enjoy tenure and can count on the protection of the law, such measures would constitute a condemnation difficult to cope with, which, of course, can only be appreciated by someone to whom membership in a definite community of faith is important. Until now excommunication, suspension, and the withdrawal of the authorization to teach have not happened in the new infallibility debate and are also unlikely to happen in the future. This is not merely due to the fact that certain critical theologians presumably command so much popularity, influence, and power that they could not be penalized. The reason is rather that in the entire Catholic Church, and in Rome as well, it has been noted that the issue and situation are complex and difficult. The number of those who have their doubts is too large. Polls would show that, in many countries, only a minority in the Catholic Church believes in papal infallibility. Thus, it has not hitherto been possible to brand as un-Catholic the critics of infallibility before the world, any more than in the past the critics of the Papal States, who were threatened with excommunication, yet were proved right in the end, some, of course, only after their death.

It is not un-Catholic to turn against the *Roman system* (Roman Catholicism) which, in the 11th century, gained control in matters of doctrine, morals, and Church government, and which in Vatican II and in the post-conciliar period has been criticized again and again by numerous Catholic bishops, theologians and lay persons because of its centralism, absolutism, triumphalism and imperlialism. The contention, which assigns to the bishop of Rome a special position linked to Peter and to the great Roman tradition and which understands that position as a pastoral ministry to the Church as a whole, cannot be dismissed on the authority of the Gospel. Whereas that absolutistic Curial system which regards the Catholic community of a faith as a "spiritual" Roman Empire does indeed contradict the spirit of the Gospel and is mainly to blame for the schism with the Eastern Churches, as well as for the Protestant Reformation, and the torpidity within the Catholic Church herself.

It is un-Catholic to intend to turn away from the *Catholic Church,* that is, the entire, universal, all-encompassing Church. More precisely: it is un-Catholic to relinquish the continuity between faith and faith-community (Catholicity in time), a continuity which endures in spite of all breaches and the universality of the faith and of the faith-community (Catholicity in space), a universality which encompasses all groups. One would thus lapse into a "Protestant" radicalism and particularism having nothing to do with genuine evangelical radicalism and community spirit. More so today than in the past, the question that clearly emerges is whether propositional infallibility (like the Papal States in the past) does not belong to the Curialist system rather than to the Catholic Church herself, as she understood herself at the beginning.

The author of this new book on infallibilty should, of course, be aware that anyone who, in this capacity as a Catholic theologian, chooses to take the road of discriminating criticism, travels a narrow and dangerous road. Reproaches will come his way from two sides. A theology that leaves no critical questions unasked will undoubtedly be taken to task by unenlightened preservers of the faith. For reasons which, to some extent, can be appreciated, a theologian is disliked if he recites his piece in a novel way. The teaching authority of the Church could be impaired, should anyone think and speak of God and Church while departing from conventions endorsed by ecclesiastical tradition and officialdom.

A theology which, through all the negative criticism, makes its way again and again toward constructive answers will undoubtedly be taken to task also by seemingly enlightened despisers of the faith. Here, for reasons which again can, to some extent, be appreciated, people feel that, in the world and society of today, the theologian should not speak of God and certainly not of the Church. It has not occurred to these flatly one-dimensional people that it is precisely enlightened persons who today can think and speak about transcendence, about God and the Church in a way which is different, new and better.

Anyone who seeks to travel this critical road becomes an unecclesial heretic in the eyes of the first group and an ecclesial opportunist in the eyes of the second. Both groups say, the first pastorally solicitous, the second cynically aggressive: Be consistent. Either you come over to us or go to the other side. There is no such thing as partial identification. But isn't there? As if, when one notices that serious shortcomings and wrong-headed developments occur in a democratic state, one should have no choice except either to conform or to get out. Not at all! Genuine consistency has nothing to do with this business of jumping to extreme conclusions, and jumping to extreme conclusions is just a mistaken kind of consistency. Even if the road is rough and even if one is exposed to misunderstandings from both sides, there is a consistent road between conformism and escapism, between uncritical adaptation and hypercritical sectarianism, namely, loyalty to the Church to which one is committed, and yet always a critical loyalty, one that finds expression in loyal criticism. In this sense, the commitment to a Church and her message is no more prejudicial to the critical theologian than the commitment to a state and its constitution is prejudicial to the critical jurist. Loyalty and criticism, commitment and freedom, sympathy and impartiality, faith and understanding, do not exclude but include each other.

I do hope that the author of this book too will consistently follow the path of critical loyalty, unswayed, if not untouched by well-meaning Church verdicts and not so well-meaning journalistic malevolence, with honest commitment to scholarship and an unshaken faith in the cause to be advocated and in the hope that fairness will prevail in the resolution of conflicts.

In the hope that fairness will prevail in the resolution of conflicts, the French theologian Yves Congar, who, more than anyone, has provided the theological preparation for the understanding of the Church which appears in Vatican II, advocates a "re-reception" of the papal dogmas of Vatican I. Historical studies (Aubert, Torrell, Schatz), theological-historical studies (Thils, Dejaifve, Pottmeyer), radical questions (Küng), the very happening of Vatican II, the revitalization of local and particular Churches, the renewal of the principles of Eastern Ecclesiology, all this, according to Congar, evokes in us a keener realization of the historical conditions which affected Vatican I and calls on us "in our Catholic fidelity" to "re-accept" the Vatican dogmas and especially the dogma of papal infallibility. In the light of a genuine understanding of the "Magisterium," in the light of the best exegetical, historical and theological studies of this decade, in the light of the ecumenical dialogue which theology conducts under such new conditions with the reality of local Churches, we should, according to Congar, reconsider and reformulate what was defined in Vatican I in 1870 and received by all Catholics in keeping with the circumstances and conditions prevailing at that time. According to Hasler, such a "re-reception" would, in fact, amount to a *revision* of the stipulations of Vatican I, and this revision would in turn afford the Catholic Church, theology, and also the whole Christian world a way out of an indefensible situation and an opening toward a new future.

May I be permitted to subscribe to Congar's proposal, and to make it more specific, not in order to unleash a new infallibility debate, but to liquidate the old debate once and for all.

Under the new pontificate, the infallibility issue should be researched again exegetically, historically, theologically, with objectivity, scholarly honesty, fairness and justice.

As was done earlier for the birth control issue, an *ecumenical commission* should be established for the infallibility issue, a commission composed of internationally recognized experts in the various disciplines (exegesis, history of dogmas, systematic theology, practical theology, and pertinent non-theological disciplines).

As the key points are researched, less importance than hitherto should be attached to negative and critical aspects and more to those which are positive and constructive. The question to be asked would then be whether the *permanence of the Church in the truth* in spite of all errors is not better substantiated by the Christian message and the great Catholic tradition, and whether it should not therefore be better lived in the Church even today.

An application: In the opinion of Rome, the ban on birth control issued by Pope Paul VI was justified in the name of the authority, continuity, traditionality, universality of traditional doctrine, hence, for all practical purposes, in the name of the infallibility and irreformability of that doctrine. Since that time, in this issue as in a few others, Rome seems to be blocked. To this day, we are being told "we cannot" ("nonpossumus"), as we were told in the past with regard to the renunciation of the Papal States. Only a resolution of the infallibility issue could allow for a resolution of the birth control issue. The Church's leadership which all too often limits itself to imparting admonitions to the whole world should itself actively help, humbly and self-critically, through the courageous revision of the doctrine of the alleged immorality of any kind (!) of birth control methods, advocated by *Humanae Vitae.* What represents a severe burden on the conscience of numberless people even in our developed countries with their declining populations represents for people in many underdeveloped countries, especially in Latin America, an incalculable hardship for which the Church becomes co-responsible. Poverty and illiteracy, unemployment, starvation and ill health are causally related to birth rates. During the past two decades, the not inconsiderable rate of growth in the production of foodstuffs in the Third World has been swallowed up to a large extent by higher birth rates.

Pope John Paul II has just returned from South America, where he has collected new experiences and spoken clearly against poverty, underdevelopment, and the plight of children. He would also like to work for the achievement of ecumenical agreement. Are we hoping too much if we expect him to take a decisive step toward the honest resolution of the pressing infallibility issue in an atmosphere of mutual trust, free inquiry, and fair discussion?

Tübingen
February 1979

Hans Küng
Director of the Institute
for Ecumenical Research
at the University of Tübingen

Enclosure 56

PROFESSOR KÜNG'S THEOLOGICAL MEDITATION, "THE CHURCH — HELD IN THE TRUTH?" 1979

POSTSCRIPT

This theological meditation is *not* intended to provoke a *new infallibility debate.* Surveyed from a certain historical distance, the latest debate has shown a number of different things:

1. No one, no theologian and no ecclesiastical authority has been able to produce a proof that there are propositions guaranteed to be infallible. Rather, the impasses to which infallible propositions lead have now surfaced more clearly than in the past (cf. *Fehlbar ? Eine Bilanz,* 1973).
2. Ecclesiastical authorities have hardly taken notice of the negative outcome of the debate. With only slight changes, they have reiterated the doctrinal utterances which had been called in question (cf. the various Declarations of the Roman Congregation for the Doctrine of the Faith and of the Conference of German Bishops, 1973-1974).
3. It is possible to pursue a constructive theology which does not operate from within a system and does not start from defined propositions only to revert to these, but is capable of bringing out the relevance of the original message about God and His Christ for the benefit of today's people (cf. *Christ sein,* 1974; *Existiert Gott ?,* 1978).
4. The traditional doctrine of infallibility continues to be called in question also within the Catholic Church and theology (cf. most recently A. B. Hasler, *Wie der Papst unfehlbar wurde,* 1979).

Yet this debate on infallible propositions and authorities will not be prolonged here. On this subject, I have made remarks in the Preface to Hasler's book. We should rather tabulate here the positive results of the infallibilty debate which have been hitherto too little noticed (cf. the last chapter of *Fehlbar ? Eine Bilanz*), in order to set forth positively and non-polemically in what way a permanence of the Church in the truth can be believed and understood today. For the majority of thinking people are not wondering today whether in some cases (in fact, very rare) error can be excluded a priori by appealing to the Holy Spirit (infallibility of individual propositions or authorities). A much more fundamental question emerges in view of the fact that new problems in the First, Second and Third Worlds assail the Churches because of the many ideologies of the left and of the right. The question is whether we can still credit to the Church a permanence in the truth or whether we are seeing the end of this Church and of her truth. In other words, the question is no longer about the infallibility of certain ecclesiastical propositions of faith and of certain authorities, but rather about the indefectibility of the Church herself.

A "re-reception of the papal dogmas of Vatican I" has been advocated by the French theologian Yves Congar, a theologian who more than any other provided the theological preparation for precisely the new understanding of the Church in Vatican II. Historical studies (Aubert, Torrell, Schatz), theologico-historical studies (Thils, Dejaifve, Pottmeyer), radical questions (Küng), then the very happening of Vatican II, and the revitalization of local and particular Churches, as well as the renewal of the principles of Eastern Ecclesiology, all this, according to Congar, evokes in us a keener realization of the historical conditions which affected Vatican I and calls on us, "in our Catholic fidelity," to "re-accept" the Vatican dogmas and especially the dogma of papal infallibility. In the light of a genuine understanding of the "Magisterium," in the light of the best exegetical, historical and theological studies of this decade, in the light of the ecumenical dialogue which theology conducts under such new conditions with the reality of local Churches, we should, according to Congar, reconsider and reformulate what was defined in Vatican I in 1870 and received by all Catholics in keeping with the circumstances and conditions prevailing at that time. According to Hasler, such "a re-reception" would, in fact, amount to a *revision* of the stipulations of Vatican I, and this revision would in turn afford the Catholic Church, theology, and also the whole Christian world a way out of an indefensible situation and an opening toward a new future.

Once more, the point is not to provoke here a new infallibility debate, but rather to liquidate the old one as soon as possible. This is the reason behind the proposal to establish an ecumenical commission.

Enclosure 57

LETTER OF PROFESSOR KÜNG TO BISHOP MOSER, February 19, 1979

Tübingen
February 19, 1979

His Excellency
Dr. Georg Moser
Bischof-von-Keppler-St. 7
7407 Rottenburg

Your Excellency:

In the next few weeks, the publishing house Piper, which has also published various writings of mine, will issue the book of my fellow-countryman Dr. August B. Hasler, *Wie der Papst unfehlbar wurde. Macht und Ohnmacht eines Dogmas.* In 1977, Hasler had already published a historical monograph in two volumes on this subject, *Pius IX (1845-1878). Päpstliche Unfehlbarkeit und 1. Vatikanische Konzil. Dogmatisierung und Durchsetzung einer Ideologie.* The *Frankfurther Allgemeine Zeitung* had asked me to review this book. In the meantime, because of the documentation published by the bishops on the discussion concerning *Christ sein,* a confrontation emerged which I did not want to aggravate. I, therefore, withdrew my promise to review the book, a promise which had been made conditionally.

However, Dr. Hasler has now asked me for a Preface to his new book. Under these circumstances, I could not refuse this request of a fellow-countryman of mine whom I have known since his student days. I have tried to write this Preface as objectively and as unpolemically as possible. In the first part, I summarize the results of the earlier debate. I have not gone beyond what I had already extensively set forth in *Fehlbar ? Eine Bilanz* (1973). The second part concisely reviews the findings of Hasler's book. In the third part, I try once more to answer the question whether such a theological position is ecclesial and Catholic. The Preface ends with the request to the Roman authorities to establish a commission of internationally recognized experts in the various disciplines to answer the question which has now taken on new urgency because of Hasler's book.

Since it was impossible in a Preface to convincingly answer the question Hasler asked me concerning the Church's permanence in the truth, in spite of all the errors, and because I am more concerned with the positive and constructive aspect of my theory than with the critical and limiting ones, I have written at the same time as the Preface a Theological Meditation entitled "Kirche — gehalten in der Wharheit?" This Meditation, too, merely clarifies what I had already set forth in the last chapter of *Fehlbar ?*

Your Excellency, it is important that I should emphatically declare that neither the Preface nor the Theological Meditation that accompanies it were intended to provoke a new infallibility debate. Yet, now as before, I am anxious that the infallibility issue should be researched exegetically, historically, and systematically, with objectivity and honesty. For the sake of this concern, I have refused to consider inquiries concerning a separate publication of my Preface or even a publication in advance of the book itself. (Of course, I cannot prevent the reprinting of isolated passages.)

In order to supplement this information, I will send you as soon as possible pre-publication copies of Hasler's book, as well as of my own Theological Meditation.

With cordial greetings, I am,

Devotedly yours,
(signed) Hans Küng

Enclosure 58

LETTER OF BISHOP MOSER TO PROFESSOR KÜNG, April 5, 1979

Rottenburg am Neckar
April 5, 1979

Professor Dr. Hans Küng
Waldhäuserstrasse 23
7400 Tübingen

Dear Professor Küng:

I thank you for your letter of February 19, 1979, and for your publication "Kirche - gehalten in der Wahrheit?" as well as for August Hasler's book, *Wie der Papst unfehlbar wurde*, for which you wrote the Preface.

I will not conceal from you the fact that the reading of both your contributions to the papal infallibility issue have affected me deeply. There I find again, and very sharply formulated, only the positions to which the Congregation for the Doctrine of the Faith objected on February 15, 1975, and which were deemed in need of reexamination and emendation by the Conference of German Bishops on February 17, 1975. For this reason, I am absolutely unable to understand how you can possibly think that your present statements should not provoke a new infallibility debate. In my opinon, your action cannot be understood as anything but a provocation. I therefore take it for granted that an unpleasant aftermath is inevitable and that great difficulties will ensue.

Although at the moment I do not know where we should go from here, especially in view of the fact that, as a teacher of theology, you are still involved in the formation of the theologians of our diocese. I am still as prepared as ever to talk and to seek a tenable reconciliation.

With cordial greetings, I remain,

Yours,
(signed) + Georg Moser
Bishop

On December 18, 1979, the Secretariat of the Conference of German Bishops published A DOCUMENTATION ON THE ENDEAVORS OF THE CONGREGATION FOR THE DOCTRINE OF THE FAITH AND OF THE CONFERENCE OF GERMAN BISHOPS TO ACHIEVE AN APPROPRIATE CLARIFICATION OF THE CONTROVERSIAL VIEWS OF PROFESSOR Dr. HANS KÜNG. The Enclosures to follow bring this documentation up to date. They include documents relative to the efforts of the Conference of German Bishops from December 18, 1979 to December 31, 1979.

SUMMARY

1. On December 18, 1979, the Declaration of the Congregation for the Doctrine of the Faith of December 15, 1979 was presented to Professor Küng, then published. On the evening of that day, Professor Küng was interviewed by Franz Alt in the ARD TV program "Themes of the Day?" He made a preliminary statement about his position **[Enclosure 59]** concerning the Roman Declaration and on the Declaration of Cardinal Höffner relative to it. (Similar statements were made also in other TV programs and on radio.) The President of the Conference of German Bishops, Cardinal Höffner, replied on November 19 in a statement to the press **[Enclosure 60]**.

2. On December 19, 1979, Bishop Moser visited Professor Küng at his home. Professors Greinacher and Kasper of the Faculty of Theology of Tübingen, as well as the Vicar General, Dr. Knaupp, and Canon Weitmann of the Diocese of Rottenburg-Stuttgart took part in the discussion. Bishop Moser admonished Professor Küng that the time had come for him to make an unequivocal written response to the objections of the Congregation for the Doctrine of the Faith. Professor Küng agreed. Professor Küng submitted his Statement **[Enclosure 61]** which Bishop Moser conveyed the same day to the Congregation for the Doctrine of the Faith and to the Cardinal Secretary of State in Rome.

3. Returning from Rome on December 21, 1979, Bishop Moser again visited Professor Küng at his home on December 23. He explained to him the inadequacies in the Statement of December 20, 1979. Bishop Moser itemized his explanations in a letter of December 24, 1979 **[Enclosure 62]** which was conveyed to Professor Küng on the same day. Professor Küng traveled to a resort in Austria. He replied to the letter of Bishop Moser on December 26, 1979 through Dr. Hermann Häring (Tübingen) **[Enclosure 63]**. He stated that "for reasons of time it is impossible for him to submit further written explanations concerning the written Statement already submitted."

4. On December 28, 1979, at the invitation of the Holy Father, a thorough discussion was held in Rome concerning the Küng affair. On December 30, 1979, the spokesman of the Holy See disclosed the outcome of this discussion **[Enclosure 64]**.

5. On the same day, December 30, 1979, Bishop Moser made a statement on German Television **[Enclosure 65]** and Professor Küng did likewise **[Enclosure 66]**.

6. On December 31, 1979, the President of the Conference of German Bishops made a declaration relative to Professor Küng's statement **[Enclosure 67]**.

STATEMENTS OF PROFESSOR KÜNG ON GERMAN TELEVISION, December 18 1979

Transcript of Professor Küng's remarks in an interview on the television program "Themes of the Day" December 18, 1979

ALT.-"I am not a heretic," said Hans Küng the past weekend in *Die Welt.* He continued, "I am and remain a Catholic!" Mr. Küng, is this claim still valid today, after the Church has rescinded her authorization to teach?

KÜNG.- Of course, the claim stands even today. I must say that one had to be afraid that something like this might happen, since Rome has instituted proceedings against me one after another. All the same, this action, just before Christmas, has taken me by surprise. I must say, it's a scandal when a Church, which appeals to Jesus Christ and intends to defend human rights, still conducts Inquisition trials in the middle of the 20th century.

ALT.- You did not know anything about these proceedings which, obviously, have been conducted against you?

KÜNG.- The proceedings were terminated in the past. Now they take out this little book, where indeed I have said nothing new, but only repeat my inquiry once more. It's only a pretext. I have even politely asked the Pope to let an international commission conduct an investigation. If one is no longer permitted to say anything in Catholic theology, then I do not know why I and many other Catholic theologians do theology in the first place. I must indeed say, I am ashamed of my Church. The Pope has just admitted, 350 years later, that the same authority which now withdraws my credentials to teach committed a basic error against Galileo. That authority now deprives a Catholic theologian of his authorization to teach.

ALT.- Cardinal Höffner has mentioned today two arguments against you: Your criticisms with regard to the infallibility of the Pope and your doubts about the divinity of Jesus Christ. What is your response?

KÜNG.- On this I have defined my position numberless times. As far as I know, there are no proceedings against *Christ sein* or *Existiert Gott ?* There I have stated my position in detail. I haven't heard any objections to the effect that my utterances were not precise enough. It is, actually, the first time that the Congregation for the Doctrine of the Faith, this inquisitional board, speaks about this book, and to me this is all only a pretext. I say it again: the reasons are very tactical. They are mentioned in this little book, as for example birth control and other things. They try to make it impossible for a Catholic theologian to stay in his own Church.

ALT.- What are the consequences of this for you, and what consequences do you draw?

KÜNG.- I have no thought of simply identifying the Catholic Church with certain decisions which, after all, have been taken by some very determined people. I must say, however, that I find it particularly sad that German Cardinals and Bishops should collaborate with the Inquisition, while the Dutch Cardinal Willebrands personally intervenes for his theologian Schillebeeckx before the Pope and gets him off the hook, so to speak. Ours push you overboard.

ALT.- Do you have the chance to appeal?

KÜNG.- Among us this is all very poorly . . . regulated. At the moment I can only say that I will fight with all possible means to have this decision rescinded. It's a decision which, in my view, goes against everything we must stand for before the world. In the past, the decisions against Teilhard de Chardin, against de Lubac and others, who were condemned at the time of Pius XII, were rescinded by John XXIII.

ALT.- What does the prohibition to teach mean? You can still go on being a professor, or can you?

KÜNG.- I can remain a professor now as before, I also intend to do my duty faithfully as a Catholic theologian, as I have done until now.

Enclosure 60

DECLARATION OF CARDINAL HÖFFNER, December 19, 1979

With regard to Professor Küng's statements relative to the withdrawal of the missio canonica, *Cardinal Höffner, President of the Conference of German Bishops, issues the following declaration:*

1. Professor Küng speaks of inquisitional proceedings and charges the German Bishops of collaborating. In this connection, he refers to Professor Schillebeeckx who was defended by Cardinal Willebrands. It must be said in this regard that the Congregation for the Doctrine of the Faith has tried for ten years to engage in a discussion with Professor Küng. Time and again, under a variety of pretexts, Professor Küng has refused to take part in this discussion. The Congregation for the Doctrine of the Faith had no other choice except to come to a decision in his absence. The extensive exchange of letters shows plainly that there have been no inquisitional proceedings. Professor Küng knew very well what the problems were. He has disappointed the German Bishops, and especially the late President of the Conference of German Bishops, Cardinal Döpfner, and his own local ordinary, Dr. Georg Moser, as they tried to settle the conflict through dialogue. He must, therefore, take full responsibility for the present situation. The reference to Professor Schillebeeckx has a strange ring. Professor Schillebeeckx was willing to take part in a discussion with the Congregation for the Doctrine of the Faith. In contrast to Professor Küng, he conjured up the measure of humility and willingness required to dialogue. It is, therefore, inept of Professor Küng to refer to his colleague Schillebeeckx.

2. Professor Küng speaks of an operation under the cover of darkness which took him by surprise. There was no such operation. To begin with, before the end of the semester, Professor Küng had not yet gone on vacation; in other words, on December 18, it was still possible to reach him in Tübingen to deliver to him the decision of the Congregation for the Doctrine of the Faith. Besides, Professor Küng knows that, by writing the Preface to A. B. Hasler's book, *Wie der Papst unfehlbar wurde,* he has violated the standstill agreement of 1974. Because of this violation, the Congregation for the Doctrine of the Faith had to

reopen the proceedings. On April 5, 1979, in a letter to Professor Küng, Bishop Moser had written in part: "I therefore take it for granted that an unpleasant aftermath is inevitable and that great difficulties will ensue." Bishop Moser added that even after the objectionable statements had been repeated, a dialogue was still possible. Professor Küng was fully aware that he had violated the standstill agreement.

3. Professor Küng maintains that he was not fully informed about the objectionable statements. This is not so. For example, on April 22, 1977, in a letter to Professor Küng, I put to him three questions. These questions did show what objections were involved.

4. Professor Küng declares that he intends to exhaust all the possibilities to have the decision of the Congregation for the Doctrine of the Faith revoked. If Professor Küng is prepared to conform his statements, in all areas, with the doctrine of the Church, there is nothing to prevent the rescinding of the present action.

5. There can be no valid reason why anyone who fails to advocate the whole doctrine of the Church should teach priests who are entrusted with the task of handing down the doctrine of the Church. The Bishops are responsible before the faithful that this should be done.

Enclosure 61

STATEMENT OF PROFESSOR KÜNG, December 20, 1979

Statement relative to the Declaration of the Congregation for the Doctrine of the Faith on Key Points of the Theological Doctrine of Professor Küng dated December 18, 1979

I have always considered myself a Catholic theologian and will continue to do so. Now as before, I regard myself as a priest of the *Ecclesia Catholica.* As a Catholic theologian, what was and is particularly important to me is the "Catholic" Church; that is, the entire, universal, all-encompassing and whole Church. Hence, my task has always been and is to teach Catholic truth with Catholic breadth and depth. Thus, all my life, I have promoted the continuity of faith and of the faith-community, a continuity which endures in spite of all breaches. This is Catholicity in time. Likewise, I have promoted Catholicity in space; that is, the universality of the faith and of the faith-community, which encompasses all groups. It is in this spirit that I would like to continue to advocate Catholic doctrine as a Catholic theologian. I know that, in this, I am of one mind with numberless theologians, pastors, religious educators and lay persons.

With regard to the latest Declaration of the Congregation for the Doctrine of the Faith, I would like to state the following. I begin with a few general observations.

In the latest publication on the infallibility issue, my purpose was not to aggravate the issue, but to resolve it constructively and without any stubbornness ("pertinacia"). In my Preface to Hasler's book, after reporting on his findings, I have merely summarized thoughts from my "balance sheet" ["Bilanz"] on the infallibility debate published in 1973. Likewise, the little Theological Meditation entitled "Kirche — gehalten in der Wahrheit?" written at the same time states: ". . . the point here is not to provoke a new infallibility debate." My task was and is not to accuse but to inquire. I am prepared to submit my ideas to a new investigation. To this end, in the Preface as well as in the Meditation, I have made reference to the French theologian Yves Congar and submitted to Rome the proposal to establish an ecumenical commission of internationally recognized experts in the various disciplines. My theological work to date has not been characterized by "the contempt of the Magisterium of the Church," a reproach I strongly reject, but by an effort at enhancing anew the credibility of the Church's Magisterium within the Church and in the world. Nor have I in any way "given preference to my own judgment as a norm of truth," even in opposition to the Church's own "sense of faith." On the contrary, I have based my whole theological work on the Gosepl of Jesus Christ and Catholic tradition with scholarly honesty and loyalty to the Church.

I cannot conceal the fact that I still entertain strong reservations with regard to the order and mode of procedure of the Congregation. In particular, I cannot understand the fact that, before the latest gravest step, the Congregation has not even vouchsafed me the opportunity of defining and defending my position. In addition, the order of procedure is being violated when, in its Declaration, the Congregation makes severe accusations against my concept of "many key articles of the Catholic faith" (Christology, Mariology), although these points have never been the object of Roman proceedings against me.

After these general considerations, some remarks on the key issue at hand. In the Declaration of the Congregation for the Doctrine of the Faith, my concept of the *Magisterium* and *infallibility* is being perceived one-sidedly and negatively. Here, for purposes of clarification and with reference to statements of the Conference of German Bishops on February 4, 1971, may I state the following. In my earlier publications on the infallibility issue, I have never called in question the proposition that there are Church utterances which are true and can be recognized as such. Their meaning remains the same, as patterns of thinking change in history; it remains in force beyond challenge and demands an unequivocal Yes or No response.

I likewise profess that the Church has the duty and the task of proclaiming the Christian message witnessed to in Scripture and of bringing out clearly and bindingly the significance of that message. In this connection, of course, the statements of the Declaration *Mysterium Ecclesiae* (1973) relative to the historically conditioned character of all formulae of faith should be taken seriously.

In addition, I have always maintained that office-holders are in a special way entrusted with the task of making sure that the Church remains in the truth. They must make Christian truth normative for language. In certain situations, they must define the extent of that truth over (definitions of faith or dogmas) against what is un-Christian. In this respect, a special authority belongs to the ecumenical councils, as representing the whole Church, to the college of bishops, and to the bishop of Rome, as the head of that college. In view of this special significance of the ecumenical councils, I also stand fundamentally on the ground of the councils of the ancient Church, and especially so in Christological matters. I have made a special effort to make these councils understandable to people in our time.

As far as Vatican I is concerned, I have never intended to deny the definition of faith which it issued, to question the authority of the Petrine Office, to make of my own opinion the yardstick in theology, nor to trouble Catholics in their faith. On the contrary, in view of the well-known theological problems, I have merely inquired how one can substantiate, on the basis of Scripture and tradition, the possibility of propositions infallibily true in the sense of Vatican I. For me, this is not a fictitious but a genuine issue. The infallibility debate conducted internationally on this issue has had at least this result: A great many people, including Catholic theologians whose Catholicity is unquestionable, have admitted that the issue must be raised and that it is legitimate to raise it.

I, therefore, in all seriousness ask to be believed when I say that, fully conscious of the risk involved for me personally, I intended in this to be of service to our Church. In the spirit of Christian accountability, I intended to bring about a resolution of this issue which burdens so many people within and without the Church. The issue is of particular importance for the reconciliation with the Eastern Churches, a reconciliation to which Pope John Paul II has given a new and hopeful impetus by establishing a special commission. A fresh discussion of the issue is also required from an ecumenical point of view.

In making this statement, I am sustained by the confidence that the present confrontation, which is grave and fraught with unforeseeable consequences, can be positively resolved in the spirit of genuine Catholicity.

Dr. Hans Küng
Professor of Dogmatic and Ecumenical
Theology at the Catholic Theological
Faculty, and Director of the
Institute for Ecumenical Research
of the University of Tübingen

December 20, 1979

Enclosure 62

LETTER OF BISHOP MOSER TO PROFESSOR KÜNG, December 24, 1979

Rottenburg am Neckar
December 24, 1979

Professor Dr. Hans Küng
Waldhäuser Strasse 23
7400 Tübingen

Dear Professor Küng:

Over and over, I have read your December 20, 1979 "Statement Relative to the Declaration of the Congregation for the Doctrine of the Faith on Key Points of the Theological Doctrine of Professor Küng dated December 18, 1979." In our conversation on Sunday, December 23, 1979, I declared that I am grateful for this statement on your part, but that I can see in it no more than a first and minimal step which, given the situation of the hour, is not sufficient. Because I am full of worry and anxiety and because I intend to do all I can for the sake of mediation, I take the liberty of summarizing once more the questions and requests and giving my reasons in writing.

1. Your Statement deals mainly with infallibility in the Church. I notice that you consistently avoid the word "infallibility." You also overlook the declarations of the Congregation for the Doctrine of the Faith concerning the other two points mentioned there; namely, the task "to authentically interpret the one and holy faith patrimony of the Word of God, a patrimony entrusted only to the living Magisterium of the Church, and, in the end, those views which relate to the valid consecration of the Eucharist." How is it that you are not disclosing your views on these points?

2. You quote from the Declaration of the Conference of German Bishops on *Unfehlbar ?* dated February 4, 1971. Unfortunately, you did not include in your quotation the important statement in which the Declaration speaks of formulations "which help to clarify the Creed," thus providing, in fact, an interpretation of the witness intended by the Scriptures and which are set forth by the Church with truly ultimate normativeness. This is precisely what is at stake.

I find it regrettable that you do not speak about the ecumenical councils in the way the bishops do, namely, "as representing the whole episcopate." Your version is: "as representing the whole Church." Thus you embark on an interpretation of the councils which has often been challenged on historical and dogmatic grounds.

With regard to the Christological questions, you only manage to go as far as to say that you stand "fundamentally" on the ground of the councils of the ancient Church. Specifically, what does this mean? Your statement to the effect that the task of caring for the truth is entrusted "in a special way" to the Magisterium, to which there belongs a "special authority," needs to be more precisely and clearly formulated. What do you mean by "special authority"? Any teacher, for example, enjoys an authority which is special.

3. One cannot discern from your Statement whether a normative

Magisterium of the Church exists *for you yourself,* a Magisterium whose judgment you acknowledge. True, you disclaim the intention of making your "opinion the yardstick in theology." You take no position as to the form which an official assessment of your doctrines would take. Likewise the "new investigation" to which you want to submit your views, as you declare, remains very vague. What kind of investigation would it be? Who would conduct it? And to what purpose? In your Statement, you make a host of declarations as to what you did and did not intend, and yet, apparently, you do not intend to accept any judgment passed by the authority of the Church on your theological doctrines and their effects. No one has contested that, subjectively, your intentions are positive.

4. Closely examined, even your remarks on "infallibility" turn out to be disappointing. It is not clear how you stand with regard to some of your earlier statements.

a. You write in your Statement that you do not intend to deny the definitions issued by Vatican I. How can this declaration be reconciled with the following: "I only deny that this indefectibility of the Church in the truth is bound up with certain propositions and authorities." (Cf. *Hans Küng: Weg und Werk* [München, 1979, p. 168]).

b. You maintain that your "inquiry" is "not a fictitious but a genuine issue." This might well have been true earlier. Later, you have indeed declared the opposite. Already in *Christ sein* one reads: "The 'inquiry' may largely be regarded as settled" (p. 663, note 22; [ET, p. 677]). In "Kirche — gehalten in der Wahrheit?" you speak of the negative results of the infallibility debate (p. 73). The old infallibility debate should be terminated "as soon as possible" (p. 74). A few lines above, you speak of "the questioning of the traditional doctrine of infallibilty" and you pick up the fatal word "revision of the stipulations of Vatican I" (p. 74). In the Preface to A. B. Hasler's book *Wie der Papst unfehlbar wurde,* you say explicitly that "there are no solid foundations for the acceptance of such infallibly true propositions or authorities" (p. XIX), and that the Pope "can fulfill his service *better* without infallible doctrinal definitions" (p. XXXI).

As long as you insist on such statements as these, your declaration that the question is "genuine" is not credible. Please, do define your position with regard to these statements, for they cannot be objectively reconciled with your Statement of December 20, 1979. I beg of you explicitly: as you do this, do not be easy on yourself.

Dear Professor Küng, I have cited these statements of yours only by way of example. I could cite more. Please make your contribution to an unequivocal clarification and write not primarily for the eyes and ears of the public but for the authority in the Church. In the present situation, as I explained to you orally, initial and minimal steps are just not enough.

In the light of Christmas, I beg of you again from the bottom of my heart, do at least contribute to the resolution of the conflict the share which has long been expected of you; otherwise, to quote Cardinal Döpfner's words on May 6, 1975, "I would be at my wit's end."

In the discussion scheduled to take place in Rome on December 28, 1979, I can help effectively only if I am in possession of a written response from you by Thursday, December 27, 1979, at 8:00 P.M.

In spite of the Christmas holidays, I have no choice but to ask you for this response.

With cordial greetings,

Yours,
(signed) + Georg Moser

Enclosure 63

LETTER OF DR. HÄRING TO BISHOP MOSER, December 26, 1979

Tübingen
December 26, 1979

His Excellency
The Bishop of Rottenburg-Stuttgart
Dr. Georg Moser
P. O. Box 9
7407 Rottenburg a. N. 1

Your Excellency:

On Christmas eve, I received the letter you addressed to Professor Küng and opened it as previously arranged. After various unsuccessful attempts on the evening of that day, I managed to reach Professor Küng on Christmas morning around 8:00. On the evening of December 25, I had another lengthy conversation with him.

The outcome of this conversation was as follows: Professor Küng appreciates how difficult is the situation in which you, as mediator in such a grave matter, find yourself; yet, for reasons of time and substance, he feels that he is not in a position to send you a personal letter within the deadline you have set. He has authorized me to impart to you what follows as an answer to your letter. I am using notes taken during our conversation.

1. Since in the days before Christmas Professor Küng had many hours-long conversations with you; he feels that he has already given sufficient evidence that he is not unamenable to take part in a discussion. In these conversations, he made all imaginable efforts to answer the substantive questions, while making it clear to you that, for reasons of time and substance, it was impossible for him to add still further written explanations to the written Statement he has already submitted. As he has already declared, he is prepared to engage in discussions with the Church authorities. This readiness he has never denied. In his opinion, this readiness is indispensable. He regards it as essential and sees in it almost a master commandment for Catholic theology to observe. Yet he still insists that such discussions must be held under just and fair conditions. For years he has been asking himself why such conditions are not being guaranteed to him by Rome.

2. Professor Küng stated that, even in the last conversation with you on December 23, he tried to give substantive answers to substantive questions. In addition, he has sent you documentation concerning those of his views which have been questioned. He was all the more dismayed that, suddenly, he should be compelled to add further explanations to the Statement already submitted, and this on Christmas eve and on Christmas morning. He cannot understand why in Rome (where, as a rule, people think in terms of centuries) an attempt should be made to extract something from him by force in the space of a few days — and this between Christmas and New Year — and precisely in relation to questions which are theologically highly complex and fraught with political implications. For reasons of time and substance, he regards this demand as irresponsible. At any rate, after the physical and psychic aggravations to which this unexpected Roman initiative has subjected him, shortly before Christmas, he feels that, to his chagrin, he is absolutely in no position to submit a new declaration now.

3. As to the detailed questions relative to his orthodoxy, which, Professor Küng surmises, were articulated by the hand of an expert, Professor Küng regards them as downright inquisitional. He regards them as partly inadequate, the citations having been taken out of context. There is no understanding of his position, nor any willingness really to identify with his intention. On the other hand, as he explained orally, he is certainly entitled to expect that an answer should be given to his well known questions. In this connection, he made reference to the account he gave of the infallibility debate in the book *Fehlbar? Eine Bilanz* (1973) and reiterated elsewhere. As other theologians also attest, the infallibility issue is still beset with basic ambiguities in Catholic theology. For this reason, Professor Küng has urged that an ecumenical commission of suitable experts be established to remove these ambiguities. Until the unresolved problematic is further clarified, by this or any other means, it would hardly be possible for him to answer questions which, to begin with, are the ones he himself has raised. If either you or the Roman authorities are not merely interested in an act of humble submission on his part, but in a genuine resolution of the problem itself, then he is entitled to expect that his proposal be, in some form or other, acted upon.

4. Professor Küng is very much aware, as you yourself are, that the situation is serious, not only for himself but for the whole Church at large. In this situation, people in authority within the Chruch should indeed be asked how they can take it upon themselves, just before Christmas, to trigger in large segments of the Church and of the clergy so much indignation, dismay, and deep sorrow at the fact that such an action is possible in a Church which pledges allegiance to Jesus Christ. Professor Küng has drawn your attention to the fact that, should the measures decided by the Congregation for the Doctrine of the Faith be enforced with finality, the problem itself would not be settled in the Church. On the contrary, a step would have been taken toward a very difficult and critical future. He could not and would not accept responsibility for these consequences.

All the same Professor Küng reaffirms his willingness to engage in discussion. Even in this hour, he emphatically wants to abide by this willingness. He stressed that, even now, he is willing, although he must still require that the discussion be held under just and fair conditions, as he has said and specified repeatedly in earlier statements and letters. Moreover, in a personal letter to Pope John Paul II in the Spring of 1979, he offered to come to Rome any time to speak with him about all the unresolved problems, should the Pope so wish and have the time.

In addition, Professor Küng would like to ask you urgently for a favor. As you go to Rome, would you take along his request that the Pope, who is entitled to take in his own hands many extraordinary matters, should find the time, in this critical moment, to speak with a theologian of our Church who, for decades, has tried as best he knows how to work for the cause of the Christian faith both within and without.

I very much regret that, in this grave moment, I cannot impart to you any other answer. I, too, would like to hope that the conflict might be so resolved that the credibility of our Church and, ultimately, of the very cause of Jesus Christ, should not be harmed but enhanced.

With respect for the task before you in the next few days, I convey to you my greetings, and I wish you God's blessings.

Yours,
(signed) Dr. Hermann Häring

Enclosure 64

STATEMENT OF THE HOLY SEE TO THE PRESS, December 30, 1979

1. The Declaration issued by the Congregation for the Doctrine of the Faith on December 15, 1979 concerning certain tenets in the theological doctrine of Professor Küng had become indispensable to the conscientious protection of the right of the faithful that the doctrine taught by the Church be imparted to them without curtailment. Previous efforts on the part of the Holy See, the Conference of German Bishops, and the local Ordinary to induce Professor Küng to correct his erroneous views had all failed.

2. Since in a conversation with Bishop Moser, Professor Küng had declared himself prepared to clarify his doctrines further, the Local Ordinary, with great patience and personal forthcomingness, once more sought to assist Professor Küng in solving his problem. Having been informed about a "Statement" submitted by Professor Küng after his meeting with Bishop Moser, the Holy Father decided to invite to a special conference the German Cardinals, Bishop Moser, and the Metropolitan Bishop of Freiburg in Breisgau, Bishop Saier. The Cardinal Secretary of State and the Secretary of the Congregation for the Doctrine of the Faith were also to participate.

After a thorough examination of the latest statements of Professor Küng, all participants in the conference came to the conclusion that these statements did not constitute a sufficient ground for changing the decision taken in the Declaration of December 15.

3. In view of this, Professor Küng cannot, of course, go on exercising the commission to teach theology which has been entrusted to him by the Church.

The competent Local Ordinary has no choice but to draw the canonical consequences in keeping with the provisions of the Concordat.

4. For years, the Congregation for the Doctrine of the Faith has taken pains to clarify with Professor Küng the ideas he has disseminated, without finding a comparable willingness on his part. The conference of December 28 is further evidence of the fact that both the Holy See and the German Bishops have handled Professor Küng's problem with the best of good will.

The decision which has been taken with great regret after so many previous efforts is exclusively determined by a deep sense of pastoral responsibility. As already emphasized in the Declaration of December 15, that decision does not at all imply that the legitimate freedom indispensable for theological inquiry is being curtailed.

The decision does not in any way alter the attitude of the Church with regard to her efforts at promoting Christian unity, in keeping with the principles set forth in the Declaration of Vatican II, *Unitatis Redintegratio.*

5. Although Professor Küng's Statement cannot constitute sufficient grounds for changing the decision contained in the Declaration of the Congregation for the Doctrine of the Faith of December 15, the Holy See and the German Bishops do not give up hope that Professor Küng, who has more than once declared his intention of remaining a Catholic theologian, will, after reflection in depth, adopt a position which will make it possible for the Church to reinstate his canonical commission to teach.

The Holy See and the German Bishops will continue to commend this matter to the Lord in prayer and ask all the persons of good will to do the same.

Enclosure 65/1

DECLARATION OF BISHOP MOSER ON THE OCCASION OF OFFICIAL DECLARATION OF THE HOLY SEE ON December 30, 1979

1. I have tried my best to bring about an agreement.

a. This venture was welcomed by those who, without being entirely in agreement with Professor Küng, were indebted to him for help and encouragement in their faith. Others, mistakenly, objected that my efforts would resist the Pope and interfere with his decision. In Rome, I have given the reasons for the decision which, as Local Bishop, my conscience had to make, and these have been appreciated.

b. I have taken upon my own conscience the risk of mediation, with the opportunity and the danger. My task, as I always see it, is to build bridges, whenever possible. I have confidence in the significance of even small steps. I intended and will intend in the future to leave no stone unturned, and to do my part to achieve mutual understanding, reconciliation, and clarification.

c. In this case, I knew full well that, with regard to this confrontation of ten year's standing, a last minute agreement could be reached only if Professor Küng would manage to contribute adequately to achieving it. Since, in the Statement he released when the Declaration was made public, he signaled, in my opinion, a certain willingness to come to an agreement, I endeavored to stay in touch with him, visited him at his home twice, and on Christmas Eve I wrote him once more a detailed letter.

d. On that day the situation looked very grave to me, as evidenced by that letter, which ends with the following lines: "In the light of Christmas, I beg of you again from the bottom of my heart, do at last contribute to the resolution of the conflict the share which has long been expected of you; otherwise, to quote Cardinal Döpfner's words on May 6, 1975, 'I would be at my wit's end'."

e. Over and over again, I said to Professor Küng that now all depended precisely on his word, and that he had to take upon himself a great responsibility; namely, to do justice to the situation and also personally to take appropriate steps. No one wanted to force him out of the Church, but he had also to show evidence that he intended to remain in the Church in the sense of affirming and advocating the Church's teaching.

Unfortunately, Professor Küng limited himself to insignificant declarations. Thus, in Rome, I could do no more than submit these declarations and use them together with some pertinent elements which had transpired in my conversations with Professor Küng to clarify the matter at hand.

2. *The discussion of December 28, 1979 in Rome was not a tribunal bent on condemnation.*

I am not authorized to reveal the details of this discussion, but I can reflect the following impressions:

a. The fact that the Declaration of December 15, 1979 remains in force is not an act of revenge on the part of Rome, even of the Pope himself; rather, it is motivated by recent comments of Professor Küng on the pontificate of John Paul II to date.

b. For hours on end, a close examination was carried out; texts were compared and discussed. The first Statement of Professor Küng, as well as his communication of December 26, 1979, signed by Dr. Häring, were analyzed. The favorable points were noted. The statements about the situation which had come to the Pope from various quarters were calmly reviewed.

c. In this discussion it became clear that no exercise of power on the part of Rome was involved and that the *declaratio* could not be looked upon as a bolt from the blue. The statements submitted by Professor Küng, as well as texts from his works which he himself had pointed out to me, were carefully weighed.

The infallibility issue, the main topic of discussion, is regarded by many as secondary. Professor Küng holds a different view. In the book, *Weg und Werk* (1978), he states on p. 168: "What is involved in the infallibility issue is a formal question, which, precisely as such, has a decisive influence on theological method and affects practically all the doctrinal utterances of the Catholic Church in matters of faith and morals."

d. The misgivings which I had voiced orally and in writing even before the publication of the *declaratio* concerning its manner and timing, and which later were similarly set forth by others from various sides, were not ignored.

e. The foregoing shows that the prerequisites for a *missio canonica* for Professor Küng no longer hold. Hence, after my return from Rome, I prepared the appropriate letter to Professor Küng which was delivered at his home on December 30, 1979.

3. The public has already been advised as to what the *Declaratio* does and does not imply. Here I refer to these observations. I repeat: The *Declaratio* emphasizes that "the *missio canonica* bears witness to mutual trust: to the trust of the competent ecclesiastical authority vis-à-vis the theologian who in his research and teaching conducts himself as a Catholic theologian, but also to the trust of the theologian vis-à-vis the Church and her unimpaired doctrine, since it is by the mandate of the Church that he exercises his office."

Unfortunately, for the time being, this trust must be regarded as shattered. I note, in this connection, that the last paragraph of the latest decision from Rome implies also a summons to Professor Küng to reconsider his position and to take pains to correct those of his doctrines that fail to accord with Catholic doctrine.

4. *The present situation is both clear and difficult.* Much will now depend on the reactions of those who feel affected by the carefully weighed Declaration from Rome. I would like to address an appeal to all the members of the Church, since all are coresponsible for further developments. It seems to me that the situation resembles that of a family tested by trials. One thing is clear: To run away from it or to give up is no solution. All must try together to remain objective, to curb emotions, and not to give up hope that an agreement will be achieved in the future.

People close to Professor Küng have suggested that I should resign. I can only say that a flight from responsibility, a separation from the Diocese in this difficult hour, would be the worst of all solutions. When all goes well, it is relatively easy to stay and persevere. The time of crisis is the acid test of fidelity. I repeat what I have said to Professor Küng and to many others: I maintain my solidarity with the Holy Father and the College of Bishops. Even in this commotion, I remain loyal to the Diocese. I will not deny it: It is very painful that reconciliation was not achieved. Yet, even in this hour, I trust that the Holy Spirit, the principle of life within the Church, will bring together all men and women of good will.

Rottenburg am Neckar
December 30, 1979

+ Georg Moser
Bishop

Enclosure 65/2

DECLARATION OF THE CHANCERY OFFICE OF THE DIOCESE OF ROTTENBURG-STUTTGART, December 18, 1979

BISCHÖFLICHES ORDINARIAT
NO. A 10885

Rottenburg am Neckar
December 18, 1979

OBSERVATIONS ON THE DECLARATION OF THE CONGREGATION FOR THE DOCTRINE OF THE FAITH

1. The Congregation states:

— In his writings, Professor Küng deviates from the complete doctrine of the faith.

— Therefore, he can no longer be regarded as a Catholic theologian or teach as such.

2. The Congregation gives the following reasons:

— Every Catholic theologian possesses a legitimate academic freedom, which, however, should not transgress the limits set by the discipline of theology itself.

— Professor Küng disputes the infallibility of the teaching office of the Church and the normative character of the declarations of the Church.

— In essential points of the Catholic faith, Professor Küng deviates from normative doctrine. The following are mentioned: the doctrine of the consubstantiality of the Son with the Father; doctrine concerning Mary; doctrine relative to the valid consecration of the Eucharist.

— Professor Küng has not responded to repeated summonses by the Congregation to strive for conformity with the normative doctrine of the Church. His further publications have instead aggravated the contrasts even more.

3. The decision of the Congregation does not imply:

— That Professor Küng is no longer to be regarded as a member of the Catholic Church. He still stands within the community of the Catholic Church.

— That Professor Küng is impeded in the exercise of his priestly ministry or that he is relieved of priestly functions. He remains a priest with all the rights and duties connected with this office.

— That Professor Küng is no longer entitled to teach and do research as a scholar. As an objective principle of our Constitution and as an individual right of a university professor, scientific freedom makes possible for him to work as a scholar. His status as a civil servant, including his remuneration, remains unaffected.

4. The decision of the Congregation does imply:

— That Professor Küng can no longer claim to teach by mandate of the Church.

— That he can no longer function as appointee to a government position linked to the Church.

5. The decision now taken is the culmination of a confrontation of many years which, in spite of all efforts, has not led to a satisfactory solution. Pro-

fessor Küng's recent critical remarks on the person and work of the present Pope have played no part in the proceedings.

Dr. Knaupp
Vicar General

Enclosure 66

DECLARATION OF PROFESSOR KÜNG, December 30, 1979

SILENCED

A disappointed Küng speaks about the outcome of the mediation efforts

With sadness and incomprehension, I have taken cognizance of the outcome of the negotiations in Rome. The Pope is condemning a man whom he has not heard. The Roman motto *"audiatur et altera pars"* ["let the other party also be heard"] does not count in the Rome of the Pope. An irksome critic must be silenced by all the means available to spiritual might. John XXIII and Vatican II have been forgotten. Apparently, Rome tolerates no "fraternal correction," no inquiries in the spirit of solidarity, no loyal criticism, no fraternal togetherness. Human rights and Christian love are being preached for the benefit of outsiders. Inside, they are ignored in spite of all the sweet talk.

I have been struck unexpectedly by the action of Rome at Christmas time. Thanks to the Roman negotiating strategy, I have always been only the object of the proceedings, never a participant. Nevertheless, through conversations with Bishop Moser, through a declaration delivered to the Pope, and through constantly reiterated willingness to speak about all the controversial questions, I have done everything I could have been expected to do in this extraordinarily difficult and burdensome situation. It was all in vain. I was not listened to. Nor were the appeals of Christians from the whole world, nor the strong protests of numberless theologians, pastors, and lay persons of various denominations, nor even the warning of the World Council of Churches.

Roman authorities and German Church leaders have failed to recognize that what is at stake in this confrontation is not only the case of Küng, but the Church, which is about to throw away the opportunity built into her own new start since Vatican II. This is not only the case of one individual theologian, but also of all those who, known or unknown, in the past and in the future, are disciplined by ecclesiastical authorities. Nor are only individual faithful involved; the unity of the whole Church is also at stake, and the credibility of the Church's leadership. Not only is the infallibility of the Pope at stake, but his moral authority within and without the Church. We are not dealing here only with a confrontation within the Catholic Church, but with the success of the ecumenical striving for mutual agreement. I ask myself how many others among our theologians, pastors, and lay persons can now still call themselves Catholic, if I am not to be a Catholic theologian.

And yet I regard the Roman verdict not as a defeat, but as a challenge to our Church to attend to the long overdue clarification of the foundations of Catholic theology and proclamation. A compromise would perhaps have preserved my authorization to teach and secured me peace for a time, but I would not have done a service to the Church, and I would have robbed myself of my Christian identity and moral credibility.

In order to counteract the negative consequences of the Roman decision in our Church, I ask the theological faculties and other theology teachers, I ask priests and diocesan advisers, parish councils, and other representative bodies within the Church to take counsel in the next few weeks and months on the present critical development, to speak their minds openly, to address appropriate requests to the competent Church authorities, and to intercede for the reversal of the manifold disciplinary measures from Rome. As far as the future practice in doctrinal proceedings is concerned, the following requirement should be observed, which in my case was criminally ignored: ". . . In doctrinal proceedings, the person concerned should in every case have the right to choose his own defender, and be given access to all the official documents." (Decision of the General Synod of Switzerland, February 16-17)

In spite of these disciplinary measures, not only do I remain a member and a priest of the Catholic Church, but also a full professor of dogmatic and ecumenical theology. I will pursue as decisively as before my central purpose, which is to make it possible for people today to understand the message of Jesus Christ. I am willing to discuss and to learn whenever what is involved is a discussion among brothers and partners. In this I am not alone. Resisting abdication in any form, I will struggle together with the many who have supported me thus far and whom I thank from the bottom of my heart. Together we want to work for a truly Christian Church.

(Text as reported in the media)

Enclosure 67

STATEMENT OF THE PRESIDENT OF THE CONFERENCE OF GERMAN BISHOPS, CARDINAL HÖFFNER, December 31, 1979

Statement of the President of the Conference of German Bishops, Cardinal Höffner, on Professor Küng's Declaration relative to the Vatican Declaration of December 30, 1979

1. Professor Küng's contention that "an irksome critic" must be silenced is dishonest. The reason why the authorization to teach has been withdrawn is only that, despite ten years of efforts on the part of the Congregation for the Doctrine of the Faith, Professor Küng is not prepared unequivocally to profess the faith of the Church on fundamental points of Catholic doctrine. The Pope

would be unfaithful to his mission if, as supreme teacher in the Church, he should allow the defined doctrine of papal infallibility to be called in question, and faith in the consubstantiality of the Son with the Father to be passed over in silence. The faithful have "the sacred right to receive the Word of God without adulteration" (Declaration of the Congregation for the Doctrine of the Faith, December 15, 1979).

2. Professor Küng maintains that he has many times manifested his willingness to participate in discussions. However, he has at the same time with various excuses declined the repeated invitations of the Congregation for the Doctrine of the Faith to participate in such discussions. The documentation issued by the Secretariat of the Conference of German Bishops provides unequivocal evidence of this.

If Professor Küng operates with the presupposition that he would agree only to a conversation directly with the Pope, not with the Congregation for the Doctrine of the Faith, the following must be said: The Congregation for the Doctrine of the Faith acts under the direct mandate of the Pope and is the dialogue partner for Professor Küng. To date, Professor Küng has declined repeated invitations to engage in discussion. Professor Schillebeeckx did not feel that it was beneath his dignity to accept the invitation extended to him by the Congregation for the Doctrine of the Faith to participate in a discussion. In the end, he declared that he was satisfied.

Professor Küng has recently appealed to the fact that he offered to participate in a discussion with the Pope as, apparently, the only partner adequate for him. In view of his constant refusal to accept the invitations to a discussion extended to him by the Congregation for the Doctrine of the Faith, this offer can only be construed as the expression of a frightful self-conceit.

3. In 1975 the Congregation for the Doctrine of the Faith terminated for the time being the proceedings against Professor Hans Küng on condition that he would no longer teach the objectionable doctrines. Professor Küng has broken this stipulation in a provocative manner. He has no right to complain about the situation which has ensued.

4. The summons of Professor Küng to theological faculties and Church councils to intercede for "a reversal of the manifold disciplinary measures from Rome" induces me to declare the following: There are no "manifold disciplinary measures" against Professor Küng. The withdrawal of the authorization to teach was "exclusively determined by a deep sense of pastoral responsibility." I have no doubt that, after carefully examining the ten years of patient efforts on the part of the Bishops and of the Congregation for the Doctrine of the Faith, theologians, representative groups, and faithful will understand and support the measure which Professor Küng's unreasonable conduct has made inevitable.

Professor Küng contends that Rome's decision has struck him unexpectedly. This contention has been often repeated; yet it does not square with the facts. At the end of a letter of April 5, 1979, Bishop Moser stated: "In my opinion your action cannot be understood as anything but a provocation. I, therefore, take it for granted that an unpleasant aftermath is inevitable and that great difficulties will ensue." During the course of the mediating efforts by Bishop Moser, Professor Küng had, even in the last days, a sufficient opportunity to make it possible for the Congregation for the Doctrine of the Faith to withdraw its decision of December 15. The documentation presented here makes this plain.

I very much hope that Professor Küng will realize that any emotional dramatization of the confrontation will do no good either to him or to the Church.

PRESS OFFICE
OF THE CONFERENCE OF GERMAN BISHOPS
December 31, 1979, 3:09 P.M.

APPENDIX I

The following is the text of Pope John Paul II's letter to the West German Bishops Conference on the Father Hans Küng case. It was dated May 15 and released at the Vatican May 22.

Venerable and dear brothers in the episcopate,

1. The substantial documentation which you have published in relation to certain theological affirmations of Professor Hans Küng shows how much attention and good will have been employed to clarify this important and difficult problem. Both the pastoral letter read in churches Jan. 13, 1980, and the detailed "erklärung," (clarification) published recently express the pastoral and magisterial responsibility conforming to the character of your office and of your episcopal mission.

I wish, in anticipation of the coming feast of Pentecost, to confirm you in your mission as pastors in the spirit of love and divine truth and also to thank you for all the concern you have shown regarding the above mentioned problem and the cooperation you have given to the Apostolic See, in particular, to the Congregation for the Doctrine of the Faith, whose duty — always essential for the life of the church — seems to be in our times particularly burdened with responsibility and difficulty.

The motu proprio "Integrae Servandae," which during the Second Vatican Council outlined the duties and the procedure of the above-named congregation, emphasizes the necessity of cooperation with the episcopate and thus, exactly corresponds to the principle of collegiality reaffirmed by the council. Such cooperation, in the case in question, was practiced in a particularly intense manner.

There are many reasons for which the church of our times must demonstrate itself more than ever as a church of knowledge and effective collegiality among its bishops and pastors. In such a church, one can also verify more fully that which St. Ireneus said about the Roman See of Peter, describing it as the center of the ecclesial community, which must gather and unite the individual local churches and all the faithful (cf. "Adversus Haereses": pg. 7, 848).

Equally the modern church must be — more than ever — the church of authentic dialogue, which Pope Paul VI pointed out in the fundamental encyclical at the beginning of his pontificate, "Ecclesiam Suam" (His Church). The interchange which this involves must lead to a meeting in truth and in justice. In dialogue, the church seeks to understand man better and thus its own mission. The church brings to it the knowledge and truth which are communicated to it in faith.

It is not contradictory to the essence of this dialogue, however, that the church, in this, is not only what it seeks and receives but also that which it has received based on certainty, which in such a colloquium still becomes augmented and deepened but never abandoned. On the contrary: It would be in contrast with the essence of dialogue if the church would wish in this dialogue to suspend its convictions and turn its back on the knowledge which already has been given to it.

Furthermore, that dialogue which the bishops conduct with a theologian, who in the name of the church and because of his charge teaches the faith of the church, has a particular character. This is subject to other conditions, in relation to those which are conducted with men of different convictions, in the common search for a meeting point. The first thing to clarify here is that the one who teaches at the charge of the church corresponds also in act and wants to agree to this charge.

Regarding the teaching charge of Professor Küng, one must put forward the following questions: Does a theologian who does not integrally accept the doctrine of the church still have the right to teach in the name of the church and on a basis of the special mission which is received? Can he still want to do so, if several dogmas of the church are in contrast with his personal convictions? And then, can the church — in this case the responsible body — in such circumstances continue to oblige the theologian to do it despite everything?

The decision of the Congregation for the Doctrine of the Faith, taken in common accord with the German bishops' conference, is the result of the honest and responsible reply to these questions. At the base of these questions and this concrete reply, one finds a fundamental right of the human person, that is, the right to truth which must be protected and defended.

Certainly, Professor Küng has declared with insistence that he wishes to be and remains a Catholic theologian. In his works, however, he manifests clearly that he does not consider several authentic doctrines of the church as definitively decided and binding on himself and on his theology. Based on his personal convictions, he is no longer able to work in the sense of the mission which he received from the bishop in the name of the church.

The Catholic theologian, as any scientist, has the right to free analysis and research in his own field: obviously, in a manner which corresponds to the nature itself of the Catholic theologian. When, however, it is a question of the oral and written expression of results of that research and reflection, it is necessary to respect in a particular way the principle formulated by the Synod of Bishops in 1967 with the expression "paedagogia fidei" (pedagogy of the faith).

It can be advantageous and right to point out the rights of theology. However, it is necessary, at the same time, to take into rightful account also its particular responsibilities. One must not forget either the right or the duty of the magisterium in deciding what conforms to the doctrine of the church on faith and morals and what does not. The verification, the approval or the denial of a doctrine, lies within the competency of the prophetic mission of the church.

2. Several questions and several aspects connected with the discussions of Professor Küng are of a fundamental character and of general importance for

the actual period of post-conciliar reform. I would like, therefore, to deal with them a little more amply in the following section.

In the generation to which we belong, the church has made enormous efforts to better understand its nature and the mission entrusted by Christ in relation to man and the world, especially the modern world. It has done it through the historic service of the Second Vatican Council. We believe that Christ was present in the assembly of bishops, that he worked in them by means of the Holy Spirit, promised to the apostles at the eve of his passion, when he spoke of the "spirit of truth" which would teach them every truth and which would remind them of all that they had heard from Christ himself (cf. John 14, 17:26). From the work of the council was born the program of renewal of the church from within, a program of wide and courageous range, joined with a deepened awareness of the true mission of the church, which by its nature is missionary.

Although the post-conciliar period was not free from difficulty (as had already occurred in the history of the church), we believe that Christ is present in it — the same Christ who even to the apostles, at times, made storms on the lake, which seemed to bring them to shipwreck. After nightly fishing, during which they had caught nothing, he transformed this failure into an unexpected abundance of fish, when they cast their nets on the word of the Lord (cf. Luke 5, 4-5). If the church wants to be faithful to its mission in this stage of its history, undoubtedly difficult and decisive, it can only do it by putting itself within hearing distance of the word of God, that is listening to the "word of the Spirit," as it came to the church through tradition and, directly, through the magisterium of the last council.

In order to follow such work — arduous and "humanly" very difficult — a particular faith in Christ and his Gospel is necessary, because only he is "the way." Therefore, only by maintaining fidelity to established signs, preserving the continuity of the way, followed by the church for 2,000 years, can we be certain that we will achieve for ourselves that power from on high which Christ himself promised the apostles and the church which attests to his presence "until the end of the world" (Matthew 28, 20).

If there is, therefore, something essential and fundamental in the daily life of service in the church, it is the particular orientation of souls and hearts towards the fullness of the mystery of Christ, redeemer of man and of the world, and at the same time, fidelity to the image of the nature and mission of the church, as, after so many historic experiences, was presented by the Second Vatican Council. According to the express doctrine of that council, "every renewal of the church essentially consists in an increase of fidelity to its own calling" ("Unitatis Redintegratio," n. 6). Every attempt to substitute the image of the church, which comes from its nature and mission, for another, inevitably leads us away from the sources of light and strength of the spirit, of whom we have a particularly great need today. We must not delude ourselves that another model of the church — more "laicized" — can respond in a more adequate way to the demands of a greater presence of the church in the world and to its greater awareness of the problems of man. Such can only be a church deeply rooted in Christ, in the sources of his faith, hope and charity.

The church must be, moreover, very humble and at the same time secure in remaining in the same truth, in the same doctrine of faith and morals which it received from the Christ, who in this sphere gave it the gift of a specific "infallibility." Vatican II inherited from the First Vatican Council the doctrine of tradition in this regard, and it confirmed it and presented it in a more complete context, that is in the context of the mission of the church, which has a prophetic character, thanks to its participation in the prophetic mission of Christ himself. In this context and in strict connection with "the way of faith," in which all the faithful participate, this "infallibility" has a character of gift and of service.

If anyone understands it differently, he moves away from the authentic vision of faith and, even if perhaps unconsciously, but in a real way, separate the church from him who, as the bridegroom, "loved" it and gave himself for it. Endowing the church with all that is indispensable to fulfill the mission which Christ entrusted to it, could he possibily have deprived it for the certainty of professed and proclaimed truth? Could he possibly deprive of this gift especially those who, after Peter and the apostles, inherited a particular pastoral and magisterial responsibility before all the community of believers? Exactly because man is fallible, Christ — wanting to preserve the church in truth — could not leave its pastors-bishops and especially Peter and his sucessors, without that particular gift, which is the assurance of infallibility in the teaching of the truths of the faith and the principles of morals.

Therefore, we profess infallibility, which is a gift of Christ given to the church. And we cannot not profess it, if we believe in the love with which Christ loved his church and continuously loves it.

We believe in the infallibility of the church not out of respect for any man but for Christ himself. We are convinced, in fact, that even for him who participates in a special way in the infallibility of the church, it is essentially and exclusively a condition of service, which he must exericse in the church. In fact, in no case, and so much less in the church, can "power" be understood and exercised if not as service. The example of the Teacher is decisive here.

We must, on the other hand, harbor deep fear, if in the church itself the faith in this gift of Christ is put in doubt. In such a case, the roots from which the certainty of truth professed and proclaimed in it would be cut off at the same time. Although the truth on infallibility of the church can justly seem a less central truth and of minor order in the hierarchy of truth revealed by God and professed by the church, nevertheless it is, in a certain way, the key to the very certainty in professing and proclaiming the faith for the life and behavior of believers. When this fundamental base is weakened or destroyed, the most elementary truths of our faith suddenly begin to collapse.

It is a question, therefore, of an important problem in the present post-conciliar period. When, in fact, the church must undertake the work of renewal, it is necessary that it have a particular certainty of faith, through which, renewing itself according to the doctrine of the Second Vatican Council, it remains in the same truth which it had received from Christ. Only thus can one be sure that Christ is present in one's own boat and guides it firmly even through the most threatening storms.

3. Anyone who participates in the history of our century and is not unfamiliar with the various trials which the church lives in its midst, in the march of these first post-conciliar years, is conscious of these tempests. The church must confront these storms and cannot be affected by uncertainty in faith and by relativism of truth and morals. Only a church deeply consolidated in its faith

can be a church of authentic dialogue. Dialogue requires, in fact, a particular maturity in proclaimed and professed truth. Only such maturity, that is certainty in faith, is able to oppose the radical negations of our time, even when they are aided by various means of propaganda and pressure. Only such a mature faith can become an effective advocate of true religious liberty, liberty of conscience and all the rights of man.

The program of the Second Vatican Council is courageous; therefore, it asks in its fulfillment a particular confidence in the Spirit who has spoken (Acts 2, 7) and requires a fundamental faith in the power of Christ. This confidence and this faith, as a measure of our times, must be great as that of the apostles, who after the ascension of Jesus, "devoted themselves to constant prayer . . . with Mary" (Acts 1, 14) in the Upper Room of Jerusalem.

Undoubtedly, such faith in the power of Christ also calls for the ecumenical work of Christian unity, undertaken by the Second Vatican Council, if we intend it as was presented by the council in the decree "Unitatis Redintegratio" (Decree on Ecumenism). It is significant that this document does not speak of "compromise," but of meeting in an ever more mature fullness of Christian truth: "The manner and order in which Catholic belief is expressed should in no way become an obstacle to dialogue with our brethren. It is, of course, essential that doctrine be clearly presented in its entirety. Nothing is so foreign to the spirit of ecumenism as a false conciliatory approach which harms the purity of Catholic doctrine and obscures its assured genuine meaning" (n. 11; Cf. n. 4).

Therefore, from the ecumenical point of view of the union of Christians, one cannot in any way pretend that the church renounces certain truths professed by it. It would be in contrast with the way the council indicated. If that council, to achieve such an end, affirms that "Catholic faith must be explained with more profundity and exactness," it is indicating also the duty of theologians. Most significant is that section of the decree "Unitatis Redintegratio," which deals directly with Catholic theologians, emphasizing that "in searching together with separated brethren into the divine mysteries," they must remain "faithful to the doctrine of the church" (n. 11). Previously, I already pointed to the "hierarchy" or order or truths of Catholic doctrine, of which theologians must be reminded, particularly "when comparing doctrines." The council evokes such a hierarchy, given that "they vary in their relation to the foundation of the Christian faith" (ibid).

In such a way ecumenism, this great inheritance of the council, can become a more mature reality, that is only on the road of a greater commitment of the church, inspired by certainty of faith and by a faith in the power of Christ, which, since the beginning, the pioneers of this work have distinguished themselves.

4. Venerable and dear brothers of the German bishops' conference!

One can love the church only when one loves one's brothers: each and every one in particular. Therefore, this letter which I write to you in relation to recent events of Professor Hans Küng is also dictated by love for our brother.

To him, I wish again to repeat that which was expressed already in other circumstances: We continue to nurture the hope that a meeting in the truth proclaimed and professed by the church can be achieved, that he can be again called "Catholic theologian." This title presupposes necessarily the authentic faith of the church and the readiness to serve its mission in a manner clearly defined and verified throughout the centuries.

Love requires that we seek a meeting in truth with every man. Therefore, we do not cease to implore God for such a meeting in a particular way with this man, our brother, who as Catholic theologian, which he would like to be and remain, must share with us a particular responsibility for the truth professed and proclaimed by the church. Such a prayer is, in a certain sense, the fundamental word of love towards man, towards neighbor, since through it we find him in God himself who, as the unique source of love, is at the same time in the Holy Spirit the light of our hearts and our consciences. It is also the first and deepest expression of that concern of the church, in which its pastors especially must participate.

In this communion of prayer and common pastoral concern, I entreat for you at the coming feast of Pentecost the abundance of gifts of the divine Spirit and I greet you in love of Christ with my special apostolic blessing.

From the Vatican, May 15, feast of the Ascension of Christ, in the year 1980, second of the pontificate. Ioannes Paulus PP II.

APPENDIX II

DECLARATION IN DEFENSE OF THE CATHOLIC DOCTRINE ON THE CHURCH AGAINST CERTAIN ERRORS OF THE PRESENT DAY

Mysterium Ecclesiae
June 24, 1973

The mystery of the Church, upon which the Second Vatican Council shed fresh light, has been repeatedly dealt within numerous writings of theologians. While not a few of these studies have served to make this mystery more understandable, others, through the use of ambiguous or even erroneous language, have obscured Catholic doctrine, and at times have gone so far as to be opposed to Catholic faith even in fundamental matters.

To meet this situation, the bishops of several nations, conscious both of their duty of "keeping pure and intact the deposit of faith" and of their task of "proclaiming the Gospel unceasingly"[1], have, through concurring declarations, sought to protect the faithful entrusted to their care from the danger of error. In addition, the second General Assembly of the Synod of Bishops, in dealing with the ministerial priesthood, expounded a number of important points of doctrine regarding the constitution of the Church.

Likewise, the Sacred Congregation for the Doctrine of the Faith, whose task it is to "preserve the doctrine of faith and morals in the whole Catholic world"[2], intends to gather together and explain a number of truths concerning the mystery of the Church which at the present time are being either denied or endangered. In this it will follow above all the lines laid down by the two Vatican Councils.

1

THE ONENESS OF CHRIST'S CHURCH

One is the Church, which "after his Resurrection our Saviour handed over to Peter as Shepherd (cf. *Jn* 21:17), commissioning him and the other Apostles to propagate and govern her (cf. *Mt* 18:18 ff.) (and which) he erected for all ages as 'the pillar and mainstay of the truth' (cf. *1 Tim* 3:15)." And this Church of Christ, "constituted and organized in this world as a society, subsists in the Catholic Church, which is governed by the Successor of Peter and the bishops in union with that Successor"[3]. This declaration of the Second Vatican Council is illustrated by the same Council's statement that "it is through Christ's Catholic Church alone, which is the general means of salvation, that the fullness of the means of salvation can be obtained"[4], and that same Catholic Church "has been endowed with all divinely revealed truth and with all the means of grace"[5] with which Christ wished to enhance his messianic community. This is no obstacle to the fact that during her earthly pilgrimage the Church, "embracing sinners in her bosom, is at the same time holy and always in need of being purified"[6], nor to the fact that "outside her visible structure," namely in Churches and ecclesial communities which are joined to the Catholic Church by an imperfect communion, there are to be found "many elements of sanctification and truth (which), as gifts properly belonging to the Church of Christ, possess an inner dynamism towards Catholic unity"[7].

For these reasons, "Catholics must joyfully acknowledge and esteem the truly Christian endowments derived from our common heritage, which are to be found among our separated brethren"[8], and they must strive for the reestablishment of unity among all Christians, by making a common effort of purification and renewal[9], so that the will of Christ may be fulfilled and the division of Christians may cease to be an obstacle to the proclamation of the Gospel throughout the world[10]. But at the same time Catholics are bound to profess that through the gift of God's mercy they belong to that Church which Christ founded and which is governed by the successors of Peter and the other Apostles, who are the depositaries of the original Apostolic tradition, living and intact, which is the permanent heritage of doctrine and holiness of that same Church[11]. The followers of Christ are therefore not permitted to imagine that Christ's Church is nothing more than a collection (divided, but still possessing a certain unity) of Churches and ecclesial communities. Nor are they free to hold that Christ's Church nowhere really exists today and that it is to be considered only as an end which all Churches and ecclesial communities must strive to reach.

2

THE INFALLIBILITY OF THE UNIVERSAL CHURCH

"In his gracious goodness, God has seen to it that what he had revealed for the salvation of all nations would abide perpetually in its full inegrity"[12]. For this reason he entrusted to the Church the treasury of God's Word, so that the pastors and the holy people might strive together to preserve it, study it and apply it to life[13].

God, who is absolutely infallible, thus deigned to bestow upon his new people, which is the Church, a certain shared infallibility, which is restricted to matters of faith and morals, which is present when the whole People of God unhesitatingly holds a point of doctrine pertaining to these matters, and finally which always depends upon the wise providence and anointing of the grace of the Holy Spirit, who leads the Church into all truth until the glorious coming of her Lord[14]. Concerning this infallibility of the People of God the Second Vatican Council speaks as follows: "The body of the faithful as a whole, anointed as they are by the Holy One (cf. *1 Jn* 2:20, 27), cannot err in matters of belief. Thanks to a supernatural instinct of faith which characterizes the people as a whole, it manifests this unerring quality when, 'from the bishops down to the last member of the laity' (St Augustine, *De Praed. Sanct.*, 14, 27), it shows universal agreement in matters of faith and morals"[15].

The Holy Spirit enlightens and assists the People of God inasmuch as it is the Body of Christ united in a hierarchical communion. The Second Vatican Council indicates this fact by adding to the words quoted above: "For, by this instinct of faith which is aroused and sustained by the Spirit of truth, God's people accepts not the word of men but the very Word of God (cf. *1 Thess* 2:13). It clings without fail to the faith once delivered to the saints (cf. *Jude* 3), penetrates it more deeply by accurate insights, and applies it more thoroughly to life. All this it does under the lead of a sacred teaching authority to which it loyally defers"[16].

Without doubt the faithful, who in their own manner share in Christ's prophetic office[17], in many ways contribute towards increasing the understanding of faith in the Church. "For," as the Second Vatican Council says, "there is a growth in the understanding of the realities and the words which have been handed down. This happens through the contemplation and study made by believers, who treasure these things in their hearts (cf. *Lk* 2:19, 51), through the intimate understanding of spiritual things they experience, and through the preaching of those who have received through episcopal succession the sure charism of truth"[18]. And the Supreme Pontiff Paul VI observes that the witness the pastors of the Church offer is "rooted in Sacred Tradition and Holy Scripture and nourished by the ecclesial life of the whole People of God"[19].

But by divine institution it is the exclusive task of these pastors alone, the successors of Peter and the other Apostles, to teach the faithful authentically, that is with the authority of Christ shared in different ways; so that the faithful, who may not simply listen to them as experts in Catholic doctrine, must accept their teaching given in Christ's name, with an assent that is proportionate to the authority that they possess and that they mean to exercise[20]. For this reason the Second Vatican Council, in harmony with the First Vatican Council, teaches that Christ made Peter "a perpetual and visible principle and foundation of the unity of faith and of communion"[21]; and the Supreme Pontiff Paul VI has declared: "The teaching office of the bishops is for the believer the sign and channel which enable him to receive and recognize the Word of God"[22]. Thus, however, much the Sacred Magisterium avails itself of the contemplation, life and study of the faithful, its office is not reduced merely to ratifying the assent already expressed by the latter; indeed, in the interpretation and explanation of the written or transmitted Word of God, the Magisterium can anticipate or demand their assent[23]. The People of God has particular need of the intervention and assistance of the Magisterium when internal disagreements arise and spread concerning a doctrine that must be believed or held, lest it lose the communion of the one faith in the one Body of the Lord (cf. *Eph.* 4:45).

3

THE INFALLIBILITY OF THE CHURCH'S MAGISTERIUM

Jesus Christ from whom derives the task proper to the pastors of teaching the Gospel to all his people and to the entire human family, wished to endow the pastors' Magisterium with a fitting charism of infallibility in matters regarding faith and morals. Since this charism does not come from new revelations enjoyed by the Successor of Peter and the College of Bishops[24], it does not dispense them from studying with appropriate means the treasure of divine Revelation contained both in Sacred Scripture which teaches us intact the truth that God willed to be written down for our salvation[25] and in the living Tradition that comes from the Apostles[26]. In carrying out their task, the pastors of the Church enjoy the assistance of the Holy Spirit; this assistance reaches its highest point when they teach the People of God in such a manner that, through the promises of Christ made to Peter and the other Apostles, the doctrine they propose is necessarily immune from error.

This occurs when the bishops scattered throughout the world but teaching in communion with the Successor of Peter present a doctrine to be held irrevocably[27]. It occurs even more clearly both when the bishops by a collegial act (as in Ecumenical Councils), together with their visible Head, define a doctrine to be held[28], and when the Roman Pontiff "speaks *ex cathedra,* that is, when, exercising the office of Pastor and Teacher of all Christians, through his supreme apostolic authority he defines a doctrine concerning faith or morals to be held by the universal Church"[29].

According to Catholic doctrine, the infallibility of the Church's Magisterium extends not only to the deposit of faith but also to those matters without which that deposit cannot be rightly preserved and expounded[30]. The extension however of this infallibility to the deposit of faith itself is a truth that the Church has from the beginning held as having been certainly revealed in Christ's promises. The First Vatican Council, basing itself upon this truth, defined as follows the matter of Catholic faith: "All those things are to be believed by divine and Catholic faith which are contained in the written or transmitted Word of God and which are proposed by the Church, either by a solemn judgment or by the ordinary and universal magisterium, to be believed as having been divinely revealed"[31]. Therefore the objects of Catholic Faith — which are called dogmas — necessarily are and always have been the unalterable norm both for faith and for theological science.

4

THE CHURCH'S GIFT OF INFALLIBILITY NOT TO BE DIMINISHED

From what has been said about the extent of and conditions governing the infallibility of the People of God and of the Church's Magisterium, it follows that the faithful are in no way permitted to see in the Church merely a fundamental permanence in truth which, as some assert, could be reconciled with errors contained here and there in the propositions that the Church's Magisterium teaches to be held irrevocably, as also in the unhesitating assent of the People of God concerning matters of faith and morals.

It is of course true that through the faith that leads to salvation men are converted to God[32], who reveals himself in his Son Jesus Christ; but it would be wrong to deduce from this that the Church's dogmas can be belittled or even denied. Indeed the conversion to God which we should realize through faith is a form of obedience (cf. *Rom.* 16:26), which should correspond to the nature of divine Revelation and its demands. Now this Revelation, in the whole plan of salvation, reveals the mystery of God who sent his Son into the world (cf. *1 Jn* 4:14) and teaches its application to Christian conduct. Moreover it demands that, in full obedience of the intellect and will to God who reveals[33] we accept the proclamation of the good news of salvation as it is infallibly taught by the pastors of the Church. The faithful, therefore, through faith are converted as they should to God, who reveals himself in Christ, when they adhere to him in the integral doctrine of the Catholic faith.

It is true that there exists an order and as it were a hierarchy of the Church's dogmas, as a result of their varying relationship to the foundation of the faith[34]. This hierarchy means that some dogmas are founded on other dogmas which are the principal ones, and are illuminated by these latter. But all dogmas, since they are revealed, must be believed with the same divine faith[35].

5

THE NOTION OF THE CHURCH'S INFALLIBILITY NOT TO BE FALSIFIED

The transmission of divine Revelation by the Church encounters difficulties of various kinds. These arise from the fact that the hidden mysteries of God "by their nature so far transcend the human intellect that even if they are revealed to us and accepted by faith, they remain concealed by the veil of faith itself and are as it were wrapped in darkness"[36]. Difficulties arise also from the historical condition that affects the expression of Revelation.

With regard to this historical condition, it must first be observed that the meaning of the pronouncements of faith depend partly upon the expressive power of the language used at a certain point in time and in particular circumstances. Moreover, it sometimes happens that some dogmatic truth is first expressed incompletely (but not falsely), and at a later date, when considered in a broader context of faith or human knowledge, it receives a fuller and more perfect expression. In addition, when the Church makes new pronouncements she intends to confirm or clarify what is in some way contained in Sacred Scripture or in previous expressions of Tradition; but at the same time she usually has the intention of solving certain questions or removing certain errors. All these things have to be taken into account in order that these pronouncements may be properly interpreted. Finally, even though the truths which the Church intends to teach through her dogmatic formulas are distinct from the changeable conceptions of a given epoch and can be expressed without them, nevertheless it can sometimes happen that these truths may be enunciated by the Sacred Magisterium in terms that bear traces of such conceptions.

In view of the above, it must be stated that the dogmatic formulas of the Church's Magisterium were from the very beginning suitable for communicating revealed truth, and that as they are they remain for ever suitable for communicating this truth to those who interpret them correctly[37]. It does not however follow that every one of these formulas has always been or will always be so to the same extent. For this reason theologians seek to define exactly the intention of teaching proper to the various formulas, and in carrying out this work they are of considerable assistance to the living Magisterium of the Church, to which they remain subordinated. For this reason also it often happens that ancient dogmatic formulas and others closely connected with them remain living and fruitful in the habitual usage of the Church, but with suitable expository and explanatory additions that maintain and clarify their original meaning. In addition, it has sometimes happened that in this habitual usage of the Church certain of these formulas gave way to new expressions which, proposed and approved by the Sacred Magisterium, presented more clearly or more completely the same meaning.

As for the *meaning* of the dogmatic formulas, this remains ever true and constant in the Church, even when it is expressed with greater clarity or more developed. The faithful therefore must shun the opinion, first, that dogmatic formulas (or some category of them) cannot signify truth in a determinate way, but can only offer changeable approximations to it, which to a certain extent distort or alter it; secondly, that these formulas signify the truth only in an indeterminate way, this truth being like a goal that is constantly being sought by means of such approximations. Those who hold such an opinon do not avoid dogmatic relativism and they corrupt the concept of the Church's infallibility relative to the truth to be taught or held in a determinate way.

Such an opinion clearly is in disagreement with the declarations of the First Vatican Council, which, while fully aware of the progress of the Church in her knowledge of revealed truth[38], nevertheless taught as follows: "That meaning of sacred dogmas . . . must always be maintained which Holy Mother Church declared once and for all, nor should one ever depart from that meaning under the guise of or in the name of a more advanced understanding"[39]. The Council moreover condemned the opinion that "dogmas once proposed by the Church must with the progress of science be given a meaning other than that which was understood by the Church, or which she understands"[40]. There is no doubt that, according to these texts of the Council, the meaning of dogmas which is declared by the Church is determinate and unalterable.

Such an opinion is likewise in contrast with Pope John's assertion regarding Christian doctrine at the opening of the Second Vatican Council: "This certain and unchangeable doctrine, to which faithful obedience is due, has to be explored and presented in a way that is demanded by our times. One thing is the deposit of faith, which consists of the truths contained in sacred doctrine, another thing is the manner of presentation, always however with the same meaning and signification"[41]. Since the Successor of Peter is here speaking about certain and unchangeable Christian doctrine, about the deposit of faith which is the same as the truths contained in that doctrine and about the truths which have to be preserved with the same meaning, it is clear that he admits that we can know the true and unchanging meaning of dogmas. What is new and what he recommends in view of the needs of the times pertains only to the modes of studying, expounding and presenting that doctrine while keeping its permanent meaning. In a similar way the Supreme Pontiff Paul VI exhorted the Pastors of the Church in the following words: "Nowadays a serious effort is required of us to ensure that the teaching of the faith should keep the fullness of its meaning and force, while expressing itself in a form which allows it to reach the spirit and heart of the people to whom it is addressed"[42].

6

THE CHURCH ASSOCIATED WITH THE PRIESTHOOD OF CHRIST

Christ the Lord, the High Priest of the new and everlasting covenant, wished to associate with his perfect priesthood and to form in its likeness the people he had bought with his own blood (cf. *Heb* 7: 20-22, 26-28; 10: 14, 21). He therefore granted his Church a share in his priesthood, which consists of the common priesthood of the faithful and the ministerial or hierarchical priesthood. These differ from each other not only in degree but also in essence; yet they are mutually complementary within the communion of the Church[43].

The common priesthood of the laity, which is also rightly called a royal priesthood (cf. *1 Pet* 2:9; *Rev* 1:6; 5:9 ff.) since through it the faithful are united as members of the messianic people with their heavenly King, is conferred by the sacrament of Baptism. By this sacrament "the faithful are incorporated into the Church and are empowered to take part in the worship of the Christian religion" in virtue of a permanent sign known as a character; "reborn as children of God they are obliged to profess before men the faith which they have received from God through the Church"[44]. Thus those who are reborn in Baptism "join in the offering of the Eucharist by virtue of their royal priesthood. They likewise exercise that priesthood by receiving the sacraments, by prayer and thanksgiving, by the witness of a holy life, and by self-denial and active charity."[45]

Moreover, Christ, the Head of the Church, which is his Mystical Body, appointed as ministers of his priesthood his Apostles and through them their successors the bishops, that they might act in his person within the Church[46] and also in turn legitimately hand over to priests in a subordinate degree the sacred ministry which they had received[47]. Thus there arose in the Church an apostolic succession of the ministerial priesthood for the glory of God and for the service of his people and of the entire human family, which must be converted to God.

By means of this priesthood bishops and priests are "indeed set apart in a certain sense in the midst of God's people. But this is so, not that they may be separated from this people or from any man, but that they may be totally dedicated to the work for which the Lord has raised them up"[48]: namely, the work of sanctifying, teaching and ruling, the actual execution of which is more precisely specified by the hierarchical communion[49]. This manysided work has as its basis and foundation the continuous preaching of the Gospel[50], and as the summit and source of the entire Christian life the Eucharistic Sacrifice[51]. Priests, acting in the person of Christ the Head, offer this Sacrifice in the Holy Spirit to God the Father in the name of Christ and in the name of the members of his Mystical Body[52]. This sacrifice is completed in the holy supper by which the faithful, partaking of the one body of Christ, are all made into one body (cf. *1 Cor* 10:16 ff.).

The Church has ever more closely examined the nature of the ministerial priesthood, which can be shown to have been invariably conferred from apostolic times by a sacred rite (cf. *1 Tim* 4:15; *2 Tim* 1:6). By the assistance of the Holy Spirit, she recognized more clearly as time went on that God wished her to understand that this rite conferred upon priests not only an increase of grace for carrying out ecclesiastical duties in a holy way, but also a permanent designation by Christ, or character, by virtue of which they are equipped for their work and endowed with the necessary power that is derived from the supreme power of Christ. The permanent existence of this character, the nature of which is explained in different ways by theologians, is taught by the Council of Florence[53] and reaffirmed by two decrees of the Council of Trent[54]. In recent times the Second Vatican Council more than once mentioned it[55], and the second General Assembly of the Synod of Bishops rightly considered the enduring nature of the priestly character throughout life as pertaining to the teaching of faith[56]. This stable existence of a priestly character must be recognized by the faithful and has to be taken into account in order to judge properly about the nature of the priestly ministry and the appropriate ways of exercising it.

Faithful to Sacred Tradition and to many documents of the Magisterium, the Second Vatican Council taught the following concerning the power belonging to the ministerial priesthood: "Though everyone can baptize the faithful, the priest alone can complete the building up of the Body in the Eucharistic Sacrifice"[57]. And again: "The same Lord, in order that the faithful might form one body in which 'all the members have not the same function' (*Rom* 12:4), appointed some ministers within the society of believers who by the power of Orders would be capable of offering the Sacrifice and of forgiving sins"[58].

In the same way, the second General Assembly of the Synod of Bishops rightly affirmed that only the priest can act in the person of Christ and preside over and perform the sacrificial banquet in which the People of God are united with the oblation of Christ[59]. Passing over at this point questions regarding the ministers of the various sacraments, the evidence of Sacred Tradition and of the Sacred Magisterium make it clear that the faithful who have not received priestly ordination and who take upon themselves the office of performing the Eucharist attempt to do so not only in a completely illicit way but also invalidly. Such an abuse, wherever it may occur, must clearly be eliminated by the pastors of the Church.

* * *

It was not the intention of this Declaration, nor was it within its scope, to prove by way of a study of the foundations of our faith that divine revelation was entrusted to the Church so that she might thereafter preserve it unaltered in the world. But this dogma, from which the Catholic faith takes its beginning, has been recalled, together with other truths related to the mystery of the Church, so that in the uncertainty of the present day the faith and doctrine the faithful must hold might clearly emerge.

The Sacred Congregation for the Doctrine of the Faith rejoices that theologians are by intense study exploring more and more the mystery of the Church. It recognizes also that in their work they touch on many questions which can only be clarified by complementary studies and by various efforts and conjectures. However, the due freedom of theologians must always be limited by the Word of God as it is faithfully preserved and expounded in the Church and taught and explained by the living Magisterium of the Pastors and especially of the Pastor of the entire People of God[60].

The Sacred Congregation entrusts this Declaration to the diligent attention of the bishops and of all those who in any way share the task of guarding the patrimony of truth which Christ and his Apostles committed to the Church. It also confidently addresses the Declaration to the faithful and particularly, in view of the important office which they hold in the Church, to priests and theologians, so that all may be of one mind in the faith and may be in sincere harmony with the Church.

Pope Paul VI, by divine providence Supreme Pontiff, in the audience granted to the undersigned Prefect of the Sacred Congregation for the Doctrine of the Faith on 11 May 1973 has ratified and confirmed this Declaration in defense of the Catholic doctrine on the Church against certain errors of the present day and has ordered its publication.

Given in Rome, at the Sacred Congregation for the Doctrine of the Faith, on 24 June 1973, the feast of Saint John the Baptist.

FRANJO Card. ŠEPER
Prefect

✠ Jérôme Hamer
Tit. Archbishop of Lorium
Secretary

FOOTNOTES

[1]Paul VI, Apostolic Exhortation *Quinque iam Anni, AAS* 63 (1971), p. 99.

[2]Paul VI, Apostolic Constitution *Regiminis Ecclesiae Universae, AAS* 59 (1967), p. 897.

[3]II Vatican Council: Dogmatic Constitution on the Church *Lumen Gentium*, 8; *Constitutiones Decreta Declarationes*, editio Secretariae Generalis, Typis Polyglottis Vaticanis, 1966, p. 104 ff.

[4]II Vatican Council: Decree on Ecumenism *Unitatis Redintegratio*, 3; *Const. Decr. Decl.*, p. 250.

[5]*Ibid.*, 4; *Const. Decr. Decl.*, p. 252.

[6]II Vatican Council: Dogmatic Constitution on the Church *Lumen Gentium*, 8; *Const. Decr. Decl.*, p. 106.

[7]*Ibid.: Const. Decr. Decl.*, p. 105.

[8]II Vatican Council: Decree on Ecumenism *Unitatis Redintegratio*, 4; *Const. Decr. Decl.*, p. 253.

[9]Cf. *ibid.*, 6-8; *Const. Decr. Decl.*, pp. 255-258.

[10]Cf. *ibid.*, 1; *Const. Decr. Decl.*, p. 243.

[11]Cf. Paul VI, Encyclical Letter *Ecclesiasm Suam*, *AAS* 56 (1964), p. 629.

[12]II Vatican Council: Dogmatic Consitution on Divine Revelation *Dei Verbum*, 7; *Const. Decr. Decl.*, p. 428.

[13]Cf. *ibid.*, 10; *Const. Decr. Decl.*, p. 431.

[14]Cf. *ibid.*, 8; *Const. Decr. Decl.*, p. 430.

[15]II Vatican Council: Dogmatic Constitution on the Church *Lumen Gentium*, 12; *Const. Decr. Decl.*, p. 113 ff.

[16]*Ibid.; Const. Decr. Decl.*, p. 114.

[17]Cf. *ibid.*, 35; *Const. Decr. Decl.*, p. 157.

[18]II Vatican Council: Dogmatic Constitution on Divine Revelation *Dei Verbum*, 8; *Const. Decr. Decl.*, p. 430.

[19]Paul VI, Apostolic Exhortation *Quinque iam anni*, *AAS* 63 (1971), p. 99.

[20]Cf. II Vatican Council: Dogmatic Constitution on the Church *Lumen Gentium*, 25; *Const. Decr. Decl.*, p. 138 ff.

[21]II Vatican Council: *ibid.*, 18; *Const. Decr. Decl.*, p. 124 ff. Cf. I Vatican Council: Dogmatic Constitution *Pastor Aeternus*, Prologue; *Conciliorum oecumenicorum Decreta*[3], ed. *Istituto per le Scienze Religiose di Bologna*, Herder, 1973, p. 812 (DS 3051).

[22]Paul VI, Apostolic Exhortation *Quinque iam Anni*, *AAS* 63 (1971), p. 100.

[23]Decree of the Holy Office *Lamentabili*, 6, *AAS* 40 (1907), p. 471 (DS 3406). Cf. I Vatican Council: Dogmatic Constitution *Pastor Aeternus*, ch. 4; *Conc. Oec. Decr.*[3], p. 815 ff. (DS 3069, 3074).

[24]I Vatican Council: Dogmatic Constitution *Pastor Aeternus*, ch. 4; *Conc. Oec. Decr.*[3], p. 816 (DS 3070). Cf. II Vatican Council: Dogmatic Constitution on the Church *Lumen Gentium*, 25, and Dogmatic Constitution on Divine Revelation *Dei Verbum*, 4; *Const. Decr. Decl.*, p. 141 and 426.

[25]Cf. II Vatican Council: Dogmatic Constitution on Divine Revelation *Dei Verbum*, 11; *Const. Decr. Decl.*, p. 434.

[26]Cf. *ibid.*, 9 ff.; *Const. Decr. Decl.*, p. 430-432.

[27]Cf. II Vatican Council: Dogmatic Constitution on the Church *Lumen Gentium*, 25; *Const. Decr. Decl.*, p. 139.

[28]Cf. *ibid.*, 25 and 22; *Const. Decr. Decl.*, p. 139 and 133.

[29]I Vatican Council: Dogmatic Constitution *Pastor Aeternus*, ch. 4; *Conc. Oec. Decr.*[3], p. 816 (DS 3074) Cf. II Vatican Council: *ibid.*, 25. *Const. Oec. Decr.*[3], pp. 139-141.

[30]Cf. II Vatican Council: Dogmatic Constitution on the Church *Lumen Gentium*, 25; *Const. Decr. Decl.*, p. 139.

[31]I Vatican Council: Dogmatic Constitution *Dei Filius*, ch. 3; *Conc. Oec. Decr.*[3], p. 807 (DS 3011). Cf. *C.I.C.*, can. 1323, §1 and can. 1325 §2.

[32]Cf. Council of Trent, Sess. 6: Decree on Justification, ch. 6; *Conc. Oec. Decr.*[3], p. 672 (DS 1526); cf. also II Vatican Council: Dogmatic Constitution on Divine Revelation *Dei Verbum*, 5; *Const. Decr. Decl.*, p. 426.

[33]Cf. I Vatican Council: Constitution on the Catholic Faith *Dei Filius*, ch. 3; *Conc. Oec. Decr.*[3], p. 807 (DS 3008); cf. also II Vatican Council: Dogmatic Constitution on Divine Revelation *Dei Verbum*, 5; *Const. Decr. Decl.*, p. 426.

[34]Cf. II Vatican Council: Decree on Ecumenism *Unitatis Redintegratio*, 11; *Const. Decr. Decl.*, p. 260.

[35]*Reflections and Suggestions Concerning Ecumenical Dialogue*, IV, 4 b, in *The Secretariat for Promoting Christian Unity: Information Service*, n. 12 (December 1970, IV), p. 8.

[36]I Vatican Council: Dogmatic Constitution *Dei Filius*, ch 4; *Conc. Oec. Decr.*[3], p. 808 (DS 3016).

[37]Cf. Pius IX, Brief *Eximiam Tuam*, *ASS* 8 (1874-75), p. 447 (DS 2831); Paul VI, Encyclical Letter *Mysterium Fidei*, *AAS 57 (1965), p. 757 ff. and L'Oriente cristiano nella luce di immortali Concili*, in *Insegnamenti di Paolo VI*, vol. 5, Vatican Polyglot Press, p. 412 ff.

[38]Cf. I Vatican Council: Dogmatic Constitution *Dei Filius*, ch. 4; *Conc. Oec. Decr.*[3], p. 809 (DS 3020).

[39]*Ibid.*

[40]*Ibid.*, can. 3; *Conc. Oec. Decr.*[3], p. 811 (DS 3043).

[41]John XXIII, *Alloc. in Concilii Vaticani inauguratione*, *AAS* 54 (1962), p. 792. Cf. II Vatican Council: Pastoral Constitution on the Church in the Modern World *Gaudium et Spes*, 62; *Const. Decr. Decl.*, p. 780.

[42]Paul VI, Apostolic Exhortation *Quinque iam Anni*, *AAS* 63 (1971), p. 100 ff.

[43]Cf. II Vatican Council: Dogmatic Constitution on the Church *Lumen Gentium*, 10; *Const. Decr. Decl.*, p. 110.

[44]*Ibid.*, 11; *Const. Decr. Decl.*, p. 111.

[45]*Ibid.*, 10; *Const. Decr. Decl.*, p. 111.

[46]Cf. Pius XI, Encyclical Letter *Ad Catholici Sacerdotii*, *AAS* 28 (1936), p. 10 (DS 3735). Cf. II Vatican Council: Dogmatic Constitution on the Church *Lumen Gentium*, 10, and Decree on the Priestly Life and Ministry *Presbyterorum Ordinis*, 2; *Const. Decr. Decl.*, p. 110 ff, 622 ff.

[47]Cf. II Vatican Council: Dogmatic Constitution on the Church *Lumen Gentium*, 28; *Const. Decr. Decl.*, p. 625.

[48]II Vatican Council: Decree on the Priestly Life and Ministry *Presbyterorum Ordinis*, 3; *Const. Decr. Decl.*, p. 625.

[49]Cf. II Vatican Council: Dogmatic Constitution *Lumen Gentium*, 24, 27 ff.; *Const. Decr. Decl.*, pp. 137, 143-149.

[50]II Vatican Council: Decree on the Priestly Life and Ministry *Presbyterorum Ordinis*, 4; *Const. Decr. Decl.*, p. 627.

[51]Cf. Dogmatic Constitution of the Church *Lumen Gentium*, 11; *Const. Decr. Decl.*, p. 111 ff. also Council of Trent, Sess. 22: *Doctrina de Missae Sacrificio*, ch. 1 and 2; *Conc. Oec. Decr.*[3], pp. 732-734 (DS 1739-1743).

[52]Cf. Paul VI. *Sollemnis Professio Fidei*, 24, *AAS* 60 (1968), p. 442.

[53]Council of Florence: *Bulla unionis Armenorum, Exsultate Deo; Conc. Oec. Decr.*[3], p. 546 (DS 1313).

[54]Council of Trent: Decree on the Sacraments, can. 9 and Decree on the Sacrament of Order, ch. 4 and can. 4; *Conc. Oec. Decr.*[3], pp. 685, 742, 744 (DS 1609, 1767, 1774).

[55]Cf. II Vatican Council: Dogmatic Constitution on the Church *Lumen Gentium*, 21 and Decree on the Priestly Life and Ministry *Presbyterorum Ordinis*, 2; *Const. Decr. Decl.*, pp. 133, 622 ff.

[56]Cf. Documents of the Synod of Bishops: *I. The Ministerial Priesthood*, part one, 5, *AAS* 63 (1971), p. 907.

[57]II Vatican Council: Dogmatic Constitution on the Church *Lumen Gentium*, 17; *Const. Decr. Decl.*, p. 123.

[58]II Vatican Council: Decree on the Priestly Life and Ministry *Presbyterorum Ordinis*, 2; *Const. Decr. Decl.*, p. 621 ff.

Cf. also: 1) Innocent III, Letter *Eius exemplo* with *Professio fidei Waldensis imposita*, *PL*, vol. 215, col. 1510 (DS 794); 2) IV Latern Council: Constitution 1: *De Fide Catholica; Conc. Oec. Decr.*[3], p. 230 (DS 802); passage quoted on the Sacrament of the Altar to be read together with the following passage on the Sacrament of Baptism; 3) Council of Florence: *Bullo unionis Armenorum, Exultate Deo; Conc. Oec. Decr.*[3], p. 546 (DS 1321); passage quoted on the Minister of the Eucharist to be compared with nearby passages on the Ministers of the other Sacraments; 4) Council of Trent, Sess. 23: Decree on the Sacrament of Order, ch. 4; *Conc. Oec. Decr.*[3], p. 742 ff. (DS 1767, 4469); 5) Pius XII, Encyclical *Mediator Dei*, *AAS* 39 (1947), pp. 552-556 (DS 3849-3852).

[59]Documents of the Synod of Bishops: *I. The Ministerial Priesthood*, part one, 4, *AAS* 63 (1971), p. 906.

[60]Cf. Synod of Bishops (1967), *Relatio Commissionis Synodalis constitutae ad examen ulterius peragendum circa opiniones periculosas et atheismum*, II, 4: *De theologorum opera et responsabilitate*, Vatican Polyglot Press, 1967, p. 11 (*L'Osservatore Romano*, 30-31 Oct. 1967, p. 3).

DECLARATION OF THE SACRED CONGREGATION FOR THE DOCTRINE OF THE FAITH ON SOME MAJOR POINTS IN THE THEOLOGICAL DOCTRINE OF PROFESSOR HANS KÜNG

December 15, 1979

The church of Christ has received from God the mandate to keep and to safeguard the deposit of faith so that all the faithful, under the guidance of the sacred magisterium through which Christ himself exercises his role as teacher in the church, may cling without fail to the faith once delivered to the saints, may penetrate it more deeply by accurate insights, and may apply it more thoroughly to life.[1]

In order to fulfill the important task entrusted to itself alone[2] the magisterium of the church avails itself of the work of theologians, especially those who in the church have received from the authorities the task of teaching and who, therefore, have been designated in a certain way as teachers of the truth. In their research the theologians, like scholars in other fields, enjoy a legitimate scientific liberty, though within the limits of the method of sacred theology. Thus, while working in their own way they seek to attain the same specific end as the magisterium itself, namely, "to preserve, to penetrate ever more deeply, to explain, to teach, to defend the sacred deposit of revelation; and in this way to illumine the life of the church and of the human race with the light of divine truth."[3]

It is necessary, therefore, that theological research and teaching should always be illumined with fidelity to the magisterium since no one may rightly act as a theologian except in close union with the mission of teaching truth which is incumbent on the church itself.[4] When such fidelity is absent, harm is done to all the faithful who, since they are bound to profess the faith which they have received from God through the church, have a sacred right to receive the word of God uncontaminated, and so they expect that vigilant care should be exercised to keep the threat of error far from them[5]

If it should happen, therefore, that a teacher of sacred doctrine chooses and disseminates as the norm of truth his own judgment and not the thought of the church, and if he continues in his conviction, despite the use of all charitable means in his regard, then honesty itself demands that the church should publicly call attention to his conduct and should state that he can no longer teach with the authority of the mission which he received from her.[6]

This canonical mission is, in fact, a testimony to a reciprocal trust: first, trust on the part of the competent authority that the theologian will conduct himself as a Catholic theologian in the work of his research and teaching; second, trust on the part of the theologian himself in the church and in her integral teaching, since it is by her mandate that he carries out his task.

Since some of the writings, spread throughout many countries, and the teaching of Professor Hans Küng, a priest, are a cause of disturbance in the minds of the faithful, the bishops of Germany and this Congregation for the Doctrine of the Faith, acting in common accord, have several times counselled and warned him that he must carry on his theological work in full communion with the authentic magisterium of the church.

In this spirit and in order to fulfill its role of promoting and safeguarding the doctrine of faith and morals in the universal church,[7] the Sacred Congregation for the Doctrine of the Faith issued a public document on Feb. 15, 1975, declaring that some opinions of Professor Hans Küng were opposed in different degrees to the doctrine of the church which must be held by all the faithful. Among these opinions, it noted especially those which pertain to the dogma of faith about infallibility in the church, to the task of authentically interpreting the unique sacred deposit of the word of God which has been entrusted only to the living magisterium of the church, and finally to the valid consecration of the Eucharist.

At the same time, this sacred congregation warned Professor Küng that he should not continue to teach such opinions, for it expected, in the meantime, that he would bring his opinions into harmony with the doctrine of the authentic magisterium.[8]

However, up to the present time he has in no way changed his opinion in the matters called to his attention.

This fact is particularly evident in the matter of the opinion which at least puts in doubt the dogma of infallibility in the church or reduces it to a certain fundamental indefectibility of the church in truth, with the possibility of error in doctrinal statements which the magisterium of the church teaches must be held definitively. On this point, Hans Küng has in no way sought to conform to the doctrine of the magisterium. Instead he has recently proposed his view again more explicitly (namely, in his writings, "Kirche-Gehalten in der Wahrheit?" — Benziger Varlag, 1979, and Zum Geleit, an introduction to the work of A.B. Hasler entitled "Wie der Papst Unfehlbar Wurde" — Piper Verlag, 1979), even though this sacred congregation had affirmed that such an opinion contradicts the doctrine defined by Vatican Council I and confirmed by Vatican Council II.

Moreover, the consequences of this opinion, especially a contempt for the magisterium of the church, may be found in other works published by him, undoubtedly with serious harm to some essential points of Catholic faith (e.g., those teachings which pertain to the consubstantiality of Christ with his Father, and to the Blessed Virgin Mary), since the meaning ascribed to these doctrines is different from that which the church has understood and now understands.

The Sacred Congregation for the Doctrine of the Faith in the aforesaid document of 1975 refrained at the time from further action regarding the above mentioned opinions of Professor Küng, presuming that he himself would abandon them. But since this presumption no longer exists, this sacred congregation by reason of its duty is constrained to declare that Professor Hans Küng, in his writings, has departed from the integral truth of Catholic faith, and therefore he can no longer be considered a Catholic theologian nor function as such in a teaching role.

At an audience granted to the undersigned cardinal prefect, the supreme pontiff Pope John Paul II approved this declaration, decided upon at an ordinary meeting of this sacred congregation, and ordered its publication.

In Rome, at the Sacred Congregation for the Doctrine of the Faith, on 15 December 1979.

Franjo Cardinal Seper
Prefect

Jerome Hamer, O.P.
Titular Archbishop of Lorium
Secretary

FOOTNOTES

[1]Cf Conc. Vatic. I, Const. Dogm. Dei Filius, cap. IV "De fide et ratione": DS 3018, Conc. Vatic. II, Const. Dogm. "Lumen Gentium," n. 12.

[2]Cf. Conc. Vatic. II, Const. Dog. Dei Verbum, n. 10.

[3] Paulus VI, Allocut. ad Congress. Internat. de Theologia Conc. Vatic. II, 1 Oct. 1966, A.A.S. 58 (1966), P. 891.

[4]Cf. Ioannes Paulus II, Const. Apost. "Sapientia Christiana," Art. 70; Encycl. "Redemptor Hominis," n. 19., A.A.S. 71 (1979) pp. 493, 308.

[5]Cf. Conc. Vatic. II, Const. Dogm. "Lumen Gentium," n. 11 and 25; Palus VI Exhort. Apost. Quinque iam anni: A.A.S. 63 (1971) P. 99F.

[6]Cf. "Sapientia Christiana," Tit. III, art. 27, par. 1: A.A.S. 71 (1979), p. 483.

[7]Cf. Motu proprio "Integrae Servandae," n. 1, 3 and 4: A.A.S. 57 (1965), p. 954.

[8]Cf. A.A.S. 67 (1975) pp. 203-204.

APPENDIX III

STATEMENT OF G. EMMETT CARDINAL CARTER, ARCHBISHOP OF TORONTO REGARDING THE KÜNG CONTROVERSY

The condemnation of certain theological opinions of Hans Küng has aroused bitterness and controversy, not all of it expressed in weighty or weighted terms. It would appear to be important to try to examine and separate the issues with a little more light and considerably less heat.

The first issue which, to my way of thinking, requires calm reflection and self-analysis as well as objective analysis is one's position on the rights and responsibilities of the "magisterium," the official teaching authority within the Catholic Church. The knee-jerk reaction of some leads one to wonder about just what rights could be invested in such an authority without arousing an equal and indignant response.

Postulating that we are talking about the Roman Catholic Church, is there any situation in which the magisterium may and must say: "This position is faulty. It is opposed to the authentic interpretation of Holy Scripture and contrary to the defined doctrine of the Church"?

Let us suppose for the sake of the clarity of the discussion that Father X and Mr. Y maintains that Jesus the Christ is not divine but a human prophet among the prophets. Or that he rose from the dead only in a symbolical sense. Does anyone in the Catholic Church have the right and duty to say: "Stop there. This teaching is erroneous and misleading"?

We are further postulating that he(she) who holds and teaches such opinion is someone with vast prestige and penetrating influence. Perhaps even someone who is officially mandated by the Church as a theologian. Does the teaching role impose any obligation on Church authority to make it clear that this is only a personal opinion, however academically qualified its author may be, in order to warn the unsuspecting and less qualified faithful that this way lies shipwreck in faith?

I, for one, find it difficult to imagine more than one answer to the above questions in the context of Catholicism. There are many, and among them very respected theologians, who deny this right or obligation to any Church. But these very persons would be the first to insist that they are speaking out of a different context and tradition.

Integral to Catholic Christianity has been the conviction that the magisterium has the right and duty to define and defend what it understands to be essential to the truth of the Gospel.

If then, as maintained, Hans Küng has held and taught positions that cast doubt upon the divinity of Christ and that repudiate the Church's understanding of infallibility, why should one be surprised if Church authorities declare that for doing so he is no longer to be considered in any official sense a Catholic theologian?

Interestingly enough, in spite of many misleading public presentations to the contrary, the vast majority of responsible theologians both repudiate Küng's teaching in these areas and agree that the Church has the right and the duty to point out that this, truly, is not Catholic teaching.

Is then the problem somewhere else? Is there perhaps some confusion of issues. We read articles in which at one and the same time we are discussing the magisterium, the procedures used by the Congregation for the Doctrine of the Faith (always throw in "successor of the Inquisition," otherwise someone might think you were biased), the brilliance of Hans Küng and the inferiority of Roman theologians, the right of the Pope to condemn, coupled with his Polish ancestry — all rolled into one indigestible lump.

Pulling the elements apart and setting them in some kind of order is not easy.

We have already suggested that the right to condemn a theological opinion is an integral part of the Catholic Church. What now about the procedures?

In this area, real concern is both legitimate and healthy. But before we offer any positive suggestions let us make sure that here, too, we are not exaggerating.

Was Hans Küng tried in absentia? Was he informed of the charges against him? Was his trial clandestine? These are three basic and very legitimate questions. Much as we hate to introduce facts into what has been such a delightfully recreational exercise for some who have publicly commented, they might conceivably be of some value.

First, the "in absentia" question. Küng published a book entitled *Die Kirche (The Church)* in 1967. The Congregation for the Doctrine of the Faith communicated with him *on April 30, 1968* and invited him to discuss its contents. "Küng declared himself open to this in principle (but) the conversations did not take place *despite repeated invitations.*" (Emphasis ours) (Declaration, Pres. Conference of German Bishops Dec. 18/79)

In 1970 Küng published a book entitled *"Unfelbar? Eine Anfrage (Infallible? An Inquiry).* After examination the Congregation sent to Küng a series of questions. *"The voluminous exchange of letters* did not bring a response satisfactory to the Congregation." (Emphasis ours - ibid)

In 1973 the Congregation published a declaration "The Mystery of the Church" questioning and opposing Küng's teachings. The position of the Congregation was presented personally to Küng by a member and he was informed that further conversation was possible and desirable. Küng did not avail himself of the offer.

In 1974 (September 4), Küng wrote to the Congregation assuring them that he wished to take advantage of the "time for reflection" granted him and even held forth the possibility that he could come to conform his teaching to that of the magisterium. In view of his positive response, the doctrinal procedure against him was closed "for now."

The publication in 1974 of *Christ Sein (On Being a Christian)* inaugurated a new round of discussions and publications. The focus of concern was Küng's understanding of the mystery of Christ. Many German Catholic theologians as well as the German Bishops' Conference raised serious questions about the compatibility of Küng's position with the Church's traditional understanding of Jesus.

The event that seems to have led to the intervention of the Congregation was the 1979 publication by Küng of a book and an extensive article on infallibility. Far from modifying his position, he made it even more explicit. This was seen as deliberately provocative.

In the light of the above, the reader can judge whether or not there was a sincere attempt at dialogue with Küng.

The second question of his being informed of the charges requires no further elucidation. It could be maintained that never was a theologian so thoroughly informed of the charges against him.

In what way was his trial clandestine? Only inasmuch as he was not present at the meetings of the theologians in Rome who examined his works or at the meetings of the Congregation itself. He was invited repeatedly to Rome to discuss his position but he refused to go unless procedures acceptable to him could be developed.

Does all this mean that we need have no reservations in this matter? Hardly. It is a painful event from which all of us may well learn something if we are open to that learning.

The first consideration is that no one should leap to the conclusion that the Church is in some sort of regression, that we are going back to pre-Vatican II days. Those outside the Catholic Church are frequently more apprehensive about the monolithic, dictatorial myth of the Church than we are. One of the great lessons taught — or re-taught us by Vatican II is that the Church is a community of believers and that, although we accept the principle of an authenticating authority, the Church goes where the spirit leads it. No one can, no one of any importance wishes, to negate, betray or destory the work of Vatican II. And, I repeat, no one could even if he or she wished to.

Another lesson re-taught us by Vatican II is that we are a learning church. Cardinal Newman has often been described as the unseen presence in that Council. His penetrating and forward-looking ideas about the development of doctrine were a beacon-light to us. We can never pretend that we have plumbed all the depths of the "wisdom and of the knowledge of God". If Aquinas could say that all of his magnificent edifice of inquiry was "just straw," how can we possibly imagine that we will ever fully "arrive" in this world. The fact that we seek the truth means that, in a way, we have found it. But, having found it a little, means only that we must seek it much more. The Church has the right and the duty to tell a theologian he(she) has erred. The Church can never tell a theologian or all theologians to stop searching.

And here, it appears, at least to me, that we have another lesson. It seems infinitely regrettable that the general public perception, due in part to hasty and irresponsible statements by a few theologians, but most of all by the typical orientation of the media to the spectacular, is that an adversarial situation has been created between the official Church and the body of theologians. I am convinced that, as I have stated, the vast majority of Catholic theologians have repudiated Küng in the very areas where he has been challenged. There are numerous statements and even publications of many respected theologians to that intent.

But, might we not have put that integrity and orthodoxy of the main body of theologians to better use. My disquiet in this dimension is admittedly inspired by my upbringing in a Western democracy permeated by a passionate dedication to due process and the principle of appearing to be just as well as actually being so. I do not have a concrete solution to offer but I suggest that in such cases as Küng's, somewhere in the procedure, a truly representative group of theologians would be called upon for a relatively open examination and a report of findings. I could not, in our ecclesiology, postulate that this would be a final court. But what a guarantee it would constitute, what valuable assistance for the ultimate judgment of the congregation or central authority which must make the final decision — and most of all, what a help for us who know about these things only after the event and very incompletely. I know that ours is not the only model of democracy, but I believe we have something to offer in this matter.

What a pity if this unhappy incident in the history of the Church were in any way to endanger the progress we have made and are making both in the area of legitimate theological investigation and in the area of our relationships with those whose fellowship in our search for truth we so much desire and so much appreciate. But it need not be so. We would hope that a cool and clear-headed appraisal of our position on authority in teaching would be understood and respected, whether shared or not. We would hope that our growing pains in finding the best procedures, if such there be, would be sympathetically understood and even alleviated by wise counsel. This is no time for men and women of good will to return to the sterile polemics of the past.

G. Emmett Cardinal Carter

Archbishop of Toronto
355 Church Street
Toronto, Ontario, M5B 1Z8

WRITTEN FOR PUBLICATION IN *THE GLOBE & MAIL*, JANUARY 19, 1980. Reprinted with the permission of G. Emmett Cardinal Carter's office.

STATEMENT OF WILLIAM CARDINAL BAUM FORMER ARCHBISHOP OF WASHINGTON AND PRESENT PREFECT OF THE SACRED CONGREGATION FOR CATHOLIC EDUCATION, CONCERNING THE VATICAN'S DECLARATION REGARDING DR. HANS KÜNG

December 18, 1979

The "Declaration on some major points in the theological doctrine of Professor Hans Küng," issued on December 18, 1979, by the Sacred Congregation for the Doctrine of the Faith, with the approval of the Holy Father Pope John Paul II, should be seen in the light of the duty of the successor of the apostle Peter and of the rights of the faithful — indeed of all human beings.

On the one hand, the Roman Pontiff, as the successor of Peter, has the duty to confirm his brethern in the faith (cf. Lk 22, 32) and to exercise a "watchful concern" for the unity of all the Churches in this faith (cf. Second Vatican Council, Lumen Gentium, 25). On the other hand, the faithful have the sacred right — as the Declaration itself states — "to receive the Word of God uncontaminated" and to "expect that vigilant care should be exercised to keep the threat of error far from them." Indeed, all human beings have the right to hear God's plan of salvation in Christ Jesus proposed to them without ambiguity, since all human beings are "bound to seek the truth, especially in what concerns God and his Church" (cf. Second Vatican Council, Declaration on Religious Liberty, 1). But this obligation cannot be satisfied if those entrusted with the proclamation of this truth do not have the means to demand fidelity to it by those specifically commissioned to teach and research the implications of this revealed Truth.

Everywhere our Lord Jesus Christ went, his listeners were especially astonished by the fact that "he taught them as one who had authority, and not as their scribes" (cf. Mt. 7, 29). At the trial for his life he declared solemnly: "For this I was born, and for this I have come into the world, to bear witness to the truth. Everyone who is of the truth hears my voice" (cf. Jn. 18, 37). This Truth, he had said, is the power behind the liberation of human beings from death (cf. Jn. 8, 32).

We believe that those whose fortune it has been to live after the Ascension of the Lord are not deprived of the privilege of hearing His Voice proclaiming the Truth with the same authority and power. The Declaration concerning the teaching of Professor Küng insists that both his teaching and the decision of the Holy See to withdraw his canonical mission to teach deal with this fundamental human right as granted and protected by the Risen "Christ Himself exercising His role as teacher in the Church" through the Sacred Magisterium.

In his writings, Professor Küng has "at least put in doubt" the capacity of the Church to teach the Truth with such authority; the Holy Father's approval of the decision to remove his canonical mission to teach in the name of the Chruch affirms this gift given to the Church and defends the sacred rights of everyone today to hear Christ the Teacher.

The process leading to this decision has been characterized by charity, prudence and patience (cf. Declaration on Religious Liberty, op. cit., 14). We pray that this decision will move all who are entrusted with such awesome responsibilities to re-dedicate themselves to the service of the Truth which originates, not in the human mind, but in the eternal counsels of the Triune God. May our celebration this Christmas of the glorious mystery of the Word made flesh strengthen our faith in the capacity of human words and concepts — indeed of the flesh of man — to bear and communicate the Truth that is God Himself.

THE STATEMENT OF ARCHBISHOP JOHN R. QUINN, PRESIDENT OF THE NATIONAL CONFERENCE OF CATHOLIC BISHOPS CONCERNING THE VATICAN'S DECLARATION RELATING TO DR. HANS KÜNG

December 20, 1979

It is important to bear in mind at least two things with regard to the Holy See's declaration concerning some major points in the theological doctrine of Professor Hans Küng.

First, the people of the Church have a right to know what the Church teaches about the revelation of Christ.

Second, those responsible for exercising teaching authority have a duty to make clear what is and what is not compatible with Catholic doctrine. As a corollary, they have the further duty not to authorize teaching in the name of the Church which is incompatible with Catholic doctrine.

This action is theological in content but pastoral in purpose. It is not so much directed against a theologian as to the Catholic people. Its intent is to prevent or alleviate confusion concerning the content of doctrine.

It is necessary to avoid misstatements and inflammatory rhetoric in this matter. Father Küng's rights have not been violated. Rather, the magisterium of the Church has exercised its right and duty to make clear what is and is not consistent with Catholic teaching. In doing so, it has performed one of the essential services for which it exists.

I am proud of my Church.

GERMAN TITLES REFERRED TO THROUGHOUT THE DIALOGUE

1. DIE KIRCHE.......................................THE CHURCH
2. UNFEHLBAR? EINE ANFRAGE...................INFALLIBILITY
3. NACHKONZILIARE DOKUMENTATION.........POSTCONCILIAR DOCUMENTATION
4. CHRIST SEIN..........................ON BEING A CHRISTIAN
5. EXISTIERT GOTT?........................ DOES GOD EXIST?
6. UM NICHTS ALS DIE WAHRHEIT.....NOTHING BUT THE TRUTH

7. APPELL ZUR VERSTANDIGUNG.................... APPEAL TO UNDERSTANDING
8. WIE DER PAPST UNFEHLBAR WURDE........... HOW THE POPE BECAME INFALLIBLE
9. KIRCHE-GEHALTEN IN DER WAHRHEIT?......... THE CHURCH MAINTAINED IN TRUTH
10. DISKUSSION ÜBER HANS KÜNGS CHRIST SEIN..... DISCUSSION OVER HANS KÜNG'S ON BEING A CHRISTIAN
11. LEXIKON FÜR THEOLOGIE UND KIRCHE......... LEXICON FOR THEOLOGY AND CHURCH
12. DISKUSSION UM HANS KÜNG DIE KIRCHE...... DISCUSSION ON HANS KÜNG'S BOOK THE CHURCH
13. ZUM PROBLEM DER UNFEHLBARKEIT: ANTWORTEN AUF DIE ANFRAGE VON HANS KÜNG.............. ON THE PROBLEM OF INFALLIBILITY: REPLIES TO THE CHALLENGE OF HANS KÜNG
14. STRUKTUREN DER KIRCHE..... STRUCTURES OF THE CHURCH
15. UNFEHLBARKEIT................................ INFALLIBILITY
16. RECHTFERTIGUNG .... JUSTIFICATION
17. KONZIL UND WIEDERVEREINIGUNG... COUNCIL AND REUNION
18. MENSCHWERDUNG GOTTES............. GOD'S INCARNATION
19. WAHRHAFTIGKEIT, UNFEHLBAR? FEHLBAR?.. TRUTHFULNESS
20. WOZU PRIESTER? EINE HILFE?......... WHY PRIESTS? A HELP?
21. FEHLBAR? EINE BILANZ........... FALLIBLE? PRO'S AND CON'S
22. UM NICHTS ALS DIE WAHRHEIT. DEUTSCHE BISCHOPSKONFERENZ CONTRA HANS KÜNG. EINE DOKUMENTATION........ NOTHING BUT THE TRUTH. GERMAN BISHOPS CONFERENCE VS. HANS KÜNG
23. HANS KÜNG: WEG UND WERK... HANS KÜNG: WAY AND WORK
24. PIUS IX (1846-1878): PAPSTLICHE UNFEHLBARKEIT UND 1. VATIKANISCHE KONZIL. DOGMATISIERUNG UND DURCHSETZUNG EINER IDEOLOGIE............. PIUS IX (1846-1878): PAPAL INFALLIBILITY AND THE FIRST VATICAN COUNCIL. FORMULATING DOGMA AND SOLIDIFYING AN IDEOLOGY
25. WIE DER PAPST UNFEHLBAR WURDE. MACHT UND OHNMACHTEINES DOGMAS........ HOW THE POPE BECAME INFALLIBLE. STRENGTH AND WEAKNESS OF A DOGMA

INDEX

Personal Name Index

Subject Index